TURGENEV

LETTERS

VOLUME ONE

Edited and Translated by David Lowe

ARDIS

Ardis Publishers
2901 Heatherway
Ann Arbor, Michigan 48104

Library of Congress Cataloging in Publication Data

Turgenev, Ivan Sergeevich, 1818-1883.
    Letters in two volumes.

    Includes index.
    1. Turgenev, Ivan Sergeevich, 1818-1883–Correspon-
dence. 2. Authors, Russian–19th century–Correspon-
dence. I. Lowe, David Allan, 1948-   . II. Title.
PG3432   1982   891.73'3   82-18515
ISBN 0-88233-735-1 (v.1)
ISBN 0-88233-736-X (v. 2)

CONTENTS

Acknowledgments

First place in the acknowledgments belongs to the scholars who prepared and annotated the *Complete Collected Works and Letters (Polnoe sobranie sochinenii i pisem).* But for that edition this collection of translated Turgenev letters would not even have been undertaken. Among the colleagues who have been helpful in elucidating difficult passages in the Russian originals, I have especially imposed on the generous expertise of three Ninas: Professor Nina Perlina of Macalester College and Professors Antonina Filonov Gove and Nina Mitelman at Vanderbilt University. Professor James Engel of Vanderbilt University and Christina Kraus kindly checked over the translations from the German. Very special thanks are due Professor Helena Goscilo-Kostin of the University of Pittsburgh: her careful checking of the manuscript saved me from myself on more occasions that I'd like to admit. Any mistakes that remain in the translations are mine, of course.

David Lowe
Vanderbilt University

For Inna Varlamova

Introduction

Ivan Turgenev was one of the literary giants of the nineteenth century. His Russian contemporaries saw the period 1860-1880 as the age of Dostoevsky, Tolstoy, and Turgenev. Abroad, Turgenev was the first Russian author to acquire a truly international following, and by the 1870s each new work of his was quickly translated into French, German, and usually English as well. In fact, his works occasionally appeared in translation before they did in the original, a curious situation that is documented in some of the letters that follow. In short, by the time of his death in 1883, Turgenev seemed destined for a permanent position in the pantheon of literary greats. The sad truth, however, is that with each passing year Turgenev's literary stock slips a little lower.

In the twentieth century Turgenev has become something of an icon. He is the object of great deference, but only one of his six novels, *Fathers and Sons,* retains a firm foothold in the twentieth-century literary imagination. True, *The Notes of a Hunter* [*A Sportsman's Sketches*] and two or three short stories have their adherents, and the play *A Month in the Country,* with its intimations of Chekhovian mood and manner, continues to hold the boards. But by and large, the vast body of Turgenev's prose fiction, not to mention his poetry and dramatic compositions, strikes us as singularly dated. The poetic sensibility at work in Turgenev's tales of destructive passion evokes ennui in the modern reader.

It seems highly unlikely that Turgenev will be forgotten, however. His own enigmatic personality, his role as a spokesman for his age, and his position as a cultural intermediary between Russian and Western Europe continue to command our attention and interest. Significantly, Leonard Schapiro's recent *Turgenev: His Life and Times* (New York, 1978), which leaves no stone unturned in assembling the facts and events of Turgenev's biography, is the work of a historian, not a literary scholar.

If the English-speaking reader wishes to come to a first-hand understanding and appreciation of Turgenev the man and entrepreneur of culture, he must have access to Turgenev's letters, of which precious few have been heretofore available in English translation. Turgenev was a prodigious correspondent, and his more than 6,000 known letters are not only a chronicle of his life and thoughts, but an encyclopedia of nineteenth-century European culture as well. Even a superficial acquaintance with Turgenev's correspondence cannot help but impress one with the man's enormous erudition, his wide-ranging interests, and the riddle of his personality.

The arsenal of languages at Turgenev's disposal was remarkable. His letters are in four languages—Russian, French, German, and English. His command of French was as close to native as one can get without having been born and raised in Paris. Though he had qualms about writing German, he read and spoke it fluently. He could cite Shakespeare in the original, although as the letters reproduced herein demonstrate, his written English, while it communicated, was heavily if charmingly flawed. Nonetheless, he spoke and read English without any great difficulty. Additionally, he had a thorough grasp of Latin, Polish, Spanish, and Italian. Clearly, Turgenev was staggeringly well-equipped linguistically to observe and comment on the all-European scene.

The sharpness and immediacy of his impressions were facilitated by the fact that Turgenev travelled widely and frequently. He spent most of his mature life abroad, and from the mid-1850s on, any given year might have found him spending considerable periods of time in London, Paris, Berlin, Baden-Baden, Moscow, Petersburg, and his estate of Spasskoye. He was the original roving reporter.

The single most striking aspect of Turgenev's correspondence, however, aside from its sheer massiveness (surely a function of the lack of telephones in the nineteenth century), is the breadth of interests and concerns that it reveals. Many of the concerns are of a purely personal nature, of course—health, finances, negotiations with publishers, and that sort of thing. And it goes without saying that Turgenev's letters shed light on his writings, especially *Fathers and Sons,* the most controversial of his works. Nor should it surprise us that Turgenev kept a close eye on literary developments in Europe and America. His letters trace his readings and his reactions to what he read.

Turgenev's interests were hardly limited to literature, however. His academic training was in philosophy, and many of the letters that follow find Turgenev in a philosophical frame of mind. He adored music, art, and the theater. As the letters collected here show, he was present at Verdi and Wagner premieres, collected paintings (until a financial pinch forced him to sell most of them), and found Sarah Bernhardt a greatly overrated actress. Moreover, and Turgenev's protests to the contrary, he was fascinated by politics and voiced his own opinions on any number of political questions. His letters to Alexander Herzen alone testify to that.

The range of Turgenev's friends and acquaintances spanned the face of Europe and extended across the Atlantic Ocean. A catalogue of only the most distinguished of his correspondents would have to include the likes of Henry James, Prosper Mérimée, George Sand, Gustave Flaubert, Emile Zola, Theodor Storm, Fyodor Dostoevsky, and Lev Tolstoy. And that is but the cream of the cream.

Selecting the 334 letters included in the present volumes, well over 200 of them never before available in English, was not an easy task. The selection process was guided by several considerations. An irrational antipathy toward bleeding limbs led the translator to reproduce letters in their entirety. A number of objections could be raised to that decision, but in the long run it was felt that only complete letters could give a real sense of Turgenev as a letter writer. The final selection—pitifully small, but at least a start—strives to portray the major events of Turgenev's life and to illuminate as many sides of the man and his age as possible. Turgenev appears herein at his best and his worst, his least charming and his most appealing.

Two additional considerations affected the winnowing procedure. One was the desire to emphasize Turgenev's role as a link between Western Europe and Russia. This explains the choice of a number of letters that show Turgenev as a purveyor of Russian culture in Western Europe and vice versa. His activity in this respect was quite remarkable: in retrospect, Diaghilev merely carried forward a process whose initiator was Turgenev. The other consideration was the decision to include as many letters as possible that cast light on the manifold ironies of Russian history. To wit, anyone familiar with contemporary "Soviet reality," as the Russian cliché runs, will find Turgenev's correspondence redolent of *plus ça change.* Censorship, arrests, *samizdat, tamizdat,* and quarrels among dissidents at home and abroad did not begin in the twentieth century.

Since the letters contained herein have been chosen so as to outline Turgenev's biography as well as his views on life, nature, and art, there seems little point in reproducing in an introduction what the reader will discover for himself in the letters. Anyone desiring to supplement the letters with a detailed biography is urged to use Schapiro's volume as a companion piece. Critical analysis of Turgenev's works may be found in Richard Freeborn, *Turgenev: The Novelist's Novelist* (Oxford, 1960) and Eva Kagan-Kans, *Hamlet and Don Quixote: Turgenev's Ambivalent Vision* (The Hague, 1975). Readers who would like to sample more of Turgenev's letters may consult Edgar Lehrman's *Turgenev's Letters: A Selection* (New York, 1961) and Nora Gottlieb and Raymond Chapman's *Letters to an Actress* (London, 1973).

11

Technical Notes

The basic source for the letters here translated and the ensuing commentary is I.S. Turgenev, *Polnoe sobranie sochinenii i pisem* v 28-i tomax (Moscow-Leningrad, 1960-1968) [*Complete Collected Works & Letters in 28 Volumes*], an edition that represents one of the most awesome accomplishments of recent Soviet scholarship. (The ninety-volume Tolstoy "Jubilee" edition and the complete Dostoevsky still in progress belong to this same category of scholarly and editorial feats.) Although the title of the Academy edition states "Complete Works and Letters," the edition is not in fact complete: previously unpublished letters still surface from time to time and probably will continue to do so well into the twenty-first century. Recent publications have been consulted in the preparation of the present translation, but the basic source remains the *Complete Works*.

The identification of letters in the translation follows the pattern used in the Academy edition. Each letter number in the present volume is accompanied by a number in parentheses: the latter refers to numerical sequence in the *Complete Works*. The name of the addressee follows the letter numbers. Immediately beneath the letter numbers and addressee is the date on which the letter is presumed to have been written (note that this is sometimes at odds with the dating that Turgenev himself indicates). As with the letter numbers, there are two dates: the first, "Old Style," conforms to the Julian Calendar, which was twelve days behind the Gregorian Calendar in the nineteenth century. The second date, of course, is Gregorian, or "New Style." After that comes Turgenev's presumed place of residence on the given date. All of this information is to be found on the left-hand side of the page. The heading on the right-hand side is Turgenev's own.

The letters may be assumed to have been translated from Russian unless a footnote indicates otherwise. Note that in many cases the French or German originals have not come down to us, so that the English translation is third-hand, through the intermediary of a Russian one. Such cases are indicated in the notes, as are instances of incomplete texts. Where Turgenev uses "foreign" works or phrases within a letter, e.g., French phrases in a German letter, the foreign phrase has been retained and glossed, except when the English cognate is so obvious as to make an explanation insulting.

The English transliteration used herein does not conform to any single standard system. It is rather an attempt to render names and places pronounceable for readers who do not know Russian. (An exception to this practice are Russian names and places that have already achieved wide currency in a conventional transliteration, e.g., Herzen, Dostoevsky, Moscow.) The reason for adopting a non-scholarly and unsystematic scheme of transliteration is that the standard systems tend not to give the uninitiated reader any sense of what the name or word *sounds* like, while anyone who knows Russian can instantly transliterate back into the orginial Cyrillic, no matter what system has been used. Moreover, readers who have Russian at their command are not likely to need this translation anyway.

Gender distinctions in surnames, where they exist in Russian, have been maintained in the transliteration. What this means most of the time, with the exception of non-Russian names, is that masculine surnames end in a consonant or "y" and feminine last names add an "a" or "aya." Hence, Alexey Karenin, but Anna Karenina; Lev Tolstoy, but Sofia Tolstaya. Another potential source of confusion is the Russian use of patronymics, i.e., middle names derived from the father's first name (Ivan Ivanovich, Anna Ivanovna). Adult Russians usually address one another with first name *and* patronymic. The exceptions are immediate family members and close friends, but even here one occasionally encounters name and patronymic.

There are four Russian words that consistently have been left in the original, on the grounds that they both occur with some frequency and lack English equivalents. The most important of these is povest, a term generally understood to describe a literary genre midway between the short story and the novel. Even that widespread definition is full of traps, however. Turgenev refers to *Crime and Punishment* as a *povest,* for instance, and it was not until 1880 that Turgenev drew a clear dividing line between povests and novels in his own *oeuvre.* Perhaps it would be best to think of a povest as a work of prose, usually longer than a short story.

The other three untranslated words are Russian measurements. A *verst* is equal to 3500 feet; an *arshin* is 28 inches; and a *desyatina* is a measure of land equivalent to 2.7 acres.

The punctuation and sentence lengths found in the translations are largely Turgenev's own. The abundance of what we would normally consider run-on sentences, together with punctuation that relies heavily on dots and dashes, may initially strike the reader as bizarre, if not illiterate. In the long run, however, it was deemed more sensible to preserve Turgenev's punctuation than to Anglicize it. It is, after all, an essential feature of Turgenev's style. And from a Russian's point of view, there is nothing the least bit sloppy or haphazard about Turgenev's arrangement of words on the page. His style represents a nineteenth-century ideal, moreover, one emulated in the twentieth. Curiously enough, although Turgenev's stories and novels are generally felt to be dated, especially in comparison to the works of his contemporaries Dostoevsky and Tolstoy, Turgenev's *language* (and that includes notions of phrase length and punctuation) is perhaps the least dated of any major nineteenth-century Russian author's. For all of these reasons, the literate English reader is asked to show forbearance as he enters this seeming jungle of dots, dashes, semi-colons, and mile-long sentences. He will soon discover that it has its own inner logic and charm.

One last note about punctuation. In his correspondence with male friends Turgenev was not averse to using scatological turns of phrase. The editors of the *Complete Works,* shackled by a censorship that is prudish in addition to everything else that one might say about it, have omitted the offending words and phrases. Where it is obvious to a Russian speaker what the term *must* have been (usually "shit"), the lacunae have been filled in. Where there were any doubts at all, however, this translation follows the *Complete Works,* veiling the unprintable with a modest [...].

The commentary to the *Complete Works* is nothing short of fabulous. Every letter is accompanied by previous publishing information and the location of the original, if it is known. Virtually every name, incident, or work mentioned in any given letter can be explicated either with the help of a footnote or a biographical index included at the end of each volume. Superb as this annotation apparatus is, it often includes much more information than the average non-Russian reader could possibly want or need. Conversely, names and incidents requiring no commentary for the average Russian reader are passed over in silence. The commentary in the present translation hardly aims at exhaustiveness: it attempts, rather, to strike a balance by drawing on relevant information from the Academy edition and adding to it such facts and developments as would normally be assumed to be beyond the ken of the average non-Russian reader.

The first occurrence of any given name is accompanied by a footnote supplying biographical information and any specific facts essential for understanding the context of the letter. The index at the end of each volume includes all the names of people mentioned anywhere in the volume. An asterisk following a name in Volume II indicates that the name occurs in Volume I as well. The numbers following the names indicate *letter* numbers, not page numbers. Italics indicate that the person is the addressee of the given letter. If one wishes biographical information for anyone listed in the index, one need only turn to the footnotes for the letter in which the person's name first occurs.

In a few instances biographical information has not been supplied. This holds for two categories of people: those whose names are too well known to require annotation (Goethe, Verdi, Zola) and those whose identity stumped even the Academy annotators. In general, it is likely that the commentary to the letters included in these two volumes will be found inadequate for specialists in Russian literature, comparative literature, or European cultural history, but the grim alternative is two volumes of letters and four of commentary. It would require the likes of a Nabokov to justify that sort of scholarly largesse. Furthermore, it is assumed that specialists in any of the above-named fields have easy access to their own biographical and bibliographical sources.

LETTERS

Letter 1 (1). To N.N. Turgenev.[1]
March 22, 23, 24, 25, 26/April 3, 4, 5, 6, 7, 1831. Moscow.

Dear Uncle,

Excuse me for not having been able to write you a letter on Tuesday: but to make up for it I'll write a very long letter today.

I'll write it to you in the form of a journal from Sunday on. I begin.

Sunday, March 22. On that day I got up after six, dressed, and went to church. After mass we set off for Sparrow Hills in a hired sleigh; after we'd driven out of the gate we asked permission to walk along the road; it was granted; I had just gotten out and walked a little way when, because of my usual clumsiness, I slipped and fell—plop!—into the mud: I got my fur coat and pants dirty and ripped by pants!! What could I do! I got up and set off again. When we arrived at Anna Ivanovna's,[2] they took me to a room, took off my pants, and while I waited for them to be sewn up, I sat nearly two hours alone in a robe. Alone! It would have been fine if they'd put me somewhere upstairs: as it was, only an unlocked partition separated me from the room where they were breakfasting! Vexation and boredom! I was supposed to have breakfast there, and from lack of anything to do I picked up a book that was lying there. What kind of one do you think? A German prayer book; I had begun reading it when they brought me my pants; I came out and we soon went home, where, thanks to the cook, we didn't have dinner. After dinner time we went to the Gagarins[3] with Mr. Lobanov;[4] there we danced French quadrilles, old and new, the gallopade, mazurka, and écossaise. I didn't especially feel like dancing: so imagine how vexed I was when a cross-eyed, ugly, and in addition to that, spiteful lady suddenly yelled at the top of her voice: "Bravo, M. Tourgieneff, bravo!" I'm saying that she was spiteful, because in front of everyone she kept saying of her little sister that she was awkward, dull, poorly brought up, etc.; and it was all said so maliciously that looking at her, I involuntarily said to myself, as Pushkin[5] says: "A snake, a snake!"[6]

But let's finish with this material: you probably don't like it. From the Gagarins we went to Miss Yakovleva's.[7] Mama was already there; they asked us there about our health, about Papa and so on. Finally we went home and I hurried to go to bed.

Monday, March 23. I woke up early and hurried downstairs and began to prepare my lessons for Mr. Falantin.[8] You probably don't know yet that Platon Nikolayevich[9] wants to replace him with a *Gregorius something-or-other.* But don't write Platon Nikolayevich about this: after all, it's a secret. Suddenly the clock struck eight and Mr. Falantin came in, sat down, and corrected our translations. "Haben sie das Buch, aus welchem sie übersetzt haben" [Do you have the book from which you have translated?], he said. I went to the library, looked—and it wasn't there! "I looked and looked, and finally I got tired," says Krylov;[10] and that's what happened to me too. I told him it wasn't there, for which the teacher wrote in clear letters the fatal words: "I was not satisfied." What had happened was that Nikanor[11] had deigned to take the book in the morning without asking; Platon Nikolayevich forgave me. After that we had our strictest teacher, Dmitri Nikitich;[12] we recited history, grammar, and poetry for him. Here's what he gave me:

Grammar—very good.
Poetry—excellent.
History—good; but the supplement wasn't memorized.

N.B. I'm grateful to Dmitri Nikitich for the supplement: I had forgotten that I needed to memorize it; he petitioned for me, and I was forgiven.

After dinner we had Mr. Gardorf;[13] he heard my lesson and then gave me a new assignment. Then I went outside, ran around, lost one of my galoshes, but it was found; that's how Monday was spent.

Tuesday, March 24. Everything went as it should; I prepared a composition, "L'Ambition" [Ambition], for Mr. Doublet;[14] he gave me an "excellent"; after that Platon Nikolayevich came and gave a geometry lesson: I knew the material well. After dinner we had Mr. Shchurovsky.[15] We didn't receive letters that day, however. Farewell for now.

Wednesday, March 25. That day was a holiday: the Annunciation; we went to church, then started to run around the yard: we got ourselves all covered with mud and came home; we changed clothes and after dinner we went to see Miss Yakovleva: there we played blind man's buff and saw Levushka Yakovlev. We had a very good time, and we arrived home late. I just can't help thinking of the Head in "Ruslan," and how it says to him "I want to sleep, etc., it's now already night, farewell!"[17]

Thursday, March 26. Today we had Mr. Valentin, and I knew the lesson well: then we had Platon Nikolayevich . . . Here's a problem for you; try to solve it.

One fountain fills a pond in 12 days; a second one in 9; if both are turned on, how long will it take them to fill the pond?

In the evening we had Mr. Lobanov, and at eight o'clock I'm sitting in my place at a class desk and finishing a letter; Nikolenka[18] is sitting at the teacher's desk eating dried fruit and reading an almanac: across from me Nikanor is reading *The Telegraph;*[19] across from Nikolenka Mr. Meyer[20] is sitting reading *Mythology;* Mama is sitting at her table studying German words.

My journal is now finished; I'll add two or three more words.

I heard that you wrote that you're going off to the militia.[21] Uncle, I won't let you go: if you go I'll hug you so hard that then you'll either go with me or stay. But you're joking; I know you.

Here's another bit of news: Mama got a beautiful woolen jacket for you from Papa, and Mama got a lovely cup. But it's time for me to realize that I've prattled enough as it is. Farewell!

> I kiss you a thousand times and remain
> your nephew who loves you beyond words,

> Ivan Turgenev.

P.S. In your next letter tell me about Skob. Oh, by the way, Mr. Meyer asked me to convey his respects to you.

Mama will write to you tomorrow.

Letter 2 (8). To A.V. Nikitenko.[1]
March 26/April 7, 1837. Petersburg.

Dear Alexander Vasilievich,

In sending you my first, weak efforts in the sphere of Russian poetry, I beg you not to think that I have the slightest desire to publish them—and if I request your advice—then it's exclusively in order to find out your opinion, which I value very highly. I was hesitant about whether I ought to send you a *drama* written by me at age sixteen, my first work—I see so many flaws in it, and I now so dislike its entire plot that if I didn't rely on your indulgence—and more importantly—if I didn't think that one can at

19

least foretell the future on the basis of the first step, I would never have made up my mind to send it to you.[2] About a year ago I gave it to P.A. Pletnyov[3]—he repeated to me what I had already been thinking for a long time, that everything was exaggerated, inaccurate, immature...and if there is anything decent in it—then perhaps certain parts, very few in number. I consider it my duty to note (you, of course, will note this immediately) that the meter of the verses is very incorrect. It wouldn't now be worth the effort to redo them—and I was about to consign them to complete oblivion when my close acquaintance with you moved me to show them to you.[4] "An Old Man's Tale," an unfinished narrative poem that will probably never be finished, was written in 1835.[5] And lastly, "Our Age" is a work that was begun last year in the middle of February, in a fit of malicious exasperation with the despotism and monopoly of certain people in our world of letters.[6] Last year was devoted to translations—Shakespeare's *Othello* (which I didn't finish—only as far as the middle of the second act), *King Lear* (with large omissions), and "Manfred." The first two translations were destroyed by me—they seemed to me too bad after Vronchenko's and Panayev's[7]...Besides which, that was a false direction—I'm absolutely unfit to be a translator. My "Manfred" hasn't been copied—that's why I'm not sending it to you. If what I've sent you doesn't seem to you absolutely awful, then would you be so kind as to tell me. I'll deliver to you three other completed narrative poems: "A Calm at Sea," "Phantasmagoria on a Summer's Night," and "A Dream."[8] In addition, I have about a hundred small poems—but none of them has been rewritten and they're scattered all over... "Our Age" isn't finished—I'm working on it now. But whether I ought to continue will depend on your decision. One more request: don't tell Pyotr Alexandrovich[9] about this; before any acquaintance with you I promised to deliver my works to *him,* and I haven't yet fulfilled my promises. His opinions, which I very much respect, do not coincide with mine. Furthermore—I'll tell you frankly—on first meeting you I felt infinite confidence in you... And I also forgot to tell you that at the end of last year I began a drama, the first act and entire plan of which are completely finished; I hope when I return from the country to bring it to you already completed (in September).[10] In conclusion, I beg you to believe in those feelings of admiration and absolute respect with which I remain

Your most humble servant,

Ivan Turgenev.

March 26, 1837

Letter 3 (16). To T.N. Granovsky.[1]
June 8/20, 1839. Berlin.

June 20, 1839. Berlin.

I was planning to send you an answer to your first letter, dear Timofey Nikolaich, when the door swung open and in walked Stankevich.[2] I confess that I was very surprised, but he explained to me that he had come here to rest and seek advice.[3] I think that there was added to this the desire to see Werder[4]—and perhaps Berta.[5] He still doesn't know where they'll send him—to Salzbrunn or Kreutznach.[6] It seems to me that it's time for him to make up his mind and not lose time. He's lost a little weight and is coughing. During our absence disasters have descended on me like the Four Horsemen of the Apocalypse: in the first place, I received a letter about our house burning down—in Mama's quarters almost everything was burned up—they saved only the most important things—she is living in Mtsensk and wants to see me very much; my brother's been forced to go on an expedition to buy horses for the military; in the second place, a certain crafty wench whom my servant brought to me twice in November and whose face I wouldn't even recognize—à la lettre [literally] (it was dark in the room), has sued me for the birth, christening, and funeral of what was allegedly my child, for a six-week long illness and—what's funniest of all— for "defloratio." Me—the destroyer of innocence! That's a surprise! Including court costs the whole thing will cost me about 200 thalers: I hired a lawyer and—submissive to cruel fate—I indifferently lowered my brow.[7] All of this is very painful. I received your second letter and passed on the enclosure to Stankevich.

There is little literary news: two parts of *Ranke's History of Germany During the Reformation*[8] came out. He used little-known archives. The first part of *Palacký's History of Bohemia.*[9] The next installment of *Strahl's History of Russia to 1505,*[10] and *Michelet's* pamphlet *Schelling and Hegel.*[11]

I've been to the theater four or five times: *Löwe* is enchanting in *Jean de Paris;*[12] Mlle *Schlegel* from Dresden sings well in *Robert,*[13] but her face is a real pancake. At the Königstadt they've resurrected *Bäuerle's* old Posse [farce] *Der Verzauberte Prinz* [The Enchanted Prince]—Beckman is superb, Eichbaum charming;[14] I think that's all. True, you haven't seen the bayadères:[15] imagine to yourself dusky, half-nude, colorfully dressed girls; behind them stands a group of three Indians, an old man and two mature men in white from head to foot—one of them draws a dolorous note from an instrument resembling a clarinet, another beats on a kind of drum, and the third knocks two rocks together and in a nasal voice sings strange words. The bayadères hardly leave their place—bending forward at the knees, they stamp their feet with agility, they twist their whole body, wave their arms through the air in measure, turn pale, and go into a frenzy...They depressed me: they seemed to be quaking before their god the way a bird quivers convulsively at the sight of a rattlesnake—and for the very same reason—das Monstrum der Gottheit bei den Orientalen [the monstrosity of the Divinity among the Orientals],[16] as Schiller says. They are consumed by it. Goethe's "Bayadère" is much better: "Sie weiss sich so lieblich im Kreise zu tragen—Und neigt sich, und biegt sich, und reicht ihm den Strauss" [She knows how to circle around so charmingly—and bends, and bows, and extends the bouquet to him].[17] A vegetable nature predominates in the Indians: I noticed that one of them stood for a half-hour like a rock, didn't even move a finger.

Among the books and notebooks brought me from you, I found a very detailed quotation from Turner's *History of the Anglosaxons*[18]—what would you have me do with it?

I haven't read Mülner's *King Ingurd*—what you said of it can also be said of his *Schuld* [Guilt].[19] I'd like to read Grillparzer's "Sappho"—I read Borne's review of it: I believe him.[20] A few days ago I finished *Souvestre's* novel *L'homme et l'argent* [Man and money][21]—I beg you, if you can get it in Salzbrunn—*"to take it and read it"*: amen, amen—it's good. *Les Ailes d'Icare* [The Wings of Icarus][22] is very interesting so far; can it really be that your Salzbrunn is such a *Loch* that you can't even get *Journal des Débats*? By the way, I don't know whether you need the thing—it doesn't make any difference. R. Brucker, one of the people writing under the name of M. Raymond, has written a *philosophical* poem in which can be found the following stanza:

1.   Oui—d'une octave à l'autre en Dieu,
                        foyer suprême—
     [Yes—from one octave to another, in God, the supreme center]
2.   Chaque évolution de la triplicité
     [Each evolution of triple unity]
3.   Sous l'oeil, en développant la prisme en théorême,
     [Under the gaze, while developing the prism into a theorem]
4.   Déchaine, dans l'essor de son activité,
     [Unleashes, in the impulse of its activity]
5.   Des sept courbes en jeu la gamme
                        élémentaire!
     [The basic scale of seven fiery curves!]
                        (Journal de Paris)

Well, what do you think? A philosophical poem! It recently occurred to me (I had been observing my own character) that "von lauter Werden komm' Ich nie an die That"[I never move from impulse to deed]; with the French it's just the opposite—any embryo of thought immediately passes over into word and deed: it's not surprising that such stupidity occurs; stupidity is undeveloped wisdom that has become corporeal before its time—Missgeburt [miscarriage]. Isn't that so? Perhaps I'm talking through my hat, though—that often happens to me.

By the way, Werder has reached the *Grund* [first principles] in his section on *Wesen* [being]—and I can tell you that I have experienced at least l'avant-goût [foretaste] of what he calls "die spekulativen Freuden" [speculative joys]. You wouldn't believe with what avid interest I listen to his readings, how anxiously I want to achieve the goal, how irritated and simultaneously thrilled I am each time the earth, on which you think you stand firmly, collapses under your feet—that's the way it was for me with Werden, Dasein, Wesen [becoming, existence, being], etc. I think that all these sensations are familiar to you. Courses finish August 1, because of their rebuilding the University; I'll be in Moscow on about the 7th, if God will it, and we'll see each other about the 15th. Until then—get better—that's the only thing I can wish you. Good-bye, dear Timofey Nikolaye-vich—I clasp your hand affectionately—and beg you to believe in the sincere regard

of your devoted

I. Turgenev.

Letter 4 (24). To T.N. Granovsky.
July 4/16, 1840. Berlin.

Berlin, July 4/16, 1840

A great blow has befallen us, Granovsky. I can hardly gather the strength to write. We have lost a person whom we loved, in whom we believed, who was our pride and hope... On June 24, in Novi—Stankevich passed away. I could and I should end the letter here... What remains to be said—what good are my words now? It's not for you, but more for myself that I'm continuing the letter: I became close with him in Rome. I saw him

23

every day—and I began to appreciate his radiant intelligence, his warm heart, and all the beauty of his soul... already then the shadow of imminent death lay on him... We often spoke of death: he recognized in it the limit of thought and, it seemed to me, secretly shuddered. Death has profound meaning if it comes—as the last thing—from the heart of a full, developed life: to the elderly it is reconciliation; but to us, to him—it's a mandate of fate. That he should die? He so profoundly and so sincerely recognized and loved the sanctity of life, in spite of his illness he enjoyed the bliss of thinking, acting, and loving: he was preparing to dedicate himself to the work that is indispensable for Russia... The cold hand of death fell on his head, and an entire world has perished. Here is die kalte Teufelsfaust, die sich—*nicht* vergebens tückisch ballt [the devil's cold fist that is fiercely clenched *not* without reason]. I received a letter from him from Florence dated the 11th of June. Here are some excerpts: "... I sometimes have the chance to rest in Florence, people in general like me, and things *seem to be moving ahead*... It's finally been decided that I should spend the summer in Lake Como... Dyakova,[1] hearing in Naples about my illness... has arrived with her son, and we'll spend the summer together." Then he tells me how he feels about Dyakova's late sister.[2] Do you remember Klyushnikov's chorale "The Beautiful Eyes Have Closed?" *He,* too, died, and Stankevich has died![3] "In Dyakova I've found a real sister, as before; her solicitations and sympathy do more for the recovery of my strength than anything else." He was tortured by his burdensome relations with Berta: he asked me to stop by to see her, find out and so on. "I have a lot of plans in my head—but when didn't I? I'm planning to work on the history of philosophy this winter. I also have several articles in my head. God only knows *how* this will all turn out... " "Write about Werder; give him my regards; tell him that his friendship will be sacred and dear to me eternally and that everything decent in me is inseparably bound up with it... Farewell *for now!*"

There's one more excerpt: "I found the Frolovs still here. Lizaveta Pavlovna[4] was terribly sick; now, fortunately, she's begun to get better; I think that after she recovers they'll go to Naples. The Kenneys[5] have taken a house here for the whole year."

Fourteen days later he died, during the night, in Novi.

On the 12th of July, I received the following letter from Yefremov:[6]

Novi, June 27

Ivan Sergeyevich! Having pulled myself together, I hasten to inform you of the misfortune that has struck all of us. In Novi, a little town about 40 miles from Genoa, on the road to Milan, on the eve of the 25th, Stankevich died. He was on his way to Como. I don't know what to write.

24

My head is spinning. Chaos. After finishing all my business in Genoa, I was planning to go directly to Berlin if nothing stopped me. Now I'm busy arranging everything for the transfer of his body to Russia. Farewell. I hope to see you soon. Farewell.

Yours, A. Efremov

I'm awaiting him impatiently, I'll find out everything and immediately write to you. My Lord, how this blow will strike you, Neverov,[7] the Frolovs, the Kenneys, the Bakunins, all his acquaintances and friends! I couldn't bring myself to tell Werder about it: I wrote him a letter. How profoundly grieved he was! On meeting him I said: "In Ihm ist auch ein Teil von Ihnen gestorben" [In him a bit of you has died, too]. He nearly burst into tears. He said to me: "Ich fühle es. Ich bin auf dem halben Wege meines Lebens: meine besten Schüler, meine Junger sterben ab—ich überlebe sie!" [I feel that I am at the halfway point of my life: my best students, my young ones are dying—I am outliving them]. He read me a superb poem, "Der Tod" [Death], which he had written immediately after receiving the news. If he consents, I'll make a copy of it and send it to you. I look around, searching—in vain. Who of our generation can replace our loss? Who is the worthy person who will take the heritage of his great ideas from the deceased and not allow his influence to perish, but will travel along his path, in his spirit, with his strength? Oh, if anything could make me doubt the future, after outliving Stankevich I would part with my last hope. Why couldn't someone else have died, a thousand others, me, for instance? When will the time come that a more developed spirit will be an essential condition for the higher development of the body and our very life a condition and fruit of the Creator's pleasures; why can the beautiful perish or suffer on earth? Until now it seemed that thought was sacrilege, and that punishment inevitably awaits everything that exceeds the blissful mediocre. Or is God's envy aroused, as it used to be with the Greek gods? Or are we to believe that everything beautiful, sacred—love and thought—is but Jehovah's cold irony? What is our life then? But no—we must not become dispirited and give up. We shall come together, give our hands to each other and become closer: one of us has fallen—perhaps the best one. But others are arising and will arise; the hand of God does not cease to sow the seeds of great strivings in souls and, sooner or later, light will conquer the darkness. Yes, but for us who knew him, his loss is irreparable. Wasn't it Rahel[8] who said: "Wäre noch nie ein junger Mann gestorben, hätte man nie die Wehmuth gekannt" [If a young man never died, one would never know suffering]. Both grief and joy flow from the heart of the Creator. Freude und Leid [Joy and sorrow]: their sounds often vibrate with a similar ring and they merge: one is incomplete without the other. It is now grief's turn . . .

Good-bye; may *you* be well. Write me a word of response. I think that I love you even more since Stankevich's death.

Your I. Turgenev

Letter 5 (28). To Bettina von Arnim.[1]
End of 1840 or Beginning of 1841. Berlin.

My dear lady,

When you told me yesterday about that amazing association that arose in you while you observed the flickering fire, when you then spoke of nature as something animate and living and then at the end asked me whether I understood you, I answered in the affirmative: but it's very important for me to know whether I really understand it. This intimate link between the human spirit and nature is not by accident the most pleasant, most beautiful, and most profound phenomenon in our lives: only with a spiritual basis, with ideas, is it possible for our spirit and our thoughts to be joined so profoundly. However, in order to have the opportunity to enter into this union, one must be as ingenuous as nature itself, in order that each of nature's ideas and each of its movements be transformed in the human soul directly into conscious thoughts and spiritual images. But even a person who is still alien to truth feels that; the longing of evening, the quiet self-preoccupation of night and the thought-filled joy of morning alternate in his breast: he is made of flesh and blood, he breathes and sees; he cannot avoid nature's influence; he cannot live entirely in falsehood. The more intensely a person strives for the simplicity of truth, the richer and fuller will be his relationship with nature—and how could it be otherwise, since truth is nothing other than the nature of man? If you look from *this* point of view (and many people do)—then how infinitely sweet—and bitter—and joyous and at the same time painful life is! You find yourself in a constant struggle—and you can never save yourself by retreating: you must see the struggle through to the end. The profound, beautiful meaning of nature is suddenly revealed to us and disappears; these are presentiments which, as soon as they flutter out of one's soul immediately vanish; at times it seems that nature (and by nature I mean the whole living spirit made flesh) wants to speak—and suddenly it grows dumb and lies before us dead and silent;

26

the darkest night covers everything around. That we do not live in the truth is so easy to recognize!!! One need only go out into the open field or the forest—and if, in spite of the joyousness of one's soul, you nonetheless feel in its hidden depths a certain constraint, an inner enfetterment which appears just at that instant when nature takes possession of a man—then you learn your limits, that darkness which refuses to disappear in the bright light of self-oblivion, then you'll say to yourself: "You are still an egoist!" But that it is possible, as you said yesterday, to be freed of one's own personality and find it again in the spirit to which you've surrendered (*"the more multi-faceted, the more individual,"* as you say in your *Gündrode*[2])— you proved that to us yesterday—or no—you have lived it, and we observe. That you thought of Goethe while watching the wind carry the ashes away from the flame, and the *way* you thought of that was not, and I'm certain of this, a *comparison:* there was no disjunction between your cognition and your thought: the motion of nature was transformed directly into that thought: for just as all of nature, including its most hidden palpitations, is open to you, so is your spirit open to nature, your thoughts grow like plants out of the earth's soil—that is the same self-revelation of the spirit, which, like an organic image here, and the idea of that image there, like a sprout from the soul, reveals itself to the light. Every person ought to be like that: instead of doing as many do, for instance on hearing a nightingale sing, giving over to an utmost yearning, people ought to have in their breast an inexhaustible spring of thoughts full of the feeling of love—and just as multi-faceted and infinite as the focus of nature ought to be the focus of thoughts, divine and simple whether they be insignificant or great, like the word of nature, which is "God"—sometimes calm and restrained, like a deep valley at sunrise, sometimes unconstrained and wild, like a storm, as rich and varied as sound. To be one and infinitely diverse—isn't that really a miracle? Nature is *a* miracle and an entire world of miracles: that is the way every person should be—and is; and that he is, has been revealed to us by the great people of all ages. Could it really be that it is in vain that we are human beings? Could it really be in vain that everything spiritual in nature has been united in a single focus which is called "I"?[3] What would nature be without us, what would we be without nature? Both are unthinkable! A witness of the fact that you are blessed and will be blessed, that you are truthful and free, is in your love,—your compassion with nature, which grieves because it has been abandoned by humans: that is why it was frank with you, spoke to you, revealed to you its whole life—and its grief—like that brook to which you once called out, "Child, why are you weeping? What do you lack?" when it was babbling so anxiously in the reeds.[4] For that reason you have never described nature: I would say that under your pen nature was transformed into words; what that word means, what divinity is contained in it, what art and form are called—you were the first

27

to teach us that. I do not know whether you will believe it, but I want to be cognizant of what happiness I experience when I read you: I have been granted by heaven such capacities for self-oblivion that I can completely forget myself; I myself do not know whether what I have just written is also right; I don't even want to know; happiness is speaking through my lips, and I am giving it freedom to speak. When I cannot find a word, when it has been denied me, then even nature is denied me, because the word is the nature of the spirit and of the thought. But I experience myself inside: I have a premonition of blessedness, which is justified—the blessedness of truth. I have found the appropriate word: between you and nature there is no boundary; in both of you lives one and the same God, who manifests Himself in your consciousness as thought and revelation; is He great? How can you know this or express it? Does God see Himself as great? As you said yesterday: is thought really a property or a possession? Is not each of us a tool, and a spoken word—is not it the speech of God, the sense of which is revealed to you with the help of a joyous miracle? Only believe that you are always right—no matter what people say: through the simple contact with truth the genuine, the idea are revealed in every relationship. What people do not wish to admit, what frightens those hard of heart, we must admit: "He who is true is good, and free, and blessed—and wise," this is not an honor, but merely the simplest thing—and it ought to be the most ordinary and everyday of things.

Letter 6 (29). To A.V. Nikitenko.
May 27/June 8, 1841. Petersburg.

I recently (last week) arrived in Petersburg, dear Alexander Vasilievich, and was planning to visit you on Friday, but I have fallen ill and I doubt that by then I'll be in any condition to leave my room. I wanted to ask your advice about books that I am supposed to receive from abroad, and I am forced to resort to a letter. The problem is the following: I am expecting a box of books to arrive on the steamer *Alexandra* tomorrow; although I tried to select ones to which I assume censorship will not place any obstacles, yet it may be that there are some forbidden ones as well: to whom should I address myself and who has the authority to allow these books to be passed? I am a candidate in philosophy and intend to take the master's examinations:[1] these books are essential to me. If you would be so kind as to give me the name of the person on whom all this depends—I would drive out to see him tomorrow and talk things over with him.[2] I hope that you will not refuse my request and will not take offense at my having troubled you. Goodbye.

Entirely yours,

I. Turgenev

Letter 7 (35). To T.A. Bakunina.[1]
Late March/early June, 1842. Moscow.

It is impossible for me to leave Moscow, Tatyana Alexandrovna, without telling you how I feel. We separated in such a way and have become so alien to each other that I don't know whether you'll understand the reason for my taking pen in hand... You may perhaps think that I'm writing you for the sake of appearances... I deserve all of that and even worse.

But I wouldn't like to part from you that way, even for a time. Give me your hand and, if you can, forget all the painful and the illogical things of the past. All my soul is filled to overflowing with profound sorrow, and I feel disgust and horror if I look back: I want to forget everything, everything, except for your gaze, which I now see so indelibly and so clearly... It seems to me that I find forgiveness and reconciliation in it... Good Lord! How sad and marvellous I feel—how I would love to weep and press your hand to my lips and tell you everything—everything that is now pressing on my soul so tremorously.

I sometimes thought that I had parted from you forever; but all I had to do was just imagine that you no longer existed, that you had died... what profound grief would seize me—and grief not only because of your death, but because you had died not knowing me, without hearing a single sincere, honest word from me, such a word as would enlighten me as well and give me the opportunity to comprehend that strange link, profound, one that has fused with my entire being—the link between you and me... Don't smile distrustfully and sadly... I sense that I am speaking the truth and that there is no reason for me to lie.

And I sense that I am not parting from you forever... I will see you again... my good, beautiful sister. We have now lived like old people—or perhaps like children—life was slipping through our fingers and we

29

watched it as would children who do not yet have anything to regret, who still have much ahead of them—or like old people, who no longer even regret life... Just like the phantoms in Act II of *Robert le Diable*,[2] who dance and smile, but who know that all they need do is shake their heads, and their young bodies will fall away from their bones like a worn-out dress... It is so crowded, so cold, so gloomy in your aunt's house...[3] and you, poor thing, have been with them an eternity...

I stand before you and press your hand very, very firmly... I would like to pour hope, and strength, and joy into us... Listen to me: I swear by Almighty God that I'm telling the truth—I'm saying what I think and what I know: I have never loved any woman more than I do you—although even you I don't love with a complete and firm love... the reason I could not be gay and garrulous with you the way I was with others was that I loved you more than the others; on the other hand, I'm so certain—always—that you and you alone can understand me; for you alone I would like to be a poet, for you, with whom my soul is linked in some inexpressibly marvellous way, so that I almost need not see you, so that I don't feel the need to speak with you—because I can't say what I'd like to—and in spite of that—in the hours of creativity and solitary, profound bliss you do not leave me; I read you what flows from my pen—to you, my beautiful sister... Oh, if I could even just once walk alone with you some spring morning down a long, long linden-shaded lane, take your hand in my hands and feel our souls merge and everything foreign, everything painful disappear, everything perfidious evaporate—and forever. Yes, you command *all* my soul's love, and if I could express it—*before you*—we wouldn't find ourselves in such a difficult situation... and I would know *how* I love you.

Look how constantly you are with me in all my best moments: here's Serafina's song from "Don Juan"[4] for you. I'll tell you about it someday... but you'll understand for yourself. I know you won't think that Serafina is you and that the person to whom she says that is me: that would be too funny and stupid; but my regard for you...

Your image, your being are always alive in me, changing and growing and taking on new form, like Proteus: you are my *Muse;* so, for instance, the figure of Serafina developed out of thoughts about you, just as did the image of Inez and perhaps Donna Anna,—why am I saying perhaps?— everything that I think and create is connected with you in a wonderful way.

Farewell, my sister; give me your blessing for the road—and consider me—for the meantime—a rock, which though as yet mute, nonetheless conceals in its very depths of a stone heart true love and the ability to be touched.

Farewell, I am profoundly agitated and touched—farewell, my best, my only friend.[5]

Until we meet again.[6]

30

Letter 8 (36). To Alexey and Alexander Bakunin.[1]
April 3/15, 1842. Petersburg.

Petersburg, April 3, 1842.

Even though I didn't promise to write to you, o children, I'm writing, assuming that you won't be angry. In addition I'm sending you Goethe's letters to Stolberg[2]—today, but by parcel post. I've been here since March 30. Next week I have an examination in philosophy—I'm studying for it and not seeing anyone. But I did go to Rzhevsky's[3] and there I saw Klyushnikov,[4] whom I liked very much. He has become a completely different person. My brother has given over to me a beautiful room with a fireplace and *three*—N.B.—three voltaire chairs: and the number of pillows is beyond human understanding. We live on an isolated street— there's no noise at any time of the day—my brother is hardly ever at home; in the morning I drink marvellous tea (with excellent rolls) from wonderful big English cups, I even have a lamp on the table. In a word, I'm living in bliss and with agitated, secret, ecstatic pleasure I'm enjoying isolation— and I'm working—working a lot. For example, yesterday I consumed Descartes, Spinoza, and Leibnitz at a single sitting; Leibnitz is still growling in my stomach—and I helped myself to Kant—and then got down to work on Fichte: but that person is somewhat stale, and therefore I am taking a break and writing a letter to you.

I've told you a thousand times that you're children and that you've experienced nothing; for instance, you've never known the complete bliss of isolation; one ought to know how to give over to isolation too, but you... Well, enough about you—better I should write about myself, a much more interesting subject.—And so:

"I"

am sitting in an armchair before the fireplace and reading Fichte; here's my train of thought:
...Wir sollen einen absoluten Grundsatz finden [We must find an absolute first principle]...hm...hm...I ought to put some more wood on (which I do...), das *Ich* setzt sich als Nicht *Ich* [the *I* posits not *I*]...hm...Silently I sit under the prison window[5]...right after that a whole whirlwind of thoughts...(but it's no business of yours what they are). Fichte behauptet [asserts]—I read those two words 25 times in a row without understanding—finally I shake my head and try again...I yawn; get up—walk over to the window and sing: ta-ri-tam, taritam, tarita...ra-ra (a sonata by Grund[6])...I watch the falling snowflakes for ten minutes or so...I pace a little: imagine myself as a minister—"it's time, it's time,"[7]—

and I again sit down to Fichte—first I spend five minutes watching the fire and smiling—then: im Ich ist das Princip sich zu setzen und das Princip—sich auch nicht zusetzen [in the I is the principle of sitting down and the principle of not sitting down as well]...[8]

Oh, the rapture, rapture, rapture of solitary, unhurried work that allows one to dream and think nonsense and even to write it.

I have a good poem, "At the Station"[9]—I'll read it to you when I visit you in Moscow.

But forgive my nonsense. Write to me if you find the opportunity. My address is: "Grafsky Lane, Kasovskaya's house." Give my regards to Tatyana Alexandrovna[10] and please write me about her health.

I have a little song that starts like this:

> Oh you children, o children,
> Oh, dear ones, good-bye!
> If you want to—forget me,
> If you want to—think of me!

and so on.

Addio, signori miei, e voi, Alexeo (how do you say Alexey in Italian), o Allesio, o Alexiso, e voi Alessandro, e tutti quanti.

Turgenev

Letter 9 (48). To Pauline Viardot.[1]
May 9/21, 1844. Petersburg.

March 9, 1844. Petersburg.

I returned to Petersburg from Moscow four days ago, my good, dear Mme Viardot, and now, having seen a passage marked off for me in Eugène's letter, I am taking advantage of this opportunity to send you my regards, too.

My stay in Moscow was not especially pleasant. Pneumonia confined me to my room for two whole months and so on. But now I've finally returned here.

It was with great pleasure that I learned from the *Allgemeine Theaterzeitung*[2] that you arrived in Vienna in good health and I hope that after a rest in France you'll come back to us—won't you? Your "good city" of Petersburg[3] awaits you impatiently. Judge for yourself how your close friends, your "faithful" followers, your "old guard" must feel. I've seen them all.[4] We've chatted, and as Pizzo[5] says, "we've gossiped maliciously on your account." I can't say that we reminisced about a multitude of things, because we haven't forgotten anything; but we provide each other the pleasure of repeating it all to each other. I've chatted especially a lot with Pizzo: what a noble, fine fellow he is; how sincerely devoted to you he is! I made him sing until his voice was completely exhausted: everything—the final scene of *Romeo,*[6] and "Die Stadt"[7]... By the way, why didn't you ever sing me anything from your *Album?* Do you know that there are remarkable things in it?—for instance, "La Chapelle" or "L'Ombre et le Jour";[8] all of those things are permeated with a profound melancholy, gloomy and gentle, which moves one and makes one weep; and along with that, what truth of expression!... I've had the opportunity to judge about that.

Pizzo is going to Vienna the 27th, and I am staying here. There's no point in even thinking about plans for a trip of some kind...

In six weeks you'll be in France. I rejoice ahead of time at the joy that is promised by your seeing your mother, your child,[9] and all your good friends. But... if your thoughts ever take you to Petersburg—I hope that now you won't be afraid, as you were before your first trip, that you won't find sincere and faithful friends here. I must tell you that you have left a profound impression here: you are spoken of and loved...

I'll spend the summer in the environs of Petersburg;[10] all that I'm going to do from morning till night is hunt. It's so good to be out amidst the fields all day: you can dream as much as you want there, and after all, you know that I'm a little bit of a dreamer by birth. By the way, speaking of hunting—I hope that Viardot[11] had the opportunity for some good hunting. If my letter catches him in Vienna, tell him a thousand good things from me and ask him to write me a couple of words, which can be addressed c/o me at the Ministry of Internal Affairs.[12]

I wanted to take a look at our nice little rooms here, but someone is now living there.

Excuse me for talking to you about all of this. But what can I do? We unfortunate victims of starvation feed on our reminiscences...

And so, farewell or better, until we see each other. Be happy. When I speak that word, there's nothing for me to add to it, because I say it from the bottom of my heart, and I say it often, because it seems to me that such wishes must realize themselves.

Once again farewell and allow me to press your hand, as in the past.

Your most devoted friend,

I. Turgenev

Letter 10 (58). To Pauline Viardot.
November 28, December 3/December 10, 15, 1846. Petersburg.

November 28/December 10, 1846. Petersburg.

It will soon be three weeks since I wrote you. It seems to me that you wish to have news about the theater and about Petersburg, and for that reason I again take pen in hand. But if what I imagine is perhaps without foundation, I nonetheless hope that you will not deprive me of such an excellent opportunity to write you.

To begin with, I'll tell you that in all likelihood I'll have the pleasure of seeing you in mid-January of the coming year. I've more or less arranged my affairs and count on being free by the arrival of the new year. So, you are forewarned. Be in voice, for then I'll present myself to you terribly starved for good music, because, to tell the truth, the local opera "ist auf den Hund" [for the dogs], as the students say.

Since writing to Mme Garcia[1] (I kiss her hands) in the way of novelties I've seen *Gazza, Ernani,* and *La Fille du Régiment.*[2] You can't imagine with what cruelty that unfortunate *Gazza* was murdered. You remember that Mme Moltini[3] (last year's) sometimes received at least some applause; this year—none, absolutely none, quite literally. True, one has to admit that never has such a remarkable fool (excuse the expression) trod the boards of the Bolshoy Theater . . . Enormous cuts were made in the libretto of *Gazza:* the second act begins with Ninetta and Pippo's duet: then the trial scene follows immediately—so that it's impossible to understand anything . . . The audience was icy, as were the actors. That didn't prevent me, however, from finding *Gazza* a real chef d'oeuvre, full of grace and talent, and at times rising to stunning drama. That trampling of lace in the mud was all the more painful. And imagine—in addition to everything else, Mme Moltini imitates you!! You can imagine that! She must have heard you somewhere . . .

December 3/15

My letter remained unfinished. I'm hurrying to finish it today. *Ernani* is being played with a large ensemble. The singers (Mme Giuli, Guasco and Collini)[4] obviously feel closer to Verdi then to Rossini. I like the opera itself only mildly. However, the final trio makes an impression, in spite of the vulgarity of melody. It has to be encored. There's no denying that Verdi is occasionally capable of producing a feeling of greatness. And all the same I'm far from being a Verdian and don't think that I'll ever become one.

You know, of course, that *La Fille du Régiment* is just barely an opera.

Thanks to Tamburini's[5] acting, two or three attractive melodies, and the originality of the plot, the public was satisfied and made Mme Marra[6] repeat the "drum roll," which can scarcely have been flattering for the singer. *Fille du Régiment* nonetheless attracted 800 people to the theater, and that's the nec plus ultra this year. Well, that's all our theatrical news.

The most kind General Gulevich[7] has finally returned to Petersburg. He instructed me to say a thousand nice things to you and hopes that you will write to him. I saw Count M.,[8] who told me that he had received a *long* and *good* letter from you; that's how he put it. That calmed me a little: the *Allgemeine Preussische Staatzeitung* (in a report on the Italian opera) spoke of "merkliche Indisposition" [obvious indisposition], which upset me considerably. It is true, isn't it, that you're in good health? Take care of yourself, I implore you.

You will receive my letter a few days before your debuts in German opera... Need I say that my sincerest wishes accompany you there? But you don't doubt that, and that gives me great pleasure. It's wonderful to think that those whom you love know about it and rely on it.

I've been very busy all this time, and I'm still busy, thanks to our new journal.[9] But I'll try to arrange everything so that I can leave Petersburg when the New Year arrives. That's why I'm working as hard as I can. I've taken several obligations upon myself, I want to fulfill them and I will.

And at the end of these two months of intense work I see a mass of enchanting things awaiting me and giving me vigor. What a wonderful thing, after all, is just the opportunity to say "until we meet"[10] to you.

Until we meet, all you my good friends; I press your hand sincerely (I hope that your husband has already returned from Paris). Be happy. I wish you good health.

Your devoted I. Turgenev

Letter 11 (66). To V.G. Belinsky.[1]
September 5/17, 1847. Courtavenel.

Courtavenel
September 17, 1847

You're leaving for Russia, dear Belinsky;[2] I can't say good-bye to you in person—but I don't want to let you go without saying a word of farewell—(by the way, in a letter to Annenkov[3] I sent you a ticket[4] to get the fur coat, and I beg your pardon for not having done that a long time ago). Annenkov didn't write me anything about your health; he preferred to fill his note with that Attic salt[5] of his wit which sometimes amazingly reminds one of the taste of Slavic buzun, as Gogol says.[6] I hope that Dr. Tira[7] helped you: I beg you to write me about that. There's no need for me to assure you that any good news about you will gladden me; even though I'm nothing but a little boy (as you say)—and generally an empty-headed person. I do know how to love good people and I become attached to them for a long time. Lately I haven't accomplished anything useful; I wrote two more long sketches, however.[8] I rewrote the old ones and sent them to Nekrasov.[9] If they haven't yet been published by the time you arrive in Petersburg, have mercy on me and take the proofreading upon yourself. If no devilry gets in my way, I myself hope to be in Petersburg by New Year's.[10] As of yet I can't say anything for certain. What will be, will be—a great phrase for fatalists and imbeciles like me. When you arrive in Petersburg, please give my best regards to your family and all our friends—and write me a couple of words; I will be very obliged. And for Heaven's sake, pay attention to what you eat—or you'll upset your stomach again. And now good-bye. I hope with all my heart that your trip has not been useless and that it has given you new strength. I embrace you firmly. Good-bye.

Your Turgenev

Letter 12 (69). To Pauline Viardot.
November 14, 15/26, 27, 1847. Paris.

Paris. November 26, 1847.

I don't want you to leave Dresden without having received another greeting from me, but this time I can't give you much news. Your mother has been so good all along—she's been showing me your letters to her... You can imagine what pleasure they gave me. There's absolutely nothing better than receiving letters! We can only thank you for the marvellous particulars that you've been writing about your Dresden life.

Mlle Kamenskaya[1] has obviously conquered you. It would be good if we could find the same sort of little corner in Berlin! We'll ask your "star" to continue being favorable to you: it ought to try to be worthy of the honor of governing your fortunes! Jokes aside, everything is fine, yes, fine, much bien [good] so far; God grant that it remain so to the end.

Of ourselves we[2] can also say that everything is going well. We feel fine, see each other often, often think about those absent. We gather at the Spanish "brasero" [hearth] every evening and *speak Spanish*. In four months or so I'll be speaking only that language. My teacher paid me many compliments on my ability... he doesn't know that I have a bump for memorization.[3]

I'm living in a small, very clean apartment that is well-furnished. I like it very much (that's very important, you know, when you want to work). It's pleasant; it's warm, and I live there like a fly... a fly of the largest breed...

By the way, in Germany I promise to sing you some of your songs— "La Luciole" or "Chanson de Loëc,"[4] for instance.

Saturday, the 27th.

I'll move on to my little revue de Paris [survey of Paris].

Yesterday they put on Verdi's *Lombardi*, under the title *Jérusalem*, for the first time at the Grand Opera. The libretto has been redone. They've introduced a scene of the knight's devotion—for Duprez.[5] Verdi, for his part, has written several new morceaux [bits] that are absolutely revolting. I won't tell you about the music, you know it—it's the summit of awfulness. But what's unimaginable is the performance. There is no other theater in the world, except perhaps the "Académie Royale de musique,"[6] where all the singers, if they turned out to be as bad as Duprez e tutti quanti [and the like], wouldn't be buried under a Chimborazo[7] of rotten apples.

Considering the quantity of horses and singers on stage, the opera's success was not as great as one would expect. After all, it's well known that as far as music goes, the French love horses and dancers' calves most of all. And then that unending "deguelando,"[8] as your brother[9] says, whom I met on leaving the theater, furious and ready to bite. That allegedly "broad style," which is very convenient for people who don't know how to sing, those inflated recitatives, those unison choruses to gallop or polka themes... No, don't sing in Paris, this is no place for you!

It absolutely seems that the time of powerful and healthy geniuses has passed; coarse, banal strength is on the side of such facile and productive mediocrities as Verdi. And, quite to the contrary, those to whom the divine fire is given waste away in idleness, weakness, or dreams; the gods are envious: they don't give anyone everything at once. And yet—why then were our fathers luckier than we? Why was it granted to them to be present at the first performances of such things as *The Barber of Seville*, to at least see *Norma*,[10] while we poor things are condemned to *Jérusalems*. Why do our young talents, our "hopes," instead of giving us abundant works, which though perhaps not produced according to all the rules, but full of strength and sap,—why instead of that do they bring forth (at the most!) small works that are well polished, well washed, well finished... What does this premature old age mean? Why are they already copying themselves in their second work? Why do they say their farewells so soon? Take Etienne Arago, for instance, who just gave us a comedy that is definitely witty *(Aristocraties),*[11] but which is an old, stagey, artificially put together thing. Why all of this like that? Why is there no longer anything original, direct, and strong? How can this absence of blood and sap be explained?

I haven't had the chance to see *Cleopatra* yet. Rachel[12] is ill. I'm now looking over the second volume of Michelet, where there are many excellent things.[13] George Sand has published a very laudatory article about Louis Blanc[14] in *Siècle.* It makes an impression of unpleasant exaggeration. She is now consumed by a passion for Louis Blanc... We know how that usually ends with her.

I'm having a "party" tomorrow. The whole "family"[15] will be here. The fact is that my room will accommodate ten people—I assure you.

My Spanish is coming along excellently. I repeat: everything is going well, even very well, bien, très bien, mais très bien [well, very well, but very well], as M. Tampoux says.[16] Your mother is a little surprised not to have received a letter from you today... True, the mail here is very bad. It takes five days for letters to get from Dresden to Paris, but when they arrive, you can imagine how "wilkommen" they are!

A thousand regards to your husband, a nice kiss to your daughter. I press your hand affectionately and beg you not forget me.

Are you going to Hamburg? Bon voyage! Be healthy, all of you.

Your devoted Iv. Turgenev.

Letter 13 (75). To Pauline Viardot.[1]
December 23/January 4, 1847/1848. Paris.

Paris. January 4, 1848.

Ah! Madame, what a lovely thing long letters are!—such as the one you just wrote to your "grandmother",[2] for instance! With what pleasure one begins reading! It's as if one were entering a long, verdant, cool pathway in summer. "Ah, it's wonderful here," one says to oneself; and one walks on quietly, one hears the birds warbling. You warble much better than they. Madame; please continue to do so; be assured that you will never find more attentive and appreciative listeners. Imagine, Madame, your mother sitting by her fire, making me read aloud your letter which she has already had almost enough time to memorize. Right now would be the time to paint her portrait!...[3] By the way, I haven't yet seen her portrait; she doesn't want to show it before it's finished, but that will be soon. I want to ask M. Léon[4] to do my portrait too, in pencil. Also, wilkommen in Berlin [and so, welcome to Berlin]? I know where you're staying—not far from the Brandenburg Gate? Excuse me if I allow myself to speak of certain details of your apartment: why is it that certain places in it, which can be mentioned only in English—probably because the English are the most modest in their expressions—why is it that those places are subjected to the mercy of the elements and the severity of the cold? Please, take care of yourself and somehow correct that flaw; this is more serious than it might seem at first glance, considering that it's the season for flu and rheumatism.

You'll probably laugh at me and at what topics I include in my letter. I can see you smiling from here, raising your right shoulder a bit and inclining your head in the same direction (that's your usual gesture; and I don't advise you to part with it, because it's very beautiful, especially when accompanied by a certain facial expression). I see your friend Müller's reddish beard dropping.[5]

And so, you made your debut in *La Juive*?[6] Just the title *La Juive* resurrects before me a mass of images and summons up many reminiscences. M. Kraus with his outstanding upper teeth, his laugh, and his leaden-colored fingers; M. Lanz—so honeyed, so restrained, so tenderly moved by his own merits. The married couple Pille-au-Nid, the fat M. Dalwatie, etc., etc.

And have you widened your circle of acquaintances this season?

Once again—willkommen in Berlin. Be healthy, cheerful, and happy. If you could find another Countess Kamenskaya there or make the real one part with Dresden for a while!

I should chat with you a little about Paris, however, and about what's going on here. As regards myself, time is not passing very quickly for me. And meanwhile we've had no lack of events: the death of Mme Adélaïde,[7] Abd-el-Kader's capture[8] (there's a person who didn't manage to die in time), the New Year, the opening of the Chamber of Deputies, the closing down of Michelet's lectures,[9] and so on and so forth. But your husband has probably already told you about that.

On New Year's Day we dined en famille at your mother's. In the evening we played salon games, and Gui kept proposing such tasks for the loser...hm...hm...At the conclusion he even embraced Mlle Antonia around the waist and loudly kissed her on the cheek...Although I'm mistaken, he couldn't kiss her loudly, since he doesn't have any teeth. In general we had a very good time.

The day before yesterday Leroy[10] took me to see a certain Mme Noirfontaine...I was very bored there! And even there, to my surprise, I noticed a certain scent of Petersburg society, which hardly enchanted me. True, the hostess' husband was a bureaucrat, and all bureaucrats are alike.

I heard *Elisir d'Amore* at the Italian Opera.[11] It was very funny. Mme Persiani[12] swims in her role (as far as the voice is concerned) like a fish in water. I assure you, ganz objectiv gesprochen [quite objectively speaking] as our German friends say, you're better in that role—much better! Mme Persiani must be a spiteful woman: when Nemorino[13] comes to her in the third act with his ardent requests, she makes a gesture that reminded me of one of my mother's maids—the coldest, most spiteful creature that I've ever had occasion to know. There seemed to rise in her throat the acute pleasure of vengeance—the desire to do evil. It was disgusting—ugh! I remember that you also seemed very pleased by the chance to take revenge on Nemorino, who had been forced to ask for your mercy; but with you that was only a slight bit of dark embroidery on a white background. When a person is kind at the bottom of his soul—he can allow himself these little pleasures. Long live the devil, when we ride him!

Yesterday I saw Auber's new opera *Haydée*. It's a comic opera with all the devices of grand opera. Grand duets, grand phrases, grand words—and not a single melody. Perhaps that's the explanation for its success...The very title is boring and false. It's the story of a person, a certain Guden, who had performed one base act in his life: he'd cheated at cards. The person he was playing with committed suicide; and the murderer is plagued by pangs of conscience. He sees himself in a dream; his enemy makes use of that and so on. At the conclusion virtue triumphs, but in this case, though, it's not virtue, but repentant vice, and malice is conquered. Two women are involved in the story. The denouement is strikingly untrue to life. It's exaggerated Scribe.[14] There are some nice things in it every so often. But when will this reign of old folks come to an end? We're fed up with these toothless delights and their wit, which was appropriate when they were twenty. What on earth are the young and the strong doing?

Mlle Grimm has a small, very fresh and wobbly voice. Mlle Lavoye[15] is so-so. I think she looks like Karatygina (facially).[16] They both pull up their lower lips, arch their brows, and throw back their heads when they want to take high notes easily; that gives them an amazingly funny appearance; they begin to resemble a goose when you take it by the bill. I sat close to the orchestra; a book lay in front of me—a history of Paris—and during the intermissions I read excerpts from contemporaries' stories about Bartholomew's Night, about the murder of the followers of Armaniac and

other delights.[17] Cruel passions, torrents of blood, unnecessary bestiality—
and suddenly the curtain rises, and I see Mlle Lavoye, all got up, with her
little finger thrust out just like this...[18] What an amusing contrast!

Man is a very strange creature!

But on this new thought I take my leave. Thank you very much, very
much[19] for the several words addressed to me in your letter to Mme García.
I was very glad to receive a letter from M. Louis. I send you the most
amicable greeting. I thank Lizochka for her remembering me and I repay
her in the same way.

Goodbye. I wish you everything that's best in the world.

Your devoted

Iv. Turgenev.

Letter 14 (98). To Pauline Viardot.[1]
May 29/June 10, 1849. Paris.

Sunday morning.

Rayer[2] just left; and not for anything does he want to allow me to go
out earlier than tomorrow afternoon, and even at that he has given
permission only for a short ride in a carriage.

By the way, Bugeaud[3] died last night. I am terribly alarmed by what I
read in the papers: there is a cry of displeasure all the way around! All of
them—including *Presse,* and *National* and *Siècle*—all of them are calling
the French to arms. And they're right. How much incompetence and
arrogance has been revealed, how much perfidy and cynicism! They expect
an explosion today or tomorrow.

I've learned of two items of news from reliable sources: Haynau was
crushed by the Hungarians at the walls of Presburg, and things were much
worse than the newspapers report.[4] But on the other hand, the Russians
shattered Dembinski.[5] To hell with all nationalistic feeling! For a person
with a heart there is only one fatherland—democracy, and if the Russians
are victorious, it will be delivered a mortal blow...

I'll write to you tomorrow. I can't come to Courtavenel earlier than
Wednesday or Thursday. So until then—be healthy and may God bless you
a thousand times.

41

My cordial regards to all the inhabitants of your estate. I press your hand firmly. Auf Wiedersehen!

Your I. Turgenev.

Letter 15 (118). To A.A. Krayevsky.[1]
October 22/November 3, 1849. Paris.

Paris.
October 22/November 3, 1849.

Vague rumors have reached me, dear Krayevsky, that you have published my *The Bachelor* in *Notes of the Fatherland.*[2] I hope that the Russian public likes it. But that's not the point—here's what it is: I received a letter from my brother in which, after an eloquent description of the disorder of our affairs due to my mother's illness and similar circumstances, he informs me of sad news, namely: I not only won't receive from him the 6000 rubles owed me for the current year, but I should not to hope for any assistance from the parental home at all. That news has perturbed me in the extreme—and that's why I'm turning to you with the following urgent request? How much do I owe you after *The Bachelor?* Let's assume: X; add to that 300 silver rubles, and I'll owe you 300 silver rubles + X. I can assure you that I'll soon earn all of that (after all, it's not my fault that *The Hanger-On* was decapitated).[3] I agree with you that I ought to include with this letter a literary piece—but you also must understand that right now I don't even have a farthing in cash—and instead of 6000 rubles that I was awaiting like manna from heaven—zero!—And therefore the sooner you send me that money, the more I will respect you and the more ardently I will act to fill *Notes of the Fatherland* with original pieces, as you gentlemen of the journals say in your announcements à l'adresse des [intended for] inhabitants of other cities. As for *Notes of the Fatherland,* I've already lost all hope of seeing it with my own eyes—you might at least send me one copy of *The Bachelor!* My address: Rue et Hôtel du Port-Mahon, No. 9. I shall be awaiting your answer with eagerness, and I hope to God not with hunger.[4] I wish you all the best, press your hand, and remain

Devotedly yours,

I. Turgenev.

Here's a list for you of the pieces intended for *Notes of the Fatherland:*

1. "The Diary of a Superfluous Man," sort of a story.
2. *The Party,* a comedy in one act.
3. *The Governess,* a comedy in five acts.[5]

And, by the way, write me a few words about the state of our literature, which for me has become unusually mysterious and extremely unfamiliar.

Letter 16 (120) To A.A. Krayevsky.
December 13/25, 1849. Paris.

Paris.
December 13/25, 1849

    I just this minute received your letter, dear Krayevsky, with the 300 silver rubles enclosed,[1] and I am answering immediately. This money has positively saved me from death by starvation—and I'm intent on proving my gratitude to you. In the first place, I'm sending you a rewritten third of "The Diary",[2] a piece long since finished, but because of my unforgivable laziness and sloth, as yet not completely recopied; I'm sending it to prove to you that this "Diary" is not a myth; I'll work day and night on the rest of the things—and may I be a Bulgarin[3] if within two weeks you don't receive the conclusion, *along with a report on "Le Prophète."*[4] As regards *The Governess,* that comedy is absolutely separate from *The Student*—and on this point I must ask your forgiveness. I had forgotten that I'd promised you *The Student* and promised it to *The Contemporary;*[5] but you won't lose anything because of this; because I give you my word of honor not to send *The Student* to *The Contemporary* any earlier than I send you *The Governess. The Student* is up to the fourth act, *The Governess* to the third (both comedies are in five acts). Again, I beg your pardon if any misunderstandings arise because of this. *The Party* is absolutely finished, but I don't know whether I shouldn't rewrite it, because the censor will surely maim it. That's the accurate and true *"state of affairs."* Supporting evidence for my activity may be found in the fact that my break with Mama is now final, *and that I have to earn my daily bread.*[6] As a result of that you won't blame me if I tell you that my price per printer's page[7] is 200 paper rubles. I take 50 silver rubles a page from *The Contemporary*—and you

43

know yourself the difference between your page and *The Contemporary*'s. That means that instead of owing you 610 silver rubles 85 kopeks—I subtract 28 rubles 57 1/2 kopeks (100 rubles—25 per page)—that leaves 582 silver rubles 27 1/2 kopeks. A decent sum—but you'll see how fast I earn it. Your advice about my returning is extraordinarily sensible—and I'm very grateful for your concern; but even without it I was firmly resolved *to return in the spring.* It's time—as you say. I'll be in your office at the beginning of May.[8]

I thank you for your promise about *Notes of the Fatherland.* I hope that you are well and in good spirits—I wish you all the best. I would hope that you like "The Diary": I wrote it con amore [with love].

I press your hand firmly and remain

Your devoted

I. Turgenev.

P.S. Please keep my manuscripts until I arrive. In two weeks—the conclusion of "The Diary."

Letter 17 (123). To A.A. Krayevsky.
March 23 (April 4), 1850. Paris.

Paris.
March 24 (April 4), 1850

You perhaps have not forgotten, dear Krayevsky, that I had planned to return to Russia in May;[1] I now wish to return more than ever before; there's only one thing I lack for that: money. I feel guilty talking about this to you, to whom I am much obliged as it is; but I'm only asking for a little: 200 silver rubles. In return I offer you, besides my gratitude—(1) *The Hanger-On* which has at last been *allowed* in Moscow (as far as I can tell from a letter from there); (2) my short one-act comedy *Breakfast at the Marshal's,* which the esteemed editors of *The Contemporary* will entrust to you—(their censor wouldn't let it by for some reason—although it was passed for the theater);[2] (3) a piece entitled "A Correspondence," which I'll

44

either send you before my departure or bring with me[3]—and finally, (4) my full-scale comedy *The Governess,* which I'll finish in Russia. I plan to leave here in mid-May—and I'll sail to Petersburg on the first steamer out of Stettin. I'm leaving Paris in a few days and I'll be staying in Brussels until my final departure.[4] If you are of a mind to help me, then send the 200 rubles to Brussels poste restante—*before* May 10th (New Style).[5] After I arrive in Petersburg we'll settle up—and I'll even be able to return your money right then—if you need it, because my family, which hasn't sent me so much as a farthing for half a year, will probably be generous when it learns of my return. My request is very important—and you can earn my intense gratitude. And therefore, relying on you, I remain your devoted

I. Turgenev.

P.S. How soon I clasp your hand depends on you. Don't forget my address (*before* May 10th [New Style])—Brussels, poste restante.

Letter 18 (124) To Pauline Viardot.[1]
May 4/16, 1850. Courtavenel.

May 16, 1850

I am at Courtavenel. I assure you that I'm happy as a child to be here. I went to say hello to all the places that I'd said good-bye to before my departure. Russia awaits; that immense and somber figure, immobile and mysterious as Oedipus' sphinx. She will swallow me up later. I seem to see her happy, lifeless gaze fixed on me with that icy attention so appropriate for eyes of stone. Be calm, sphinx, I'll return to you and you will be able to devour me at your pleasure if I fail to divine your enigma. But leave me in peace a little while longer! I'll return to your steppes!

It has been very lonely weather today. Gounod spent the whole day walking in the Blondureau woods searching for an idea; but inspiration, capricious as a woman, didn't come, and he didn't find anything. At least that's what he himself told me. He'll take his revenge tomorrow. At this moment he's lying in labor on a bear skin. He displays an obstinacy and tenacity in his work which excite my admiration. Today's wasted afternoon makes him very unhappy; he is unable to distract himself from his preoccupation. In his desolation he has set to work on a text. I tried to cheer him up and he seems better. It is very dangerous to allow oneself to slip down that incline: one ends up by crossing one's fingers over one's stomach and saying: "But this is all atrocious!" I found it a little funny to listen to his complaints, since I know that all these little clouds will dissipate with the first breeze, and I'm very flattered to be privy to these little pangs of creation . . . [2]

Iv. Tourguéneff.

Letter 19 (126). To A.I. Herzen.[1]
June 10/22, 1850. Paris.

Paris.
June 10/22, 1850

I arrived from the country, dear Alexander, an hour after your departure[2]—you can imagine how vexed I was—I would have been so glad to see you once before returning to Russia. Yes, brother, I am returning; all my things are packed, and the day after tomorrow I leave Paris and in a week, on Saturday, I'll board a steamship at Stettin. You may be assured that all your letters and papers will be delivered intact—and although you didn't even deign to notify me of your place of arrival—I'll fulfill all my promises; I'll send you books and journals c/o Miss Erne at Rothschild's;[3] I'll go see him today and inform him of this. God only knows when I'll have the chance to write to you again, God only knows what awaits me in Russia—mais le vin est tiré—il faut le boire [the wine has been drawn—it must be drunk]. In case of any important development—you can notify me by placing in the *Journal des Débats* an announcement que M. Louis Morisset de Caen, etc. I will be reading that journal and will understand what you want to tell me.[4] Farewell, dear Herzen; I wish you all the best; I'll embrace all your friends for you—we'll be talking a lot about you. Via the same address I'll try to send you information about Ogaryov[5] and the others. Be healthy and do whatever you can. I press your wife's hand firmly and kiss your children. Regards to Herwegh[6] and his wife. I embrace you once more and remain

Your

I. Turgenev.

46

Letter 20 (132). To Pauline Viardot.[1]
October 23/November 4, 1850. Petersburg.

St. Petersburg, Monday, October 23 O.S., 1850

Here is little Pauline,[2] dear Mme Viardot, and this note will be delivered to you by Mlle Robert,[3] who has kindly taken the girl's care upon herself. I've entrusted her with 400 francs (100 rubles) for travelling expenses; please give her another 50 francs on my behalf as a sign of my gratitude. Please be so good as to inform me of her arrival. I thank you beforehand from the bottom of my heart for your kind treatment of the girl; I can only reiterate my profound devotion to you. I'll write you tomorrow: this is just a note that I'll send via Mlle Robert.

Be happy; may Heaven bless every step of your life.

Your I.Turgenev.

Letter 21 (133) To Pauline Viardot.[1]
October 26, 28, 30/November 7, 9, 11, 1850. Petersburg.

St. Petersburg, Thursday, Oct. 26 (Nov. 7), 1850.

My dear, good Mme Viardot, theuerste, liebste, beste Frau [dearest, most beloved, best woman], how are you? Have you already made your debut? Do you think of me often? A day doesn't pass without the precious recollection of you coming to mind hundreds of times; a night doesn't pass without my dreaming of you. Now that we are separated, I feel more than ever the strength of my ties to you and your family; I'm happy that I enjoy your sympathies, and I'm sad that I'm so far away from you! I implore Heaven to send me patience and not to delay too long that moment, which I bless a thousand times beforehand, when I will see you again.

My work for *The Contemporary* is finished and has turned out better than I had expected. It's a supplement to *Notes of a Hunter*, another story where, in a slightly prettified form, I have portrayed a competition between two folk singers at which I was present two months ago.[2] The childhood of all nations is similar, and my singers reminded me of Homer. Then I stopped thinking about that, since otherwise my pen would have fallen out of my hand. The contest took place in a tavern, and there were a lot of unusual types there, whom I attempted to draw à la Teniers[3] . . . Damn it! What thunderous names I quote at any convenient opportunity! You see, we minor literati who are worth two sous need strong crutches in order to move.

In a word, I like my story—and thank God!

Saturday, October 28.

Today is my birthday, and you can easily understand that I couldn't let it pass without extending you both my hands. Today I am entering my thirty-second year . . . [4] I'm growing old! It is exactly seven years today since I first met your husband at Major Komarov's;[5] do you remember that funny creature? On next Tuesday it will be seven years since I was at your place for the first time. And here we have remained friends and, I think, good friends. And I'm happy to tell you that in those seven years that have passed I've never seen anything on earth better than you, that to meet you on my path was the greatest good fortune of my life, that my devotion and gratitude to you know no bounds and will die only together with me. May God bless you a thousand times! I pray to Him for that, on my knees, with my hands pressed together. You are everything that is best, noblest, and the nicest on this earth.

This evening there will be a large gathering of friends at Tyutchev's to celebrate his birthday and mine: we were born on the same day. He's an outstanding fellow, and I love him with all my heart, his wife—too. By the way, don't forget to check to see whether you can arrange what I asked you to do for them.[7]

At this moment Pauline should be en route from Warsaw to Berlin.[8] I hope that she arrives safe and sound. There is little to add about her personality to what I've already said; I think, though, that she is more receptive than I used to think; during the two weeks she spent at the Tyutchevs' she apparently changed very much for the better. I don't as yet feel any great tenderness toward her; perhaps that will come later. But I've firmly decided from this time forth to do everything for her that will depend on me.

I need to make a correction to what I wrote in my last letter. Yesterday morning I was at Count Mikhail Vielgorsky's and I saw Count Matvey there;[9] they both take the liveliest interest in you, peppered me with questions about you, about Fidès,[10] about your plans and so on. I talked a lot about you as well as about Gounod, who can now count two more friends and admirers in Russia. Count Mikhail asked me to *implore* him to send them something (for instance, "Sanctus" or the *Requiem*); they agree to have whatever is sent performed with the help of all the enormous means at their disposal. Say a couple of words about this to Gounod; why shouldn't he do it? He can be certain that everything will be done to assure a worthy performance of the task. It seems that nothing was done in England. You would have mentioned it. Petersburg does not approach London as regards music, but nonetheless the public here deserves attention. You know that well.

Monday, Oct 31 (November 12).

I just received your letter dear, kind, Mme Viadot: how it saddened me! Your eyes hurt and the neuralgia pains in your ear have returned again, you poor thing! Why must you suffer? If only I could take your suffering upon myself, with what pleasure, with what joy I would do it! I want to hope that this letter will find you recovered; but I will be calm only when you yourself tell me that. Please calm me down, as soon as possible! Since this morning I've been unable to think of anything except that horrible day in Paris when you so exhausted yourself with suffering... I would gladly allow my arm to be cut off if only that could help you; it really irritates me that I am healthy while you suffer. Get well soon, dear friend, and notify me of that with all haste. What you say in your letter about the reception given you by the orchestra would have given me much more pleasure if the bad news about your ill health hadn't spoiled it. The news deprives me of the courage to speak of anything else. All the same, I'll mention that I'm now busy writing a one-act comedy for the talented actress Samoylova.[11] I have yet to see a single one of my comedies on the stage. They keep putting on benefit performances, practically without a break, and therefore they keep needing new plays; but one of my comedies is announced for the day after tomorrow. I'll let you know my personal reaction to them. Another comedy,[12] in five acts, that was sent here and forbidden by the censors, is now enjoying fairly great success in the salons. Tomorrow I'll start a new letter, No. 1, and I'll pray to God that the number of letters not exceed 50. But the main thing is—get better soon.

Mein Gott, ich möchte mein ganzes Leben als Teppich unter Ihre lieben Füsse, die ich 1000 mal küsse, breiten [My God, I could lay my whole life, like a carpet, under your dear feet, which I kiss 1000 times]. A thousand regards to you, and as regards you, Sie wissen, dass ich Ihren ganz und auf ewig angehöre [you know that I belong to you entirely and forever]. I kiss Gounod. All of you be happy and content.

Your I.T.

Letter 22. To Pauline Viardot.[1]
November 16/28, 1850. Petersburg.

Thursday, November 16/28, 1850

Dear and kind Mme Viardot!

I only have time to write you these couple of words in haste: I just received a letter with the news that my mother is on her death-bed[2]—I'm leaving for Moscow this very evening. I'll write you the day that I arrive. I'll probably have to endure some very painful moments and decide many difficult questions. Give me both your hands so that I may find strength in their firm, cordial embrace. Farewell! God bless you. I'll write you from Moscow in three days.

Your I. Turgenev

P.S. Write me at the same address: Yazykov's[3] office.

Letter 23. (139) To Pauline Viardot.[1]
November 22/December 4, 1850. Moscow.

Moscow, November 22 O.S., 1850.

Dear, kind Mme Viardot!

I arrived here last night and found my mother no longer among the living; she died last Thursday, the same day that I was notified of her illness.[2] My brother[3] is here with his wife. I'll write to you tomorrow; I'm too upset today. I only wanted to inform you of this news and clasp your hand oh-so-firmly. Until tomorrow! May Heaven bless you and keep you.

Your I. Turgenev

Letter 24 (140). To Pauline Viardot.[1]
November 24, 26, 28/December 6, 8, 10, 1850. Moscow.

Thursday, November 24/December 6, 1850.

It's now three days that I've been here, dear and kind Madame Viardot, and I scarcely have the time to take pen in hand to write you a few words in haste. It's not that my brother and I have so many things to *do*— the seals won't be removed for a week[2]—but we have so many things to discuss and prepare. It is a terrible responsibility that has just fallen on our shoulders.

My mother died without having made any sort of provisions; one could say that she left the whole multitude of creatures who depended on her out on the street; we have to do what she should have done. Her last days were very sad. God save us all from such a death. She did nothing but attempt to stupefy herself—on the eve of her death when the death rattle had already begun—an orchestra was playing polkas in the next room—by her order. One ought to have nothing but respect and pity—so I won't say anything more. However, how impossible it is for me not to confide in you everything I feel and know—I'll only add a word—and that is that up to her last moments all she thought of—I'm ashamed to say it—was to ruin us— my brother and me, and that the last letter that she wrote to her manager contained a precise and formal order to sell everything dirt cheap, to put the torch to everything if necessary, so that nothing—But I must forget that, and I'll do that in all sincerity, now that you know, you who are my confessor. And nonetheless—I feel this—it would have been easy to make us love her and feel sorry for her! Oh yes, God save us from such a death! I'll spare you a mass of other details—what's the good? May God grant her peace.[3]

My brother, his wife, and I are staying here until New Year's to try to arrange our affairs as well as possible. The property that my mother left is hardly in a prosperous state—and unfortunately the harvest has been almost nil this year. We have to try to restrain ourselves as much as possible until next August. I proposed to my brother that we immediately pay all my mother's personal debts (of which there aren't many), recompense all the employees—use all the available cash for that. Once this burden falls from our shoulders, we will move more easily and quickly. I plan to return to Petersburg in six weeks, go to the country in April, and stay there until the month of November. Then—we shall see. I am, as you know, hardly suited to business affairs; I intend to entrust the management of my property to my good and fine friend Tyutchev; my brother is certainly a thoroughly

51

honorable man and I would like nothing better than to leave him in charge of all this; but I'm afraid of misunderstandings—he is terribly thrifty, almost stingy—he'd like to be so for me—he would never consent to the sale of property, no matter how necessary it might be—I would like to avoid such family cross fire. I've decided to divide our property. That is to say, it is he who will do the dividing—and he'll certainly do it a thousand times better than I. I'll never have an income of less than 25,000 francs; and with that one is *rich*. I'll talk to you about this again; but please tell me what you and your husband think of my decision.

Dear and kind friend, I think of you very often!

Sunday.

Good day, dear and kind friend, meine theuerste, liebste Freundin [my dearest, most beloved friend]. Yazykov's office[4] has just sent me your kind and charming letter—I fall on my knees in gratitude. Little Pauline has arrived—and you like her—and already love her! Dear, dear friend, you are an angel. There isn't a single word in your letter that doesn't breathe kindness, sweetness, an inexpressible tenderness.

How could I end up other than loving that little girl insanely? You have such a joyous and serene way of doing good, which makes one happy as a child to acknowledge it. One has a feeling of having rendered you a great service when one gives you the opportunity to oblige someone. I really don't know what to say in order to make you feel how much your dear letter moved me and touched me . . . I search for the words—I'll simply have to repeat that it is with adoration that I prostrate myself before you. Bless you a thousand times over! Lord—how lucky she is—that little girl! She is really in Jesus' pocket—as a Russian proverb says in regard to fortunate people. It will be so much the better if she doesn't have just intelligence—her character would have to be really bad, for her, living with you, not to be infected by your goodness. I still hope that this great change will save her. Embrace her for me, I beg you. Now that I've become more wealthy, I'm not afraid of going up to a thousand francs a year: have her learn to play the piano. I'll send you some money in a couple of weeks. I'm very happy that you have found a resemblance to me in her and that that resemblance pleased you. Send me a little pencil portrait of her done by you. I repeat that I'll end up being completely attached to her as soon as I find out that you love her . . . Your success in *Les Huguenots*[5] pleases me infinitely—I await the details impatiently . . .

Tuesday.

52

Guten Morgen, theuerste, liebste, beste Freundin. Ich küsse mit Anbetung Ihre schönen Hände. [Good morning, dearest, most beloved, best friend. I kiss your beautiful hands reverently.] Good day, dear Madame Viardot. We're beginning to see our affairs a little more clearly. My mother gave 50,000 rubles to the young person whom she adopted.[6] We hurried to recognize that debt—she'll stay at my sister-in-law's until her marriage—and we'll pay her 8% per annum for her expenses. On marrying she'll receive her 50,000 francs. My mother didn't make any other bequests, we have provided for them, and I think people will be satisfied with us.

Dear friend, I haven't stopped thinking of you—and of little Pauline— the whole time here. I feel her becoming dear to me, since she is in your hands. I don't know how many times I've reread your letter. It is impossible for me to express everything that I feel when your image, which never leaves me, arises in my memory, even more vivacious. May you be blessed a thousand times! Give me some details about the little girl. Are you still pleased with her—and what does Madame Renard[7] say? What last name have you given her?[8]

With all my heart I thank the good Mme García and my dear Mme Sitchès[9] for their kindness to her. There's no other way to say it—you're all angels—and I love you all madly.

Everyone here receives me with open arms, especially dear papa Shchepkin.[10] I can't make many visits—yet—during the week that I've been here I've been at his place two or three times—and at the Countess Salias',[11] a charming woman who has great intelligence, much talent, and who, in spite of the fact that she's a writer, is not a bluestocking. Unfortunately, she is very ill. The last thing that I wrote—"The Singers at the Tavern"[12] is having a great success here. I'm finishing my letter so that I'll be able to send it to you today. I'll start another one tomorrow. Tell Viardot that I embrace him with all my heart, that for several days I've been doing nothing but re-reading Montaigne in the volume that he made a gift of to me in Petersburg. Embrace Gounod for me—don't forget to tell me about *Sappho*.[13] A thousand greetings to everyone—for you—I fall on my knees. Bei Ihren lieben Füssen will ich leben und sterben. Ich küsse sie *stundenlang* und bleibe auf ewig ihr Freund [I want to live and die at your feet. I kiss them *for hours on end* and remain your friend forever].

I. Tourguéneff.

Letter 25 (152) To Ye.M. Feoktistov.[1]
April 2/14, 1851. Petersburg.

St. Petersburg.
April 2/14, 1851.

If I didn't answer your first letter, dear Feoktistov, please don't attribute it even to laziness—I would have overcome that—but I was ill the whole time (with my old illness) and was in a very bad mood. Even now I won't write you a lot—I'll only say that Botkin[2] and I will probably go our separate ways—(I'll be in Moscow around the 15th)—and it's with unusual pleasure that I'll see the Countess[3] and you. Everything that you tell me is intelligent, nice, just, and flattering—I give you my word of honor that *Notes of a Hunter* is finished forever—I intend to refrain from publishing for a long time and devote myself as much as possible to a large work, which I'll write con amore [with love] and at my leisure—and without any arrière pensées [hind thoughts] about censorship—God knows what the result will be![4] I am very glad that people in Moscow like my article about Poznyakov[5] (it passed unnoticed here). The censor crippled it severely—and in some places there are horrible misprints . . . In one place a whole line is missing and so on. Pisemsky's novel[6] is fine—but too objective, pardon my saying so! As far as Botkin is concerned, my opinion has been formed for a long time—he is in essence simply garbage—and uninteresting garbage.[7] That's just between us, though, as you say. About ten days ago I spent the evening with the Countess' sisters,[8] but didn't drop in to see them—all because of my bad mood. I'm fed up with my body—it's clumsy, old, ugly, and in addition, it aches. It's shitty, I tell you, shitty.

I haven't continued my comedy *The Scarf,* and I doubt that I'll finish it. Inform Shchepkin and Shumsky[9] of this sometime and give them my best regards.

It's impermissible to write—for anyone—in such a mood as I am now in—but I didn't want to delay my answer even longer. And therefore—be well and cheerful—I heartily wish you every blessing—and I love you and the Countess as much as is possible for a man who practically hates himself.

Your I.T.

I so wish myself malice that, honestly, I'd marry the disgusting Bodisko with the greatest pleasure.

I hope that the Countess won't leave for anywhere before the 15th. My regards to all, beginning with Granovsky.

54

Letter 26 (154). To Ye.M. Feoktistov.[1]
Second half of June, O.S., 1851. Spasskoye.

What a strange, though you seem to think very serious letter you wrote me, dear Feoktistov![2] I have to admit that I hardly expected such a prank from you, but it's true that even the most decorous people cannot escape the influence of the milieu in which they find themselves: it's not for nothing that you are an inhabitant of Moscow, a city in which everyone is possessed by the desire to stick his nose into other people's business. What is this senile, morbid, purely Muscovite passion for sticking one's fingers in "between the tree and the bark"; I have no intention of offering a defense in regard to Botkin's relations with Yelizaveta Alexeyevna[3]—that would only mean enlarging the snowball—the more so as I was a complete outsider in this matter; I'll just say that the letter, which was intercepted, in Botkin's words, "in a completely inexplicable way," was presented by Yelizaveta Alexeyevna's maid to her brother, Mikhail Alexeyevich, that Mikhail Alexeyevich (there's no need for me to tell you that I don't approve of this) presented it, in his turn, to Uncle Pyotr Nikolayevich,[5] as the oldest member of the family, that my sister-in-law[6] had the temerity to get herself involved in this matter from the point of view of morality and family relations (which, of course, is completely absurd), and that I personally did not get at all involved and don't intend to. As regards Yelizaveta Alexeyevna, my opinion of her is based on information known to me, and I wish her all the best; there is only one thing you can be assured of—she is not being persecuted. I'm very sorry that you'll find some sharp words addressed to you in this letter, but it can't be helped...

Letter 27 (160). To K.N. Leontiev.[1]
December 3/15, 1851. Petersburg.

St. Petersburg. December 3/15, Monday.

I have some unpleasant news to convey to you, dear Konstantin Nikolayevich: the censor has forbidden your comedy from the first word to the last.[2] I confess that I didn't expect that at all, though I did think they'd mangle it a little. In a few days I'll get it back from Krayevsky and will await your further instructions in this regard. I'm very vexed that from your very first step onto the literary stage you should encounter obstacles: but that musn't deprive you of vigor: it's right here that a respectable person should show himself; in such cases spitefulness is allowed, but not apathy. I should even tell you that in accordance with the principle of extracting maximal good from evil, that to a certain extent I'm not completely upset by this failure. Your comedy is an excellent work, but in the other thing you showed me[3] there are more conditions for success, and it probably won't seem so dangerous to the censorship. Just be sure to write without a loss of spirit, and let me know how you're working. There's one other unpleasant side of this prohibition: you were perhaps expecting money—and now you shouldn't count on it. But even in this disaster there is the possibility of help: the editors of *The Contemporary,* with whom I'm on friendly terms, are prepared to send you a certain sum of money in the middle of this month as an advance on your future works. Write me directly, without mincing words, how much you would like, and I'll arrange it for you. But the main thing is not to be depressed, but to go forward boldly and cheerfully.

My address is: the corner of Malaya Morskaya and Gorokhovaya, the Gillerme house, Apartment 9.

Be well. Awaiting your answer, I press your hand firmly and remain

Your devoted

Iv. Turgenev.

Letter 28 (162). To M.P. Pogodin.[1]
December 4/16, 1851. Petersburg.

St. Petersburg
December 4/16, 1851.
Tuesday.

I received your letter, my dear Mikhail Petrovich—and hasten to answer you. Your proposal was made in such a friendly fashion that I can't but thank you for it. I would be very happy to participate in *The Muscovite,* although—(following that noble candor, of which you provide me an example—and which, in your words, ought to exist, especially between men of letters)—in many ways I depart from your journal's opinions.[2] But I have absolutely nothing written now—and to tell the truth, I don't even feel any particular desire to write. For some reason I feel not so much like resting—(I've nothing to rest from)—as being quiet a while, listening, looking, and studying. Whether after this epoch of passive observation will come a new epoch of activity—or whether I'll ultimately be pacified, having recognized that I've exhausted the small store of what I ought to say and do—I don't know. But in any event I am leaving the ranks of the active for the time being. I can assure you that I'm telling you the pure truth—the stories announced in *The Contemporary* are really nothing, they're written indifferently—and there are only two of them.[3]

I've already begun to ask about Novitsky[4]—and as soon as I find out, I'll let you know immediately. In any case, I'm pleased that we have begun a correspondence—I hope that it won't cease.[5] If you see Gogol, don't forget to give him regards from one of his lesser disciples. Will he ever give us a continuation of *Dead Souls?*

Farewell—be healthy and accept the assurance of the sincere respect with which I remain

Your most humble servant,

Iv. Turgenev.

**Letter 29 (166). To S.T. Aksakov.[1]
February 2/14, 1852. Petersburg.**

St. Petersburg.
February 2, 1852.
Saturday.

Your letter made me extraordinarily happy, dear and respected Sergey Timofeyevich; and the main thing is that it was pleasant for me to think that if your wonderful *Notes*[2] will make their appearance earlier than you supposed, then readers will be partly obliged to me for that.[3] For Heaven's sake, publish them this winter; don't compare them to your book about *Fishing,*[4] which, good as it is, is of interest to too few among us; here in Russia people mainly fish with nets—there are really few fishermen—but—

thank God!—there is a great multitude of hunters. Besides which, your *Notes* will be valuable not only for hunters; they will give real pleasure to anyone who doesn't lack a poetic sensibility; and for that reason I am ready to answer for their literary—and material success. And I repeat—it will be simply a holiday for me to write a review of them.[5]

I certainly am not devoid of hypochondria; but this time I have a disease which, if not dangerous, is real and unpleasant: a stomach fever that visits me every day from 12 to 7. Thanks to a very strict diet, though, it seems to be passing—but I'm still home all the time. I hope to be in Moscow around the beginning of May—and if I don't catch you in Moscow, I'll definitely drive out to see you for a few days. You are so kind and write that you regret that you got to know me so late; please be assured that that regret is no less strong from my side, especially when I recall that we could have been long acquainted . . . but each person has his own fate, which leads him along his own paths . . .

Give my regrets to your children,[6] whom I love sincerely—although with a different love. I think I could easily become very close with the one who shares my name. I think of our spring meeting with pleasure. I hope that their almanac gets published—and I regret that I couldn't be a contributor to it.[7] For some reason I'm unable to write—at least anything respectable—and I'll tell you frankly that I respect their publication too much to give them, for instance, such an empty piece as the one which will appear in the second issue of *The Contemporary*.[8]

Your idea of continuing *A Family Chronicle* is an excellent one. Undertake its realization.

Good-bye—be healthy and cheerful—I wish you all the best in the world and with sincere attachment remain

Respectfully yours,

Iv. Turgenev.

Letter 30 (171). To I.S. Aksakov.[1]
March 3/15, 1852. Petersburg.

. . . I must tell you without exaggeration that for as long as I can remember nothing has made such an impression on me as Gogol's death—

everything that you say about it speaks to me directly from the heart. This horrible death, a historical event, isn't immediately comprehensible; it's an enigma, a painful, fearful enigma—one needs to try to unravel it ... but the person who does unravel it will find nothing joyous in it ... we all agree about that. Russia's tragic fate is reflected in those Russians who stand closest to her inner essence—there's not a single person, even if he possesses the strongest spirit, who can maintain an entire nation's struggle on his own—and Gogol has perished! True, it seems to me that he died because he made up his mind that he wanted to die, and that his suicide began with the destruction of *Dead Souls*[2] ... as far as the impression that his death has made here ... it will be enough for you to know that the director of the university, Mr. Musin-Pushkin, did not feel it beneath him to publicly proclaim Gogol a trashy writer. That happened a few days ago apropos of a few words that I wrote about Gogol's death for the *St. Petersburg News* (I sent them to Feoktistov in Moscow).[3] Mr. Musin-Pushkin could not get over the brazenness of people who felt regret about Gogol. It's not worth an honest person's wasting his honest displeasure at this. Sitting up to their necks in filth, these people have decided to eat that filth—bon appetit! Honorable people must hang on to themselves and to each other more firmly now than ever. May Gogol's death at least be useful in this way ...

Letter 31 (172). To V.P. Botkin.[1]
March 3/15, 1852. Petersburg.

... I thank you from the bottom of my heart for sending the copy of Gogol's letter to Prince Lvov.[2] That letter explains a lot about the sad catastrophe of his demise. Wouldn't it be possible to try to print what I wrote about Gogol (unsigned, of course) in *The Moscow News,* as an extract from a letter from here?[3] Je voudrais sauver l'honneur des honnêtes gens qui vivent ici [I would like to save the honor of honest people who live here]. Couldn't it pass just like that, and we didn't say anything to you? Did Feoktistov show you my article about him? Musin-Pushkin forbade it for *The Petersburg News* and was even amazed at the brazenness of writing about Gogol like that—a trashy writer ...

Letter 32 (180). To Louis and Pauline Viardot.[1]
May 1/13, 1852. Petersburg.

St. Petersburg, May 1/13, 1852.

To *Monsieur and Madame Viardot.*

My dear friends,

This letter will be delivered to you by a person who is leaving here in a few days... or else he will send it to Paris after having crossed the border, so that I may have a little talk with you frankly and without fearing the curiosity of the police.

I will begin by telling you that if I didn't leave St. Petersburg a month ago, it was entirely against my will. I am under arrest at a police station, by order of the Emperor, for having had an article published, a few lines about Gogol in a Moscow journal. That was only a pretext, the article in itself was absolutely insignificant. I have been looked at askance for some time. They latched onto the first occasion that presented itself. I have no complaint with the Emperor, the affair was presented to him in such a vile way that he could not have acted otherwise. They wanted to forbid anything's being said about Gogol's death, and they were not sorry to put an embargo on my literary activity at the same time.[2]

In fifteen days I'll be sent from here to the country, where I will have to remain until a new order comes. None of this is very cheerful, as you can see; I must say, however, that I'm being treated very humanely; I have a good room, books; I can read. I was able to see people during the first days. Now that's been forbidden, because too many people were coming. Misfortune doesn't make one's friends flee, even in Russia. The *misfortune,* to tell the truth, is not so great. The year 1852 won't have had a springtime for me, and that's all. What is saddest in all this is that I have to say a definitive farewell to any hope of taking a trip outside the country; but I never had any illusions on that score. I knew well, when I left you, that it was for a long time, if not forever. Now I have only one desire, that I be permitted to come and go inside Russia. I hope that I won't be refused that. The heir apparent is very kind, I've written him a letter from which I expect some good to come. You know that the Emperor has left.

My papers have been sealed, or rather, they sealed the doors of my apartment, which they opened ten days later without having examined anything. It's likely that they knew that they wouldn't find anything forbidden there.

60

I have to admit that I am reasonably bored in this hole of mine. I'm making use of the enforced leisure by working on Polish, which I began studying six weeks ago. I have fourteen days of incarceration left. I'm counting them, believe me!

So, my dear friends, that's the news, hardly pleasant, that I have to give you. I hope that the news you give me will be better. My health is good, but I've aged ridiculously. I could send you a lock of white hair, that's no exaggeration. But I'm not losing my courage. *Hunting* awaits me in the country! Then I'm going to try to put my affairs in order. I'll continue my studies of the Russian people, the strangest and most astonishing people in the world. I'll work on my novel with all the more freedom of spirit, since I won't think of its passing through the claws of censorship. My arrest is probably going to make the publication of my work in Moscow impossible. I regret that, but what can I do about it?

I beg you to write me often, my dear friends, your letters will play a large role in giving me courage during this time of trials. Your letters and the memory of days spent at Courtavenel, those are all my worldly possessions. I won't linger on this topic for fear of being too moved. You know well that my heart is with you, I can say that, now especially... My life is finished, the charm in it is gone. I've eaten all my white bread; we'll chew what's left of the brown bread, and we'll pray that heaven be "very kind," as Vivier[4] said.

I have no need to tell you that all of this must remain a complete secret; the slightest mention, the slightest allusion in a newspaper, would be enough to do me in.

Farewell, my dear and kind friends; be happy, and your good fortune will make me as happy as I can be. Be of good health, don't forget me, write me often, and be assured that my thoughts are with you always. I kiss you *all,* and I send you a thousand blessings. Dear Courtavenel, I salute you, as well! Write me often. I kiss you again. Farewell!

Your

Iv. Tourguéneff

Letter 33 (191). To K.N. Leontiev.
October 6/18, 1852. Spasskoye.

Village of Spasskoye.
October 6, 1852

I have not written for a long time and it isn't because I've forgotten you, dear Konstantin Nikolayevich, that I haven't answered your letter; on the contrary, the interest aroused in me by you has never waned, but various cares crowded all other thoughts out of my head, besides which, I went out hunting almost every day. Now the snow has fallen—the birds have all flown away—and like a drunkard after a spree, I'm again coming back to human feelings and concepts, to the desire for human intercourse. I'm writing to you in Moscow, at the university, on the assumption that you've recovered your health and have again returned there. In the first place, I ask you to send me the piece[1] of which you spoke in your letter. I'm extremely anxious to know how you'll begin your novel. I consider you very capable of a novel or a povest;[2] that is your real calling. Your subtle, gracious, occasionally morbid, but often accurate and powerful analysis comes in handy here. As I recall, I expressed the same opinion in regard to your comedy.[3] The censorship did not pass it, and after the events of this year[4] there is no reason to suppose that it will become more lenient; but that is no tragedy, at least not for you—not because I think that your comedy is weak, but because it seems to me that there's no sense in a truly talented person's rushing. Writing for money—that's something to be done only in an extreme case. By the way, excuse my frankness, but do you by any chance need money? I promised you some earlier—and wasn't able to fulfill my promise, to my great regret. I hope that you won't stand on ceremony with me and that you'll tell me straight out whether you need any money or not. Young talents often conceal the desire to appear in print under the pretext of financial necessity, and the pretext is a very good one—what young person doesn't need money? Some people do that unconsciously, but in view of your subtly developed consciousness, it's impossible to imagine this in you, and therefore, if you really desire to be published, tell me straight out—even though I myself am a literary invalid in retirement, I can still help you, but in any event, send me your work. If you need money, take it from me directly and completely independent of your literary activity.

What is there to tell you about myself? All this time I've done nothing; I have a lot of plans, but the Lord alone knows whether anything will come of them. I wish you good health and happiness—both in life and in your creative work, and while awaiting a quick reply from you, I press your hand in friendship and remain

Your devoted

Iv. Turgenev.

My address is the same: Oryol Province, the city of Mtsensk.

Letter 34 (193). To K.S. Aksakov
October 16/28, 1852. Spasskoye.

Village of Spasskoye.
October 16, 1852.

I thank you heartily for your letter, dear Konstantin Sergeyevich. I'll tell you straight out that to a large degree I myself share your opinion of my *Notes*[1]—and I say that not at all out of a desire to flaunt my modesty—but because I feel that way myself—and have for a long time. "Why did I publish them?" you may ask—in order to be done with them, with that *old manner*.[2] Now that burden has been cast off my shoulders... But whether I'll be able to go on ahead—as you put it—I don't know. Simplicity, calm, clearness of line, the eagerness for work, that eagerness which comes with assurance—all these are as yet only ideals that flash before me. The reason, by the way, that I haven't yet gotten down to work on my novel,[3] all the elements of which have long been fermenting in me—is that I don't feel in myself either that radiance or that strength without which you can't say a single solid word. The example of Grigorovich at least ought to frighten people—and he's not lacking in talent![4] On the other hand, life hurries us and drives us on—and teases us and beckons... It's difficult for a contemporary writer, especially a Russian one, to be tranquil—neither from outside nor inside is he bathed in tranquility...

While I agree completely with your remarks about my *Notes*—and *taking note* of them for my future works—I can't share your opinion about "ape-people, who are no good for art..."[5] Apes are free and more importantly—self-satisfied, yes... But I can't deny either history or *my own right* to live; it's disgusting pretentiousness—but I empathize with

63

suffering. It's difficult to explain all of this in a short letter ... But I know that it's exactly on this point that you and I diverge in our views on Russian life and Russian art—I see the tragic fate of a tribe, a great societal drama, where you find reassurance and the refuge of the epic ... But I repeat—one can talk about this and argue—but it's difficult to write about it.[6]

I admit with shame that I haven't yet read your article in *The Collection*[7]—but for the whole summer I've taken neither pen nor book in hand. I wish you success in your new work. I'm happy to hear that the second issue of *The Collection* will come out.[8] Regards to all of yours— Heaven knows when we'll have occasion to see each other, but I'd like that. Don't forget to write and tell me whether you'll be in Abramtsevo[9] for long.

Farewell—I press your hand firmly and remain

Your sincerely loving and respectful

Iv. Turgenev.

Letter 35 (194). To S.T. Aksakov.
October 17/29, 1852. Spasskoye.

Village of Spasskoye.
October 17, 1852.

Your letter made me very happy, dear and respected Sergey Timofeyevich, and I hasten to answer it. But first I must ask you whether you received the letter I sent to you June 7th in answer to your triple letter. I would be very upset if it has gotten lost—I thanked you in it for your concern—tell me in your next letter whether you received it. I really will spend the whole summer in Spasskoye—and therefore I hope to correspond with you often. And winter has already come—and what a winter! No one can recall such an early winter. It has cut short my hunting, as if with an axe. On the 1st of October there were still a lot of woodcocks—by the 2nd they had almost completely disappeared. However, during the last year I made 304 kills with my rifle, specifically—69 woodcocks, 66 snipe, 39 great snipe, 33 black grouse, 31 partridges, 25 quail, 16 rabbits, 11 corncrakes, 8 moor-hens, 4 ducks, 1 small snipe and 1 curlew. My two hunters killed about 500. These figures seem large, but if you consider how much and how far I drove, then one cannot say that I hunted successfully. I drove to Kozelsk and Zhizdra for black grouse, and to Karachev and Epifan for swamp fowl. I feel very bad for you when I see this blindingly white, dead snowy tablecloth—they say that it's good for people with poor eyes to wear a black veil when they go walking in the winter.

I'm so happy that my predictions about your *Notes* have turned out to be true—and you're already preparing a second edition![1] I just finished my review of your wonderful book (I got down to it on the day of the first snowfall—I hadn't taken pen in hand all summer long)—and I'm sending it to Petersburg with today's mail. You wouldn't find anything in my review that would cause you to correct anything in your book—I only express regret that since you ceased hunting 10 years ago, you were not able to give your articles on rifles, dogs, and so on, that fullness of detail that we find, for instance, in E. Blaze's *Le Chasseur au chien d'arrêt*—an exemplary book for *French* hunting, which I know from personal experience. But the main merit of your work is not in its serving as a guide for the beginning hunter, although every page is sprinkled with many useful comments and recommendations; your book will remain at a more respected rank in Russian literature—we have not yet had *such* a book—and I will be very glad if my review proves that once again to the Russian public, which nonetheless did not wait for that proof to buy up all the copies of your book.

Everything you have to say about my literary activity is very dear to me and flattering—I value your opinion very highly—I'll try not to disappoint your expectations—I will arrange things so that anything that I write will be delivered to you, and I intend to work.

I've attached to this letter a few words to Konstantin Sergeyevich[2] about his remarks, the greater part of which I find just—although we diverge in our fundamental view of Russian life, and hence, of Russian art. I think that he knows that—but what he perhaps does not quite know is the passionate sympathy I feel toward his noble, sincere nature. They say that Ivan Sergeyevich[3] was going to write me, but I haven't received a letter from him.

I understand very well the difficulties that you'll have in compiling a biography of Zagoskin[4]—but nevertheless it will be a gift for all lovers of literature—and you must finish that work as soon as possible.

Farewell, my kind Sergey Timofeyevich. How I'd love to say: until we meet again . . . But I'm not free to say so. I wish you health and happiness and remain

Your sincerely loving

Iv. Turgenev.

65

Letter 36 (195). To P.V. Annenkov.
October 19/31, 1852. Spasskoye.

Village of Spasskoye.
October 19, 1852.

Dear Annenkov, why haven't I heard anything from you? I wrote you about a month ago and invited you to visit me here on your way back to Petersburg. You would surely have notified me, at least if that had been impossible, and I took your silence as a pledge of your visit. But perhaps my letter didn't reach you. I decided to write you a second time and ask you in any event to tell me whether you're coming or not ... Thoughts of you came into my head this morning for many reasons: in the first place, there is a terrible whirling blizzard outside, which gives me an excellent avant-goût [foretaste] of coming winter pleasures, and in the second place, I read your letter about the Tatar banker and his crossing the Kama River.[1] I hadn't read it until now, and I became very irritated that in Petersburg I didn't say anything to Arapetov when he, in his usual kind way, would begin making heavy fun of you, specifically in connection with that letter.[2] I liked it very much, and the end of it (Yura and especially crossing the Kama) is simply superb. The beginning is too lengthy—and more importantly—too detailed in the analysis of the motives for each thought. Thoughts, like time and space, are divisible ad infinitum, there's no way to exhaust them, nor is there any reason to. For Heaven's sake please come visit—at least for a few days—I so much want to talk with you. The Tyutchevs are wonderful people, but for some reason it's difficult talking with them. Alexandra Petrovna is completely swallowed up by her husband—he's busy—and you just can't talk to the rest of them. I'm beginning to sense what it means to live in the provinces—it's only now that I understand how it's possible to await an issue of a Russian journal impatiently and read it from cover to cover.

In case you didn't receive my first letter, you should know that I live ten versts from Mtsensk, a city that lies on the Oryol highway, and that in Mtsensk all you need to do is ask where Spasskoye-Lutovinovo is, and anyone will tell you.

I feel that it's very impolite to invite you for a common sharing of rural ennui—but I hope that you won't refuse to sacrifice a few days to us, which we will try to fill in every possible way, but you yourself ought to bring the main filler—the Pushkin biography.[3]

Farewell or until we meet—in any event write me a couple words. I clasp your hand firmly.

Your loving Iv. Turgenev.

Letter 37 (196) To Pauline Turgeneva.
October 21/November 2, 1852 (?). Spasskoye.

For Paulinette.[1]

Dear Paulinette, your sweet letter made me blush at not having written you for so long. Don't think because of this that I've forgotten you or that I have less affection for you; I truly love you, and everything that people write about you makes me more attached to you; but I've had a host of preoccupations of all sorts, which, however, hasn't prevented me from thinking of you often. Here you are already a big girl, as they tell me. I will be very happy to see you and I very much hope that we'll see each other someday, but that's still very uncertain.[2] For the time being be good, work, and more importantly—love your two mamas[3]—and don't forget me. ˑ Never doubt my affection. Your Uncle Nicholas is well—he's in Moscow with his wife. I ask Mme Viardot to send me your daguerreotype—tell her to do that, if it's possible. Farewell, my dear little one, be well. I hug you with all my heart.

Your father,

I. Turgenev.

Letter 38. (197). To P.V. Annenkov.
October 28/November 9, 1852. Spasskoye.

Village of Spasskoye.
October 28, 1852.

If my letter made you happy, dear Annenkov, then you can imagine how happy yours made me. I received it yesterday and am answering on my birthday, when I turn—not, as you think, 28, but a whole 34. Your letter is so intelligent and sensible and there is such true concern in it for me and my works that I must thank you for it from the bottom of my heart. Everything that you say—I feel just as clearly as you do—that's the unquestionable truth—and I endorse your every word. I need to take another road—I need to find it—and part with the old manner forever.[1] I've had enough of trying to extract the essences—triples extraits [triple extracts]—of human

characters in order to then pour them into little glass jars—as if to say—
have a sniff, respected readers—open it and take a whiff—doesn't it really
smell like a Russian type? Enough—enough! But here's the question: am I
capable of anything large and tranquil? Are simple, clear lines in my
power . . . I don't know and won't know until I try—but believe me—you'll
either hear something new from me—or you won't hear anything at all. For
that purpose I'm glad for my winter confinement—I'll have time to collect
myself—and more importantly—in solitude a person stands far away from
everything—but especially from literature—not just the journals, but all
kinds, and something can come of me only after the destruction of the man
of letters in me—but I'm 34—and it's difficult to be regenerated at that age.

 Well, we shall see.

 Solitude is good, there's no argument about that—but in order for it to
be of any use—it's necessary, however, for it to be enlivened at least
occasionally by conversation and confrontation with an intelligent person
whom you like and believe. You're such a person—and if you really take an
interest in the future of my talent—then you should definitely drive out
from Moscow to see me for five days. The Tyutchevs (who, I mention in
parentheses, remember you and like you very much) are wonderful
people—but they're poor judges in literary matters, although they're frank
and unhypocritical, but I can't learn anything either from their praises or
their denigration. And other than them, there's no one—there are the
_____,[2] who can't be of any use for anything at all. That's
why I'm definitely expecting you and I implore you to stop out here in
November.

 I understand how difficult it must be for you to finish the Pushkin
biography—but what can be done? Among us an honest biography of an
historical person can't yet be written quickly, not only because of
censorship, but even because of so-called decency. If I were you, I would
end it ex abrupto—I'd perhaps include Zhukovsky's story about Pushkin's
death, and that's all.[3] Better to knock off a statue's feet than to make him
tiny and out of proportion. And as far as I'm able to judge, your torso will
turn out a superb one. I can tell you frankly that I wish I could change my
manner as happily as you have yours in this biography. Surely under the
influence of the great Pushkinian spirit, genuinely classical in its severe and
youthful beauty, you have written a marvellous, intelligent, warm, and
simple work. I very much want to hear it all the way through. One more
reason for you to come here.

Farewell, dear Pavel Vasilievich. Guests are already beginning to pile in. In another letter I'll tell you about our life here. Did you receive my second letter? I clasp your hand firmly and remain

Entirely yours,

Iv. Turgenev.

Letter 39 (200). To A.A. Krayevsky.
November 15/27, 1852. Spasskoye.

Village of Spasskoye.
November 15, 1852

I'm very grateful for your remembering me, dear Krayevsky. I'm not dead yet, but the profound solitude in which I live gives me some intimation of the silence that awaits me in the grave.[1] But I'm not complaining. As of yet I haven't felt bored for even so much as an instant, I work and read—besides which my stay in the country in the winter is helpful for putting my somewhat jumbled affairs in order; I can't boast of absolutely good health—that's what's bad.

You are mistaken in supposing that the author of the truly remarkable povest "Childhood" and the person who wrote the comedy that the censorship did not pass for *Notes of the Fatherland* are one and the same person.[2] The former's name is Count Tolstoy—and as far as I've heard, he's an officer serving in the Caucasus; the latter's name is Leontiev, and is a student in Moscow. I don't know Tolstoy at all—and I have no contacts with him; I've written Leontiev two letters this year and haven't received any answer. But that doesn't prevent me from keeping your wish in mind—and if anything good comes into my hands, you'll learn of it.

It will probably be a long time before I publish anything myself, and my works aren't the sort that need to be printed; but since I owe you a respectable amount of money, I will ask you to wait until the new year—we have no transportation, thanks to eccentric weather—and I have yet to sell a kernel of wheat.

You'll soon receive "Lakoon," which I've looked over, and an indication of the cited passages.[3]

Be well and cheerful—I clasp your hand and remain

Your devoted

Iv. Turgenev.

Letter 40 (214). To P.V. Annenkov.
January 10/22, 1853. Spasskoye.

Village of Spasskoye.
January 10, 1853

Thank you, dear Pavel Vasilievich, for your letter from Moscow about "The Inn." It made me very happy—and saddened me by the news about the impossibility of seeing you here in the country. What can be done about it? I realize that it's not profitable for you to lose time now. I wish you complete and quick success in your publication.[1] As for me, here's what I've decided on: I'll have a copy made of the five chapters I've written of a novel[2] and have them delivered to you in Petersburg—on the condition that you *don't show them to anyone*—and return them to me with your comments and advice. I feel that they are essential for me—because I'm writing and working here practically in a foreign land—no one can tell me whether what I'm doing is good or bad—and after all, the only people who can work without that sort of response are people like Gogol. For people like me it's hard without it.

I'll say a few words about "The Inn." I am convinced of the importance of the mathematical accuracy of reality—in such works—and as far as I can tell, it has been followed. It will be easy to correct the error about the district police officer.[3] A serf *does not have* the right to acquire property other than in his master's name (no more than a week ago I gave one of my wealthy peasants in Tambov the power of attorney to buy 150 desyatinas[4] with his money—and in my name), moreover, the whole story that I related took place 25 versts[5] from here—and "Naum" is alive and thriving up to this day. I agree with you about one thing: it's likely that sales of that sort are sniffed out ahead of time and no measures are taken against them—because there aren't any measures you can take—but pressure of a sort is

70

exerted. I didn't mention them because I was afraid of retarding and complicating the course of the drama for no good reason. Everything that you say about the very nature of such dramas is superb and absolutely accurate—and I'm very glad that I 'really succeeded in giving the story that clarity and that free current without which the whole thing would make a painful and non-artistic impression.

In my present—very ugly—situation (it has recently become especially graphic—I think you understand what I mean)[6] my only salvation is intense literary activity—and in order to function with pleasure, you have to feel that you're moving ahead—and the approval of people in whom you believe is extremely beneficial. And for that reason I can't help thanking you a second time for your letter—I'll be curious to know your opinion about my novel. I beg you to write in all candor from Petersburg and tell me how Mme Viardot's voice strikes you. They say that people liked it very much—but I'll only believe you.

Write me about Nekrasov[7] and other friends. I sent the *Contemporary* a small piece on S.T. Aksakov's book.[8] Aside from two or three thoughts about nature and ways of describing it I don't think there will be anything remarkable for you in that article.

Write me as well about Mérimée's *False Dmitry* in *Revue des 2 Mondes*—what is it? About a month ago I wrote my good friend Chorley— one of the editors of *Atheneum*—about the mysterious Shenstone or Chenston[10]—as soon as I receive a reply—I'll send it to you.

Everyone here is well and sends regards to you. I caught a cold three days ago, have a cough, and don't leave my room—I hope that this will soon pass.

Leontiev visited me for a few days; he's the author of that comedy that I gave you to read in Petersburg—remember?[11] He brought me a good piece, which I'll send to Krayevsky in a few days; he's preparing another work for *The Contemporary*.[12] He has talent, but he himself is a thoroughly rotten little boy, touchy and spoiled. In his voluptuous delight over himself, his reverence for his "gift," as he puts it, he far outdoes the half-deceased Fyodor Mikhailovich,[13] apropos of whom your eyes grew so big and round. Furthermore, he's sick and irritable—whiny, like a little girl.

The weather here is disgusting—it's been a month since we've seen the sun.

Please write me—and you may rely on my conscientiousness. Give my regards to all our friends, be well and happy and don't forget

Your

Iv. Turgenev.

71

P.S. One more thing: You say that if Akim knew that Mrs. Kuntse could sell his inn—then that was not a surprise for him.[14] In Yaroslavl Province there isn't a single peasant who doesn't own a little parcel of land in his master's name (consequently, it doesn't belong to him)—our merchants continue to transfer enormous sums via their stewards—without a receipt, but do you think that the loss of land or capital isn't an unforeseen occurrence for them? That's just what makes for our Russian chic. One can't even imagine a preliminary deal, and I think that even if it were possible, it wouldn't even occur to anyone.

Letter 41 (217). To K.S. Aksakov.
January 16/28, 1853. Spasskoye.

Village of Spasskoye.
January 16, 1853.

Dear Konstantin Sergeyevich. I've been planning to write to you for a long time, but I kept putting it off until I could read your article in the *Moscow Collection*.[1] Now I've read it very carefully—and as far as I can judge in these matters—I agree with you about a "patrimonial way of life." That patrimonial way of life—the way Solovyov[2] and Kavelin[3] present it—has always seemed to me to be artificial, systematic, somehow reminiscent of our past secondary-school exercises in the field of philosophy. Any system—in the positive and negative sense of that word—is a non-Russian thing; nothing sharp, defined, and limited suits us—that's why, on the one hand, we're not pedants, but on the other hand...

I only know Russian history in the way a person who hasn't studied the sources does; my judgements about it are based more on my feeling for what is now happening in Russian life; one has only to take a good look at contemporary rural mores to realize the impossibility of Solovyov's patrimonial way of life.[4] The facts that you gathered were interesting and new to me, your view accurate and clear—but I confess frankly that I can't agree with your conclusions: you paint an accurate picture—and when you've finished it you exclaim: "How beautiful this all is!" There is no way that I can repeat that exclamation after you. I think that I've already told you that in my opinion the tragic side of the life of the people—of any nation—escapes you—while our songs themselves speak loudly of it![5] We

72

deal with the West, just as Vaska Buslayev (in *Kirsha Danilov*) does with the dead head—we kick it—but we ourselves...Do you remember— Vaska Buslayev went to the top of the hill but jumped and broke his neck. Please read the dead head's reply.[6] I have Kirsha Danilov in Sakharov's edition—the song that you speak of is not there, but I remember reading it....I'll order myself a special edition of Kirsha Danilov from Moscow.

I'll be curious to know your opinion of my last work. What conclusion will you draw from it? It's frustrating that it's impossible to discuss all these things on paper; you can say more and learn more from an hour's conversation than from a year's correspondence. My situation here is quite exceptional—via the Governor I asked the Minister of Internal Affairs whether I could visit *my own* villages that are outside the Oryol Province— a few days ago the reply came—a refusal. There's nothing to do but sit by the sea and wait for fair weather. At any rate I'm at least not being lazy here: I've gotten down to work on my novel and have written five chapters.[8]

Good-bye, my good Konstantin Sergeyevich. Will God someday allow us to see each other? I clasp your hand in friendship and remain

Your

Iv. Turgenev.

Letter 42 (246). To I.F. Minitsky.[1]
May 12/24, 1853. Spasskoye.

Village of Spasskoye.
May 12, 1853.

I didn't answer your letter immediately, dear Minitsky, because I wasn't home—I went hunting about 150 versts from here—and didn't return until the day before yesterday. I'll begin my reply with what is the most unpleasant thing for me—the necessity of turning down your request for help. You know that I'm always ready to serve everyone—and you more than anyone; but my affairs absolutely do not allow me even to think of any extra expense. I hardly have enough money for living expenses—there is a mass of debts—in a word, to my great regret, I find myself absolutely unable to help others now. I can't even pay out the promised pensions—

that's very painful for me—but there's nothing to be done about it.

I don't know whether I should be happy about the position you received—it's somehow very difficult for me to imagine you as a supervisor—but if you can get a decent number of lessons through this position, then fine![2] Have patience for a year or two. The main thing is not to neglect your health. If in time I'm allowed to leave Spasskoye, then I'll definitely descend on the South and I'll visit Odessa. I'd like to see you healthy, cheerful, and as happy as is possible. Perhaps I'll be in Odessa this winter.

The end of your letter touched me very much. Yes, Minitsky, the best time in a man's life is his youth—not just because he sleeps and eats better then and has more energy—but because it's then that the "sacred flame"—which is laughed at only by those in whose heart it has either been extinguished or never flared up, is ignited and burns. Maintain in yourself that noble decisiveness that now breathes in your words—and know that without faith, without profound, strong faith it's not worth living, living is detestable; know that this is being told you by a person of whom it is perhaps thought that he is permeated through and through with irony and criticism—but without ardent love irony is garbage and criticism worse than abuse. If we penetrate the poetry of evil embodied in the Satanic type, then we'll find infinite love as its basis—remember Consuelo.[3] In any event our calling is not to be devils—let's be people—and let's try to be them as long as we can—"God be with you on the difficult journey!"[4]

Here's what I can tell you about myself: my health, which went almost completely to pieces this spring, is now back to normal. I've worked a lot— I finished the first part of my novel[5]—12 Chapters—about 300 pages. Perhaps I'll be able to read you all of it in Odessa—sooner than we think.

The author of the delightful povest "Childhood" is a certain Count L.N. Tolstoy—he lives ten versts from Turgenevo[6]—but he's in the Caucasus now.

I'll send you a copy of my *Notes*[7] with the next parcel post—in memory of our living together. My *Notes* now seem a very immature work to me—but I'm nonetheless happy about their success. All the copies were already bought up three months ago.

Farewell, dear Ivan Fyodorovich. Everyone here sends his regards. You can't imagine how painful it is for me to turn down your request— especially in view of the circumstances...Let's not talk about that. Be healthy—and believe in the sincere devotion of

Your

Iv. Turgenev.

Letter 43 (252). To P.V. Annenkov.
May 30/June 11, 1853. Spasskoye.

Village of Spasskoye.
May 31, 1853.
Saturday.

Dear Pavel Vasilievich. Just a couple of words today—specifically, I wanted to tell you that I give you the full right to read my novel[1] to whomever you deem it useful (Korsh,[2] for instance?), for gathering opinions. Just don't read it from the point of view of journalism or publishing, you yourself can imagine why I don't want that.

Yesterday I made the acquaintance of Fet,[3] who is passing through here. He has a poetic nature, but he's a German, a systematician, and not very bright—that's why he holds the second part of Goethe's *Faust* in such reverence. He's amazed, he says, that all humanity is depicted there—it's neater than studying a single person. I assured him that no one thinks about gastronomy in general when he wants to eat, he just puts a bit of food in his mouth. He read me a comedy in verse—it was bad—that's not his kind of thing; he also read translations from Horace—superb. He hasn't yet lost his talent completely.

Don't forget to inform me about the arrival of the package.[4]

The weather here continues to be disgusting—you might as well wear a fur coat.

Farewell—be healthy and "enjoy it, this easy life," etc.[5]

Your

Iv. Turgenev.

Letter 44 (255). To K.N. Leontiev.
June 9/21, 1853. Spasskoye.

Village of Spasskoye.
June 9, 1853.

I hasten to answer your letter, dear Konstantin Nikolayevich. I'm glad that you've met Krayevsky in person, but please allow me, as a person more experienced in literary matters, to make the following observations: in the first place, for you yourself, for the future of your talent, please don't think that you can joke with the public—by writing, as you say, "something full of falsehood and flattery" for money, and later show yourself in your true light. Understand this: you can't dupe the public by so much as a hair—it is smarter than any of us; understand as well that while bringing it all of yourself, all your blood and flesh, you must be grateful to it as well if it realizes and appreciates your sacrifice, if it pays attention to you; and that's understandable, and what's more—it's just. It's not the public that needs you, but you who need it. You want to conquer it, all right then—harness all your energies. I don't mean by this that you ought to try to please it or serve its tastes; no, be what God has made you, give everything that's in you, and if your talent is original, if your personality is interesting, the public will recognize you and take you and will use you, just as for instance, in another sphere of activity it accepted guttapercha, because it found guttapercha a useful and handy thing. Don't distort your sincere thoughts and plans in censored form, but seek to find inoffensive topics. I don't think that "Summer on a Farm"[1] can offend anyone. I'm very sorry that "The Germans" wasn't passed—it's a good work; we must hope that it won't drop out of sight completely and that with time it will be published. My second request consists of the following: don't agree to do any *feuilleton* work. Besides the fact that it's a matter for dilettantes, I can't see in you—I won't say those qualities, but those faults which are essential for a feuilletonist. You're too young, fresh, and, in the happy sense of the word, inexperienced for it. And Krayevsky will be pleased to extract anything useful from you. He's a very clever entrepeneur, but you shouldn't fall into his hands. Finish your "Summer," refine it lovingly, without haste, and give it to *Notes of the Fatherland.* That will be very good and useful, and very profitable for you as a beginning.

I wish you good health—that's the main thing: everything else will take care of itself. I think that I've already written you that there's no reason for you to regret that you're late in beginning to publish. How much I would give if only not just my first bad poems, but even a lot of things in my later works had remained unpublished!

But taking money right off the bat, as they say, is difficult and awkward. Remember that even Menshikov didn't manage to take anything in Constantinople right away.[3] Time is necessary everywhere. Sow only good kernels—the harvest will come in its own time.

I can tell you about myself that my stomach is really torturing me. Everyone has his own cross.

Well, farewell, once again I wish you good health and I beg you to forgive me for my tone of counsel. That's a privilege of graying heads. I remain

Your sincerely devoted

Iv. Turgenev.

Letter 45 (264). To P.V. Annenkov
September 1/13, 1853. Spasskoye.

Village of Spasskoye.
September 1, 1853

Your last letter is so intelligent, dear Annenkov, that I can't even tell you, honest to God. And I'm not saying that as a result of your approval of my work[1]—no—your letter is a delight all by itself. Right now I don't have the chance to answer you properly—Tyutchev is leaving me. For all his remarkable honesty, he is a most impractical person—and in two years has brought affairs to such a state that my income (excluding payment to the trustee council) *did not even cover his wages*—and there wasn't even a kopek for my living expenses. When I saw that, I, to my great regret, felt it necessary to part with him, and now—this entire enormous mass of business and management, like a vault which the supports have been pulled out from under, has collapsed on my defenseless head. At the first instant I was very much at a loss; now, however, I'm getting used to my situation, and perhaps in time I'll extract some pleasure and usefulness from it. In any case there was nothing else I could do. I'll stay here until December—i.e., until the Oryol elections—because I can't go anywhere, since I don't have even a kopek. I'll have many occasions to recall Pushkin's verses to his nurse—remember?—"Let's drink a toast, my good old woman."[2] It's all right—I'll endure a little and grow to like it. Other than Pushkin and Gogol there's nothing Russian I can read—the Eastern poems delight me beyond description—for my sake read the poem, "Perplexed, the prophet frowned"[3] and tell me whether it isn't the summit of perfection.

77

We've had winter here ever since August 1—all we lack is snow. The stones crackle, there's a draft from the windows, the tips of your fingers freeze, noses turn blue—it's a miracle! I drove around to all my villages and must have seemed a foolish young fellow to my peasants.

I'll get down to the novel as soon as I get my bearings. My heroine is very surprised by all the changes that I'm making in her. I'll redo the chapter about Dmitry Petrovich's upbringing con amore [with love]—I'll throw out a great deal. I also received the Aksakovs' opinion—all in all they're not completely dissatisfied—but K. Aksakov is strongly upset that love was introduced; I was forced to explain in my letter that according to my plan, Dmitry Petrovich was supposed to conceive a hatred for Yelizaveta Mikhailovna just as capriciously as he came to love her—but in petto [in his thoughts]. I thought just then how right my friend Annenkov was that I shouldn't have sent everyone just the first part. But about that some other time—now it's time to set off for the fields and watch how ten peasants, not walking in a straight line, wave their arms in a special way. This operation is called *sowing*.

Farewell, dear Annenkov—I'll probably write you before next Tuesday without waiting for your answer. Our correspondence is a great delight for me. Be healthy—and give my regards to all our friends.

Your

Iv. Turgenev.

Letter 46 (280). To N.N. Turgenev.
November 23/December 5, 1853. Spasskoye.

Village of Spasskoye.
November 23, 1853.

Dear Uncle,

The reason I have taken so long to respond to your joyous news about the birth of my cousin, and your daughter, is that I kept waiting for your promised visit to Spasskoye, but now I'm sending you a courier with the news that a letter came for me today from Count Orlov with the announcement of my freedom and permission to enter the capitals.[1] They also write from Petersburg that I need to appear there at least for a short time to deliver my personal gratitude. As a consequence, I beg of you, if it's possible, to come here as soon as possible to discuss things with me and take over for me. Please come for at least 10 days. I no longer need the house in Oryol, because if I go there, then it will be only for the elections. I hope that all of your people are well and prosperous, I embrace you and everyone in absentia—and I kiss my cousin.

Hoping to see you soon,

Your

Iv. Turgenev

Letter 47 (292). To S.T. Aksakov.
May 31/June 12, 1854. Peterhof.

Peterhof.
May 31, 1854.
Trinity Day.

I'm writing you, dear and esteemed Sergey Timofeyevich, after both May Michael's Days (do you remember?), on which nothing special happened to me.[1] I'm ensconced here in a small colonial house[2] two versts from Peterhof and half a verst from the sea, which I can see from my windows, over the tops of the pine forest. I've acquired a horse and a cabriolet—and I propose to live here until the fall. Unfortunately, the weather here is so indescribably foul that I can't even find words for it. It's cold and rainy, the wind howls and whines—what ennui! What happened to the lovely days that comforted us in Abramtsevo?[3] I'll have to arm myself with patience. I literally have to sit by the sea and wait for good weather. I still haven't gone to Kronstadt, which is only five versts from here. They say the English are nearby—but they haven't yet shown their noses here.[4]

Let's talk a little about literary news. In the first place, I'll tell you that I made the acquaintance of Baratynsky's widow[5] (an absolutely wild woman—just between the two of us)—and she entrusted me with an album

79

in which she entered everything that was left of her husband's, his letters and so on. It will be possible to write up a rather interesting article.[6] Tolstoy, the author of "The Story of My Childhood," has sent a povest, a continuation of his first one, under the title "Adolescence"—they say it's superb. In Paris there has appeared a translation of my book[7] with a long preface—full of nonsense, I'm sure.

Baratynsky isn't a poet in the only true sense, the Pushkinian one—but one can't help respecting his noble artistic honesty, his continual and disinterested striving for the highest ideals of poetry and life. Konstantin Sergeyevich would like him, in spite of his Westernizing. He had much wit, taste, and perspicacity, perhaps too much—every word of his carries the trace not just of the chisel—but of the file as well—his verse never rushes, it doesn't even pour forth. Here's one of his unpublished poems for you (don't let anyone copy it)—all the major characteristics of his muse are expressed rather accurately:

When your voice, oh poet,
Is stilled at its highest sounds by death,
When impatient Fate catches you
In the flower of your years—

Who will be touched at the bottom of his heart
By the sunset of powerful days?
Who will cry out from his constrained breast
In response to your demise?

And [who will] visit your quiet coffin,
And weeping over the silenced muse
Honor your ashes
With an unhypocritical requiem?

No one! but a canon will be composed for the singer
By a former critic
Who already flatters the deceased
In order to bathe the living in incense.[8]

An echo of our great classical era can be heard in the form of Baratynsky's verse.

Nekrasov—whom you so dislike—has written several good poems, especially one—an old peasant woman's lament for her dead son.

My address is very simple: Peterhof. I've already made arrangements here at the post office—letters will be delivered. Please write me a couple words about yourself, about your life in Abramtsevo, which I have come to love so sincerely. Please give my regards to your wife and all your family. I clasp your hand and Konstantin Sergeyevich's[9] and remain

Your devoted

Ivan Turgenev.

Letter 48 (308). To Ye. Ya. Kolbasin.[1]
October 29/November 10, 1854. Spasskoye.

Spasskoye.
October 29, 1854.

Dear Kolbasin, I congratulate you from the bottom of my heart on finishing your examination and on your triumph over Musin-Pushkin.[2] Apparently failure is not to plague you in everything. Taking into account several other similar instances, I am beginning to think, on the contrary, that you are an extraordinarily lucky young man. God grant that be so in the future as well!

I'll arrive in Petersburg by November 20. I wrote your brother[3] and asked him to see about an apartment for me—would you be so good as to help him? (Did he receive my letter to Obolensky? I wrote immediately.) We'll find something for you to do for the winter—don't worry. I'm very happy about the success of "Adolescence."[4] God grant that Tolstoy live a little longer, and I very much hope that he will yet amaze us all. His is a talent of the first rank. I've made the acquaintance here of his sister (she too is married to a Count Tolstoy).[5] A very sweet, charming woman.

My health is most satisfactory—and my stomach hardly plays any pranks at all. I play chess here rarely—but successfully. The local fellow won't move ahead. Do you remember the hallowed games at Peterhof?[6]

Good-bye, be well and cheerful. Give my regards to everyone, Fumeli and the others.[7] I'll write to Minitsky with the next post. He's a very nice person.

Your

Ivan Turgenev.

Letter 49 (309). To N.A. Nekrasov.
October 29/November 10, 1854. Spasskoye.

Village of Spasskoye.
October 29, 1854.

I was boasting when I said that I'd gotten down to work—that is, I was about to get down to it—but now I've gotten lazy again. I'll try, however, not to leave the first or second issue of *The Contemporary* without a povest.[1] I'll bring with me a short but very good povest by Karatayev[2] (whom you saw when you were visiting me). I made the acquaintance of the Tolstoys here. Count Tolstoy's wife—my neighbor—is the sister of the author of "Adolescence"—a very nice person—intelligent, kind, and very attractive. I found out many details about her brother. He's now serving in the 12th Gunnery Battery and is probably in Kishinyov. I saw his portrait. His is an ugly but intelligent and remarkable face. By the way, why is it you won't tell me what kind of impression his povest is making? Tomorrow Countess Tolstaya and I will be at a christening done by the Turgenevo priest. I'll be the godfather to her child. It's too bad that it's about 25 versts from here to their place. I like her very much.

Bubulka (knock on wood) is getting visibly fatter—and her character isn't changing. Your dogs are doing well. Kashtan is a real little wolf—he's careful and incredibly mischievous. His illness has cleared up completely.

I don't know for certain when I'll be leaving here. For some reason I'm not especially anxious to. But it won't be later than in three weeks. This monotonous life has its own sort of charm.

How can it be that "our good one"[3] made a mistake? I recall his showing me a beautiful format. You didn't write me whether Mukhartov got married.[4]

Give my regards to all our friends—and give Druzhinin[5] a handshake. I've gotten to like him very much ever since our last trip to see him. Have you heard anything about Fet?

Delvig, the poet's brother,[6] lives near Tolstoy. He promised to get me Baratynsky's letters to his brother.

Farewell, be healthy and don't be lazy like me.

Your

Iv. Turgenev.

Letter 50 (316), To N.M. Shchepkin.[1]
November 29/December 11, 1854. Petersburg.

Petersburg.
November 29, 1854.

Dear Nikolay Mikhailovich, do me the favor of letting me know by the first mail whether my comedy *The Student* (or *Two Women*)[2] was forbidden just by Snegiryov[3] or was it subjected to examination by the censorship committee? I very much need to know that. Here's my address: by the Anichkov Bridge, on Fontanka Street, Stepanov's house. Give my request to your father—and convey to him my regrets that I couldn't be of use for his benefit performance. I hope to see him and you at the beginning of January. Be well and be assured of the sincere attachment

Of your devoted

Iv. Turgenev.

Letter 51 (326), To O.A. Turgeneva[1]
January 6/18, 1855. Petersburg.

Dear Olga Alexandrovna, I am sending you my forbidden povest.[2] Please be so kind as to read it today, because I'm leaving tomorrow and I want to take it with me. But I'll see you tomorrow anyway and say good-bye to you before my departure for Moscow.

I remain

Your devoted

Iv. Turgenev.

**Letter 52 (327). To O.A. Turgeneva.
January 6/18, 1855. Petersburg.**

Olga Alexandrovna,[1] allow me first of all to thank you for your decision to write me. I've been wanting to have a frank talk with you for a long time, but without your letter our relations would have probably ended mutely and hollowly.

I thank you for your faith and confidence—I especially thank you for giving me the opportunity to express to you those feelings of sincere admiration and heartfelt friendship with which you have inspired me and which I hope to keep forever.

You ask *my* forgiveness... but of the two of us, Olga Alexandrovna, of course I alone am at fault. I am older than you, it is *my* duty to think for both of us; I should not have allowed myself to yield to an uncontrolled enthusiasm—and I especially ought not to have let you notice it until I myself realized clearly what sort of enthusiasm it was... I shouldn't have forgotten that you were risking much—I nothing at all. And nonetheless— I did all of that! At my age it's absurd to use the rashness of my first inclinations as a justification—but I can't imagine any other justification— because it's the only real one. When I became convinced that the feeling that was in me had begun to alter and grow weaker—even then I behaved badly. Instead of indulging in those idiotic splenetic pranks which you endured with such simplicity and gentleness, I should have left at once. You see that I alone am to blame—and only the feminine—moreover, only the virginal magnanimity of a pure soul could even go so far as not to reproach a person who had done all of this—and practically blame herself!

You ask me not to *hate* you... but I would consider myself the most worthless person if only I didn't respect you! Believe me—I am able to appreciate your worth—and in spite of everything that happened, I still consider my acquaintance with you one of the happiest incidents of my life. Now my main duty is to avoid frequent meetings and close relations with you. We must put a stop to the rumors and gossip, the cause of which was my conduct.[2] But I would be sincerely grieved if you attributed my present estrangement from you to any other reason... On the contrary, I dare to hope that when all of this settles down—we'll again grow close, if only you yourself desire that. Believe me—no matter what your and my future fate may be, the feeling of profound attachment to you will never die in me. Forgive me, Olga Alexandrovna—and I will forgive myself only when I see you surrounded by the happiness of which you are so worthy. Give me your hand, allow me to clasp it firmly—and together with my profound gratitude, please accept the expression of the sincere devotion

Of your

Iv. Turgenev.

Letter 53 (332). To M.N. and V.P. Tolstoy.[1]
February 8/20, 1855. Petersburg.

St. Petersburg.
February 8, 1855.
Tuesday.

Imagine, my dear friend, that after leaving on Thursday[2]—it wasn't until yesterday, i.e., five days later, that I arrived here. Thanks to a snowstorm and uncleared roads we sat in Zavidovo for more than three days—we were cold, had God only knows what to eat, gave ourselves up to the bedbugs to be devoured and so on. There is unfortunately no post house at Zavidovo, just two small barns. The whole thing was thoroughly revolting—and if any of us had fallen ill, that would have been the end of him, because there was no communication beyond the snowdrifts! But everything turned out all right—true, my cough has gotten worse—but there's nothing inflammatory in it. I'm just horribly tired—and I intend to stay home today and tomorrow. As soon as I leave the house, I'll arrange things for Mlle Vergani[3] and let you know. "The Inn" was left with you—keep it until I need it—and give the proofs of "A Correspondence" to Botkin when he shows up for them. He's now here—he's staying with me—and he's not altogether well—he also has a cold.

I've thought of you often since the trip—and now I keep having visions of your apartment with its fantastic chairs and horrible pictures. I hope that the Countess is well and cheerful. I'll write more next time—right now my head is splitting. Regards to you and I clasp all your hands. Until we meet in two months,

Your

Ivan Turgenev.

Letter 54 (344). To A.A. Krayevsky.
Mid-March (O.S.), 1855. Petersburg.

Dear Krayevsky,

The difficult times in which we find ourselves force me to turn to you with a request: could you pay for my last povest[1] and count the money that I owe you as an advance for other works? (By the way, please write and tell me how much I owe you.) There are just over two signature pages in "Pasynkov"—I think it won't be asking too much if you give me 125 silver rubles for it. *The Contemporary* gives me 75 silver rubles per signature— but I want to prove to you that I remember your service and my long inaction.

See you this evening.

Your Turgenev.

P.S. If you could give me 200 rubles—adding 75 to what I owe you, that would be marvellous—but I do not wish to abuse your generosity.

P.P.S. You can entrust the money to the messenger.

Letter 55 (352). To A.K. Tolstoy.[1]
13/25 May, 1855. Spasskoye.

Dear Count,

In the first place, I'm taking advantage of this opportunity to recall myself to you, and secondly, I'm addressing myself to you with the following request (you have spoiled me). I have a friend of long standing, Mikhail Alexandrovich Yazykov, a wonderful, honest, nice person whom I love from the bottom of my heart. He now finds himself in very strained circumstances, is afraid of losing the minor government post on which he depends—and in general his fate is acquiring a not very attractive look.[2] Allow me to recommend him to your attention; I will consider any favor that you can do him as much more than a personal favor. I feel guilty about troubling you with requests so often—but what else can I do? You have only yourself to blame—if you were other than you are, you wouldn't be bothered so often.

I'm living in the countryside—and giving myself over to all the pleasures of "rural quiet"—as far as is possible under the present circumstances. The weather is marvellous. What are you doing and where are you? I'm writing to you in Petersburg in any event. Please write me about yourself. Where is your regiment going—and are you beginning to get used to military duty? Give my most respectful regards to your mother—and also give my regards to all our good friends, beginning with Sofia Andreyevna.[3] Be well and don't forget

Your sincerely devoted

Iv. Turgenev.

Letter 56 (356). To S.T. Aksakov.
June 2/14, 1855. Spasskoye.

Village of Spasskoye.
June 2, 1855.

I've been planning to write you about ten times, dear and respected Sergey Timofeyevich, but I had a house full of guests who left only yesterday after staying three weeks—and I didn't have a moment's free time. Your letter, which I received a few days ago, made me blush—I felt ashamed of my laziness and hastened to take up my pen—my guests were Grigorovich, Botkin, and Druzhinin; we spent the time very merrily—we performed a home-grown farce in our home-grown theater and so on and so forth. Now the house is all empty again—and I'm not against having a rest. I ought to give you an account of my hunting adventures. I arrived here April 12—and to my amazement I didn't find a single woodcock— they had already passed on—this year everything is happening two weeks earlier than usual—even the rivers flooded in mid-March, bringing a lot of destruction and losses. On April 18 I set off for the bands of the Desna 200 versts from here to hunt spring great snipe and snipe. We found the great snipe and snipe sitting on their eggs already, although there were still birds—and the hunting turned out to be not bad at all. Using four rifles for five fields we killed 220 birds. My share was 52. I shot rather poorly, but my dog made me very happy. The weather was superb, and I thoroughly enjoyed the spring. In one of my fields I killed a strange bird: a cross between a moor-hen and corncrake. Her height and whole shape were that of a corncrake—the feathers on the back were the same; the feathers on the breast, stomach, and sides were like a moor-hen's, the nose all red and longer and sharper than on a corncrake. Unfortunately, I couldn't keep the body.—Up until now I didn't have the least idea how a cat catches a fish—and I was always surprised even that the cat so wants to—now I understand it. Live and learn. I'm very happy that Count Sollogub[1] finally delivered "The Inn" to you—and it's even nicer that it gave you cause to recall me and write to me; I think it unnecessary to tell you how much your approval and your remembering me are dear to me.

For the time being I'm not doing anything, but I'm planning to get down to work on my novel[2] again and rework it completely. My health is fine.

For Heaven's sake publish your book[3] in Petersburg and no later than the first days of October. That is absolutely necessary. What is Ivan Sergeyevich doing?[4] Thank Konstantin Sergeyevich[5] for his regards.

I'll leave here in mid-October—as soon as the fall woodcock season is over—and I'll definitely drop in on you on my way from Moscow. But I hope that we will exchange several letters before that.

Give my earnest regards to your spouse and all your family; be well and don't forget

Your sincerely devoted

Iv. Turgenev.

Letter 57 (359). To I.I. Panayev.
June 13/25, 1855. Spasskoye.

Village of Spasskoye.
June 13, 1855.

Dear Panayev,

In response to your letter I can tell you that since the departure of my guests (Grigorovich, Druzhinin, and Botkin) I have gotten down to work—and I'm writing a povest[1] for *The Contemporary*, a long one, for the September or October issue—but there is no story as yet—and if I write one, it will be very short—and so I can't promise you anything for certain. I must tell you that I am glad for Beketov's refusal;[2] if he had passed "A Correspondence"—and it had appeared in your journal—I would have been put in a thoroughly false and unpleasant position in regard to Krayevsky, to whom that povest belongs *as of now*.[3] Botkin seems to be finishing Carlyle.[4] I didn't have time to read all of the fifth issue of *The Contemporary*, but it seems to me successfully and nicely put together—and to judge by the contents page, the sixth issue is even better. But please do something to make certain that the issues arrive here at least simultaneously with those of *Notes of the Fatherland*—because they always arrive about ten days later—and in the provinces that's extraordinarily important. "You haven't received your journal yet? I already got mine!" and so on.

Tell Annenkov that I'm now counting on his arriving in the fall—and in 12 days I'm going 250 versts away for a month. From July 25 to August 10 I will be home again—and there from September 8 until November.

Be well. I'll definitely have a povest for you—but right now I simply can't write a story—maybe I'll still manage and send one to you. I clasp your hand and send regards to all our friends.

Your

Iv. Turgenev.

P.S. Ask Bazunov[5] (I've already written him about it, but you repeat it) why he's not sending me *The Muscovite*.

Letter 58 (361). V.P. Botkin.
June 17/29, 1855. Spasskoye.

Village of Spasskoye.
June 17, 1855

Dear Botkin,

Heartfelt thanks to you and your two fellow travellers[1] for the amusing and detailed description of your journey to Dulebino. I laughed myself sick—and was carried in my thoughts to you and your visit here. Now everything here is as calm and quiet as in a monastery: at first there was such a heat wave and dry spell that we almost lost our minds, just sat in the dark and had difficulty breathing: but fortunately the rains came and Kolbasin and I got down to work. This time I would like to justify at least a tiny part of the hopes that you have placed on me; I've written the detailed plan of a povest, thought over all the characters, and so on. Will anything come of it? Maybe just nonsense. We'll see whether this latest attempt is at all successful.[2]

I read the article on Pushkin with the greatest pleasure. It is noble, warm, sensible, and accurate. It is the best thing that Druzhinin has written. But nonetheless he is wrong about Gogol...[3] That is, he is absolutely right in what he says—but since he can't say *everything,* the truth emerges as falsehood. There are eras when literature cannot be *just* art, when there are interests higher than poetic interests. The moment of self-knowledge and criticism is just as essential for the development of a nation's life as for the life of an individual—but you know what I mean. And all the same the article is marvellous—and when you write Druzhinin, give him my sincere thanks. Today's writers ought to take note of much of what he says—and I know as well as anyone où le soulier de Gogol blesse [where Gogol's shoe pinches]. After all, Druzhinin was referring to me when he spoke of a certain writer who would like a *counterweight* to the Gogolian tendency...all of that is true;—but he speaks of Pushkin with love, while he only gives Gogol his due, which never actually turns out to be fair.

I've only seen the Countess[4] once since your departure; she asks me to send you her regards. Karateyev didn't come...Remember "O Vasily, o Vasily!"

There's nothing more to write for the time being.

"Après tant de malheurs, Rhadamiste, est-ce vous?" [After so many misfortunes, is it you, Rhadamiste?][5]

Did you see our old housekeeper, Praskovya Ivanovna? They say that as soon as she heard our play, she threw up her arms and exclaimed: "But he (i.e., me) wrote it about himself, made fun of himself!" What opinion do you suppose my subordinates have of me? But the triumph remains yours.[6]

Farewell, be well and write when there's nothing to do. I received a letter from Panayev in which he begs me to help *The Contemporary;* he asks me to remind you about Carlyle and so on. We'll have to help the braggart.

In a few days my messenger F. Lobanov, or someone else, will turn up at your place. Please drop in at Arlt's[7] and ask whether he has any books for me—and if he does, take them and give them to my messenger.

I'm leaving here the 26th and will be gone until July 20—I'm going to hunt grouse in the Zhizdrensky district.

Your

Iv. Turgenev.

P.S. Send me Druzhinin's country address—I don't recall whether it's Gdov or Luga. My messenger will give you the copy of Alfred de Musset that you forgot here.

Letter 59 (366). To P.V. Annenkov.
July 1/13, 1855. Spasskoye.

Village of Spasskoye.
July 1, 1855.

Dear Annenkov,

I'll be brief, since in the first place, I don't know whether my letter will find you in Petersburg, and in the second place, cholera is raging here—and that strongly effects my abilities.

(1) Thank you for what you did for the Belenkovs; everything stays just as you have arranged it.[1] That's marvellous.

(2) Kolbasin will give you 15 rubles. He is the one taking care of Feoktista.[2]

(3) *Narskaya's* povest in the July issue of *The Contemporary* is a delight[3]—for the first time a woman has spoken in literature—but Chernyshevsky should be publicly stigmatized for his book.[4] It is unheard of *vileness* and impudence.

(4) I didn't go hunting because there was cholera where I was going—but since it's raging here, too, it doesn't make any difference—I'm going tomorrow.

(5) Let me know your country address and write. I hope you won't forget to send me all of Pushkin.[5]

(6) As for the Countess, everything is finished and done with.[6]
Farewell—be well. Until we meet—if the cholera allows it.

Your devoted

Iv. Turgenev.

Letter 60 (373). To I.I. Panayev.
July 10/22, 1855. Spasskoye.

Village of Spasskoye.
July 10, 1855.

Hello, dear Ivan Ivanovich—the cholera is so virulent here (especially where I wanted to go hunting) that I've been forced to sit home and brood. But I'm working too. I received your letter and I'll answer it in a few words. First of all, congratulations on Narskaya's povest[1]—it's a fresh, merry, lively piece—it has much immaturity in it—a tendency to gab—but there are superb pages—and I like its whole coloration. Who is she? I won't conceal the fact that I'm a little angry with you as well. Chernyshevsky's book, that vile rot, that spawn of spiteful stupidity and blindness, ought not to have been reviewed the way Mr. Pypin did it.[2] Such a direction is disastrous—and *The Contemporary,* more than anyone else, ought to protest against it. Fortunately, the book is so dry and lifeless that it can't do any harm. Tolstoy's article about Sevastopol is a marvel.[3] I wept while reading it and cried, "Hurrah!" I'm very flattered by his desire to dedicate his new story to me.[4] I read *The Contemporary*'s announcement in *The Moscow News.* It's fine—God grant that you can keep your promises, i.e.,

92

that the articles arrive, that Tolstoy not be killed and so on.[5] That will help you very much. Tolstoy's article has created a general furor here. The summer issues of *The Contemporary* have been good, interesting, and sensible so far. I'd like to know about the Nekrasov line (in the poem "To a Russian Writer"):

Serve not glory, *not* art—

is surely a misprint for: *but* art?[6]

All of us here are very grieved by Nakhimov's death.[7] The poor man! He didn't have a chance to enjoy his glory.

I imagine that it must be stifling in Petersburg! I feel sorry for you. I wish you good health and all the best. Give my regards to Avdotya Yakovlevna.[8]

I'll definitely be in Petersburg on October 10th, if I'm still alive. As for Leontiev—you're absolutely right.[9]

Good-bye,

Your

Ivan Turgenev.

P.S. The news about Mikhailov's[10] getting a haircut had such an effect on me that I dreamed about him—no joke—and was so frightened that I rushed to kiss his feet.

Letter 61 (376). To V.P. Botkin and N.A. Nekrasov.
July 25/August 6, 1855. Spasskoye.

Village of Spasskoye.
July 25, 1855.

My dear friends, Botkin and Nekrasov—for some incomprehensible reason your letter of the 10th didn't reach me until yesterday—and, heartily annoyed at the punctuality of our mails, I decided to answer it. I warn you, however, that because of the unbearable heat and my rather bad mood, my letter will be short. My bad mood is a result of the fact that my ears have been irritated since morning by the tolling of the funeral bell and the wailing of women at the cemetery (you remember, it's right under my windows)... Cholera is raging—and because of it I can't go anywhere—to see you, to go hunting—not because of money, for the offer of which I nonetheless thank you.

Thank you, dear Nekrasov, for your kind proposal—I'm certain that we would have bagged scads of fowl, so it's all the more irritating that it's all running down our moustaches but not landing in our mouths. What's to be done, though?

I'm very glad, dear Vasily Petrovich, that you like Narskaya's povest.[1] As for Chernyshevsky's book[2]—here's my main objection to it: in his eyes art, as he himself puts it, is only a surrogate for reality, for life—and in essence it is only appropriate for immature people. You can't deny it—that idea is at the basis of everything he says. And that, in my opinion, is nonsense. Shakespeare's Hamlet doesn't exist in reality—or perhaps he does—Shakespeare discovered him and made him our common property. Chernyshevsky is taking a lot upon himself if he imagines that on his own he can always get to that very heart of life of which you speak. I imagine him extracting poetry from reality for his own use and time; no, his book is false and harmful—we'll talk about this some time at length.

I took advantage of my inability to go hunting and finished a long povest yesterday.[3] I wrote it with love and thought—what the result is, I don't know. I'll let it sit awhile, then read it through, make corrections, and when I've copied it, I'll send it to you—perhaps you'll have something to say. Perhaps Nekrasov too?

In my last letter to him I asked him to send me Burns—don't forget to do that for him.[4] Send me Fet along with the corrections as well.

I inquired about the promissory note to Belinskaya.[5] It turns out that I really haven't paid on it—I paid on another one. You'll receive 90 silver rubles with this letter. Of them 4 are for you, and the 86 are interest through May, 1855. I would send the money myself, but I don't know her address. Please see that she gets her money—and tell her that I beg her pardon and that when I see her in October I'll be ready to pay the capital if she wants— or I can continue to pay interest. Send me her address—I'll write her myself.

Farewell, friends. It's so hot that the pen falls out of my hand. I wish you all the best, good health and happiness. I press your hands firmly, thank you for remembering me, and remain

Your devoted

Ivan Turgenev.

P.S. Arlt sent me all sorts of nonsense, including books that I had already received from him. I'll send them back to him.

Letter 62 (385). To S.T. Aksakov.
September 5/17, 1855. Spasskoye.

Village of Spasskoye.
September 5, 1855.

To show my gratitude for your letter, dear and respected Sergey Timofeyevich, I was about to write you about my (wholly unsuccessful) hunting expeditions—but the news about Sevastopol,[1] which we received here yesterday, has deprived me of any vigor—and all I feel like doing is clasping your hand in silence and repeating that I'll definitely visit you in a month. May we at least be able to take advantage of this horrifying lesson, as the Prussians did with the defeat at Jena . . .[2] But no—it's impossible to write about this. I received Konstantin Sergeyevich's book and haven't yet finished it—but I thank him for remembering me.[3] I had news about Ivan Sergeyevich[4] from the Karachevsky man of wealth, Kireyevsky,[5] who gave him the hospitality of all his "troups" and got to know him. When I get my spirits back, I'll write him in Kiev. Be well. You're the first to write to me about the new Moscow journal.[6] God grant that it go well and competently. It's long past time for one. We'll talk over everything—but now I once again give my regards to all Abramtsevo and say "Good-bye."

Your devoted

Ivan Turgenev.

Letter 63 (389). To Pauline Turgeneva.[1]
September, 1855. Spasskoye.

Dear Pauline,

It's been a long time since I've written, dear Paulinette, but that ought not to make you feel bad—I think of you no less often—even more often. So there you are with a new boarding school—I'm certain that things are fine for you there—I hope that you will work very hard, that you will be nice and obedient. I'm speaking to you as to a child—and Mme Viardot writes me that you are almost as tall as she is—I would very much like to see you—I'll recognize you in spite of the changes in you since I last saw you five years ago. As regards me, I've gotten older and grayer—time is moving quickly. But when will we see each other? Ah! That's the question. I can tell you only one thing: it will happen as soon as there is the slightest possibility; unfortunately that doesn't depend on me.[2] We have to be patient—you especially should take advantage of the time so as to make me very happy when we see each other. Imagine my astonishment when I hear you play a beautiful sonata by Beethoven! That will be lovely! That's when I'll hug you very hard, very hard! Mme Viardot often writes me that you care very much for me... It's now for you to prove it. Do all you can so that Mme Harang[3] will be satisfied with you—and you'll be just as pleased with me—I promise you.

Adieu, my child—be well. I hug you tenderly.

Your father,

Ivan Turgenev.

P.S. I'm now in the country at Spasskoye, I'll return to Petersburg for the winter—and if peace comes,[4] I'll come to see you in the spring—pray to God for peace.

Letter 64 (390). To A.A. Krayevsky.
July-September, 1855. Spasskoye.

Dear Krayevsky,

I'm writing you with the following proposal: would you like to buy my novel?[1] It will consist of two parts—I can give you written assurance that I'll deliver the finished text to you by September 1st of next year at the very latest. Give me 75 silver rubles per signature—and since I need the money now—give me 500 silver rubles now, which together with the money I owe you will comprise an advance. All this can be formalized on paper. Answer me whether you agree to my proposal—and why haven't you read Kolbasin's povest yet?[2]

Your

Ivan Turgenev.

Wednesday.

Letter 65 (391). To L.N. Tolstoy
October 3/15, 1855. Pokrovskoye.

Village of Pokrovskoye
October 3, 1855.

I've long been planning to initiate at least a written acquaintance with you, dear Lev Nikolayevich, due to the momentary impossibility of any other kind; now, on leaving your sister's home in Petersburg,[1] I want to bring this long-time intention of mine to fruition. First of all, I thank you sincerely for dedicating your "Wood Felling" to me—nothing else in my entire literary career has so flattered my self-esteem. Your sister has probably written you of my high opinion of your talent and of how much I expect of you—and recently I've thought of you especially often. I feel awful when I think about where you are located.[2] Although, on the other hand, I'm also glad for you for all these new sensations and experiences—

but everything in good measure—and you ought not to tempt fate—as it is she is happy to wound us at every step. It would be very good if you could get out of the Caucasus—you have proved well enough that you are no coward—and, after all, a military career is not for you. Your calling is that of a writer, an artist of thought and word. I have decided to speak to you in this way because in your last letter, which was received today, you hint at the possibility of a leave—in addition to which I love Russian literature too much not to nurse the desire to know you in a milieu other than one of stupid, undiscerning bullets. If it should really be possible for you to come to Tula Province even for only a while, I would make a special trip from Petersburg in order to make your acquaintance in person—that can't be much of a lure for you—but really, for your sake and for the sake of literature, come. I repeat—your weapon is the pen, not the sword, and the Muses not only have no patience with worldly vanity—but are jealous as well.

I think we would become close and have very satisfying talks, and perhaps our acquaintance would be useful for both of us.

I would tell you much about yourself—about your works—but that's absolutely out of the question on paper—especially in a letter. How we all regretted Nikolay Nikolayevich's[3] departure!

It's really frustrating to recall that though close neighbors, we became friends so late.

Your reply would make me very happy. Here is my address: St. Petersburg, the Fontanka, by the Anichkov Bridge, the Stepanov house.

I press your hand in cordial fashion, dear Lev Nikolayevich, and wish you all the best, starting with your health. I remain your sincerely respectful

Ivan Turgenev.

Letter 66 (403). To V.P. Botkin.
December 3/15, 1855. Petersburg.

Petersburg.
December 3, 1855.

Dear Botkin,

I've been planning to write you nearly every day, but various things kept getting in the way. But when I received your kind letter, I immediately seized pen in hand. I'm very glad that my portrait gives you some pleasure—if it looks at you in a friendly way, that means the likeness is true. You already know from Nekrasov that Tolstoy is staying with me here. I would very much like for you to meet him. He's an extremely nice, unusual person. But who you wouldn't recognize is me, your humble servant. Imagine me riding around to frivolous suburban balls, in love with a lovely Polish woman, giving her silver services and spending nights with her until 8 in the morning! It really is unexpected and unlike me, don't you think? But meanwhile that's the way things are. But now I've had my fill—and I want to get back to usual—living like a philosopher and working—because it's shameful to fool around at my age!

I've already redone a lot in *Rudin* and added to it. Nekrasov is satisfied with what I read to him, but I still have to work on it. I hope that everything will be finished by the 15th. Please come and visit—I would so like for you to catch Tolstoy here. He would have left already as a consequence of a letter he received from the country, if circumstances hadn't arisen which have detained him. You'll like him very much—you'll see!

I imagine that you can't be having too marvellous a time in Moscow. Come visit—and you'll give Nekrasov great pleasure. His health is no worse than before—but he seems to be in the dumps.

By the way, my cook Pyotr begs me to remind you about him for the Moscow Merchant Club—because they say d'autres se mettent sur les rangs [there are other candidates]—and you won't find a better cook.

I'm anxious to see you—come for a visit—I'll show you Nadezhda Nikolayevna—you'll fall in love with her.

Good-bye—I hug you.

Your

Ivan Turgenev.

Letter 67 (405). To M.N. and V.P. Tolstoy.
December 8/20, 1855. Petersburg.

St. Petersburg.
December 8, 1855.

I'll begin, my dear friends, by announcing to everyone within hearing that I'm guilty before you, especially before you, dear Countess—but you know that the sword refuses to strike a repentant head. Moreover, I should tell you that I would surely have written you a long time ago were it not for the arrival of your brother,[1] which shook me out of my usual habits for a while, but now I'm back to normal. However, I developed some sort of carbuncle-like boil on my stomach, they cut it open, i.e., the boil, not my stomach—I screamed like a hare—it was horribly painful—but I'm better now—though I'm still not going out at all—and will stay at home about six more days. You see that I'm not just a hypochondriac; say what you want, but boils are not caused by hypochondria. Well, I'll tell you that you have quite a brother. I've nicknamed him the Troglodyte—even the Furious Troglodyte—because of his impetuousness, wild stubbornness, and idleness—which doesn't prevent me from loving him from the bottom of my heart and growling at him without surcease, like a wise uncle at an extravagant nephew.

He has managed to commit a wide variety of atrocities since he arrived here—but he hasn't gambled, nor has he given in to drunkenness. I'll describe all his acts in detail sometime—the reason he couldn't leave and so on. For now I'll just tell you that he read us some excerpts from his new works—they're superb, and in general, if he doesn't cripple his talent, he will leave us all far behind, out of sight. His health is now satisfactory—and I'm trying to contain him within four walls. Islavin[2] often comes to visit—I've gotten to like him very much—especially because he himself is quite attached to the Troglodyte, whom he and I often discuss, moreover, invariably to the accompaniment of sighs, raising our eyes to heaven, and shrugging our shoulders.

The music that you wish, Countess, will be sent to you tomorrow.

There is a lot of news here—but it's not convenient to write about it all. They gave a dinner for Totleben[3] a few days ago at the chess club, but my cursed carbuncle prevented my being present. It was very noisy and lively—speeches were pronounced and verses read—all the Sevastopol naval heroes (Shvarts, Zherve, and others) were present—Maykov[4] read poetry—I especially like the following quatrain:

Nakhimov performed a glorious feat
Like a simple soldier,
Not recognizing his childish soul,
How simple, great and
Holy he was...

Only it's too bad that toward the end there was a slight scandal: the scientist Yakobi[5] (the inventor of galvano plastics) was roughed up a little for his drunken and insolent remarks, for which he later apologized.

The Troglodyte has gotten to know all our men of literature here. In general, everyone likes him because there really are many amiable things about him; he himself will tell you how he liked the writers. He seems not to be bored here—but he's sunk in idleness, as if in a tavern eiderdown. I'll let him read this letter—in the hope that he'll repent!

What else can I tell you? I've only been to the opera twice—things are going rather poorly there. There is no superb primadonna, although Madame Bosio[6] is not bad. I liked *Trovatore* (Verdi's new opera), about which I had the strongest apprehensions, just as I do about Verdi in general—but especially one scene in the final act was surprisingly beautiful and poetic.

Kolbasin[7] is fine and sends his regards. He's now working on a long biographical article about Martynov,[8] the translator of the ancient classics. Martynov was an extraordinarily remarkable person—and it's turning out to be interesting.

I'm very sorry about the tragedy that has befallen Baron Delvig's family. But where is he? If he's here, then why doesn't he come to see me?

I send my regards to all our good acquaintances—and clasp all your hands firmly. If Nikolay Nikolayevich[9] is still at your place, embrace him for me.

Be healthy and prosperous. Until the next letter.

Your

Iv. Turgenev.

101

Letter 68 (418). To V.P. Botkin.
February 8/20, 1856. Petersburg.

Petersburg.
February 8, 1856.

I received your letter about Ladyzhenskaya.[1] Your description of her is so accurate that I can only wonder why you, with your subtle understanding of human physiognomies, have never written anything yourself? The package (i.e., her povest) has already been sent to you—and you've probably already received it and delivered it. I imagine, however, that your acquaintance with Ladyzhenskaya will nevertheless be a pleasant one: she is precisely a "+" rather than a "-."

What should I tell you about us? Things are so-so. I met Gagarina,[2] whom I liked very much. Nekrasov is recovering. I nearly broke off with Tolstoy—no, my friend, such lack of education can't help but create that reaction one way or another. The day before yesterday at dinner at Nekrasov's he made so many banal and vulgar remarks about G. Sand that I can't even tell you. The argument went very far—in a word—he infuriated everyone and showed himself in a highly unfavorable light. I'll tell you the whole story some time—it's awkward to write about it.

Fet has left. His poems have all been put in order and have already been passed on to the censor. The printing will begin in a few days.

How did Moscow like the second issue of *The Contemporary* and what was the final opinion about *Rudin?* Write me about that. And the third issue of *The Russian Messenger* is not bad. Ostrovsky[3] arrived yesterday. I'll let you know what impression he makes here and what impression is made on him.

The School of Hospitality was given in Shtakenshneider's private theater[4] yesterday—and it created a scandal—half the audience fled in disgust—I hid and got away—and Druzhinin stood amid the audience like a rock amid the waves. Grigorovich, who is still staying on here, didn't appear at all. Best of all was that this junk was attributed to me. I had some very bad moments—and did they have to drag out into the light of day that farce which is only suitable for holidays in a village in the steppe?[5]

The day before yesterday I was at the dress rehearsal of *The Bureaucrat,* a play by Sollogub. Vera Samoylova was very charming. Artificial through and through, but the play itself is artificial, just as if it were written for a Gymnase [secondary school] with a good-hearted colonel, a comic type, a generous jeune premier [first lover] and a coquettish widow. But you know *The Bureaucrat* anyway. They're putting

102

it on now at Maria Nikolayevna's[6]—and Sollogub est redevenu inar-bordable et insolent [has again become unapproachable and insolent]. To hell with him!

Farewell, friend, be well. If you yourself don't come here soon, then I'll see you at the beginning of March. Be well and give my regards to everyone in Moscow who remembers me. I doubt that you'll have to give my regards to many people.

Farewell,

Your

Iv. Turgenev.

Letter 69 (427). To L.L. Dobrovolsky.[1]
April 27/May 9, 1856. Petersburg.

Dear Lavrenty Lvovich,

Please excuse me for allowing myself to trouble you with a request, even though I have not made your acquaintance. Here is the problem. You may perhaps be aware that I intend to publish a collection of my povests. The reprinting of one of them, entitled "Mumu," has met with difficulties. My friend, General Kovalevsky,[2] however, told me that he had received a letter from the Minister of Public Enlightenment in which he makes known his intention to pass the povest; since I'm leaving here on Monday, I would very much like to know the Minister's final decision.[3] My censor, Goncharov,[4] inquired today at the Censorship Committee, and there had not yet been any decision. Please do me the favor of letting me know how the matter stands and whether I may hope to receive an answer before my departure.

I would have come to see you in person, but I hesitate to trouble you with a visit.

With ultimate respect and devotion, I have the honor of remaining

Your most humble servant

Ivan Turgenev.

Letter 70 (441). To D. Ya. Kolbasin.
May 21/June 2, 1856. Spasskoye.

Spasskoye.
May 21, 1856.
Monday.

Dear Dmitry Yakovlevich, I received your answer and, for the sake of clarity, I'll answer point by point:

(1) I'm very glad that "Mumu" was finally passed and that the printing will begin. Next week I'll send you the corrected "Three Meetings"—and I ask you to do me the favor of sending me, when you've copied them—*the added pages* in "A Quiet Spot" and "Pasynkov." I think that there are some spots that ought to be touched up there, and furthermore, it will serve as a guarantee that you have been through them.

(2) You must have long since received the Tula Marshal's certificate sent to you by insured mail—and you've probably already been to see Ignatiev.[1] But in today's mail I received notification from Princess Odoyevskaya[2] (the sister of Lanskoy,[3] the Minister of the Interior) that "the foreign passport for the Collegiate Secretary Turgenev was sent from the Ministry of the Interior to the St. Petersburg Governor-General on May 14 with No. 881." That means that my request paid off and has been set in motion, in spite of the missing paper. If that's the case, brother, then find out how things stand—and whether all I really have to do is receive the passport. If they tell you yes, then find out how soon after the day of receipt I have to leave (they say that by land, in six weeks, by sea—in three weeks)—and write me all the details. If it turns out that I have to hurry, I'll send you money to book me a place on the Stettin ship before July 21st (I took a ticket for July 21st) and the ticket—which, if they refuse to exchange, can be sold, I hope. But I admit that I wouldn't like to leave before July 21...In a word, find out all the details, using the above-mentioned information delivered by Princess Odoyevskaya, and write me punctually.

(3) Pay the money to the chess club—and Saturday I'll send you 50 silver rubles with a list of purchases that I'll ask you to make for that sum.

(4) The Tolstoys (especially the Countess) are extremely interested in their "relative"[4] and they heartily regret that he didn't come. If I'd been able to foresee how heavily they were going to sigh about him, I would definitely have dragged him here. They're waiting for a portrait of Nekrasov, for the purchase of which they've sent him money. The Countess is a little sad and has lost weight, the Count is flourishing like a peony.

(5) I've been hunting once, but besides corncrake and quail, there isn't anything.

(6) On your way past Davydov's[5] drop in on him and remind him that together with *The Contemporary* he wanted to send me the second volume of Solovyov[6] and *For Light Reading.*[7] What impression has the fifth issue of *The Contemporary* made?

If it should be necessary for me to come for the passport in person, I could do that—as it was, I was planning to be at Botkin's in Moscow around the 1st of June, and it's not far to travel from there. But I have to say that I was about to change my mind about going to see Botkin. I'm overcome by laziness.

What's with "the relative's" povest?[8] Still no answer? Why doesn't he write me? What's he doing now?

The weather here is still unsatisfactory. It's cold and there are frequent rains.

I'm loading you down with an unconscionable number of assignments—but I rely firmly on your kindness and friendship. I clasp your hands firmly and remain

Your devoted

Ivan Turgenev.

P.S. Porfiry[9] sends his regards. He too is flourishing.

Letter 71 (442). To S.T. Aksakov.
May 25/June 6, 1856. Spasskoye.

Village of Spasskoye.
May 25, 1856.

Dear and respected Sergey Timofeyevich, your wife told me when I was passing through Moscow that you would be there about a month—and therefore I'm sending this letter to Denezhny Lane in the hope that in the case of your departure they'll forward it to you at Abramtsevo. I've been in my village here for more than two weeks now—and I'm living a vegetable (so as not to wound myself, I won't say animal) life. I'm eating *everything*—

even lettuce!—and sleeping like a pug dog. I can't do anything, but I'm reading Grot's *History of Greece*[1] with great pleasure and enjoying my dear, happy Athenians. I went hunting twice—I bagged some corncrakes and quail and two great snipe—and a unique bird for us—a little *black* gull (about the size of a thrush) with huge gray wings and red webbed feet—now I'll hang my rifle up on the nail until the grouse season. I've been thinking a lot this whole time, in the first place, about the continuation of *A Family Chronicle* that I heard, and in the second place—about my talks with your son. *A Family Chronicle* is an absolutely epic work, but I'm afraid that Konstantin Sergeyevich[2] and I will never see eye to eye. He sees in the "mir"[3] some sort of all-embracing medicine—a panacea, the alpha and omega of Russian life, but while recognizing its being peculiar—if one may say so—to Russia, I nevertheless see only a basic, fundamental ground—but no more than the ground, a form, *on* which the state can be built, but not *into* which it can be cast. There can be no tree without roots, but Konstantin Sergeyevich, it seems to me, would like to see roots on the branches. No matter what you say, the right of individuality is destroyed by it—and it's for that right that I've fought up to now and will fight to the end. We'll talk about all of this in July—but the proverb says that only the grave can cure a hunchback, and he and I are both nearly hunchbacks, though in different directions. Although I belong more to "the rags," among whose numbers Konstantin Sergeyevich counts Fet, for instance—but after all, a rag too can be sturdy: it's easy to tear it to pieces—but you can pound it with a hammer as much as you like and you won't do a thing to it.

Rumors have reached me that your son Ivan has become friends with Vasilchikov and is going to the Crimea; I'm happy for him and for the business itself.[4] It was sad to think that such a person as Ivan Sergeyevich could exclaim: "When will thy time pass, o youth, o heavy burden!"[5]

Good-bye, dear Sergey Timofeyevich. I wish you all the best, especially good health. I send regards to your wife and all your family and remain

Your sincerely devoted

Ivan Turgenev

Letter 72 (449). To Ye. Ye. Lambert.[1]
June 10/22, 1856. Spasskoye.

Village of Spasskoye.
June 10, 1856.

Your letter from Revel, dear Countess, made me very happy and somewhat embarrassed: I feel that I don't deserve all those nice things with which it is filled, and I know (though I've only read 30 pages of your book so far) that the human heart is so made that even undeserved praise provides a secret sweetness for it—or at least the pleasure of humility... These are all dangerous feelings, and it's better not to even speak of them. Thank you for remembering me, and I hope with all my heart that your stay in Revel will be pleasurable.

I'll say a few words about myself. In the first place, I received the news from Petersburg that my passport has been issued—and I'm leaving Russia around the 20th of next month: we'll still have time to exchange letters. I hope that our correspondence will not cease while I am abroad. The permission to travel abroad pleases me ... but at the same time I can't help admitting that it would be better for me not to go. To go abroad at my age means to fix my course permanently on a gypsy life and to abandon all thoughts of a family life. But what can be done? Obviously, such is my fate. But that is easily said: people without firmness of character love to make up a "fate" for themselves; that relieves them of the necessity of having their own will—and of responsibility for themselves. In any event—le vin est tiré—il faut le boire [the wine has been drawn—it must be drunk].

I have no manor house here; I had one, but it burned down; I live in the old wing. But there's a large, good orchard—just neighbor ladies, and I'm hardly an Onegin![2]

The hunting season hasn't yet begun. Oh yes, there's something else I should tell you: the anecdote I told you about a woman with whom I had dinner and who involuntarily disillusioned me has nothing to do with the woman of whom you write...[3]

You write Russian very nicely—do you know that? And not a single mistake, even in spelling! But all the same, write me in French.[4] All the same one observes a certain effort in your selection of phrase—and it's as if you translate mentally from French. It will be easier for you to write French—and you'll write more eagerly.

It pleases me to think that we'll be exchanging ideas and feelings even if only occasionally; it's even more pleasant to think that there will come a time, God willing, when we shall see each other again—and—I dare to hope—become firm friends. In the life of a man, just as in the life of a woman, there comes a time when more than anything else one values calm and stable relationships. Bright autumn days are the most beautiful days in the year. I hope that I'll be able then to persuade you not to fear reading Pushkin and others. Are you still afraid of "alarm?"[5]

I no longer hope for happiness for myself, i.e., for happiness in that same *alarming* sense in which it is now understood by young hearts; there's no point in thinking about flowers when the time of flowering has passed. God grant that there may at least be some sort of fruit—and those vain backward impulses can only hinder its ripening. One must learn from nature's correct and tranquil movement and her humility . . . But when it comes to words we're all wise men: but let the first ridiculous passing thing come our way and we up and chase after it.

When I glance back at my life, all I seem to have done is chase after ridiculous things. Don Quixote at least believed in the beauty of his Dulcinea, but in our age Don Quixotes see that their Dulcineas are ugly— and keep running after them.

We have no ideal—that's why all this happens: but an ideal comes only from a strong civic environment, art (or science), and religion. But not everyone is born an Athenian or an Englishman, an artist or scientist—and religion is not granted to everyone—immediately. We'll wait and believe— and know that for the time being we're acting foolish. That realization may nevertheless be useful.

But I seem to have gotten carried away with philosophizing. And therefore—with your permission (remember, you said that I could) I clasp your hand respectfully and cordially, I wish you all the best and remain

Your sincerely devoted

Ivan Turgenev.

P.S. My sincere regards to your husband.

Letter 73 (473). To A.I. Herzen.
September 10/22, 1856. Courtavenel.

Courtavenel.
September 22, 1856.

Why haven't I heard anything from you, dear friend? I've been waiting for you to send a letter and my povest,[1] but I've finally decided to write you a couple of words. Have you moved to Putney,[2] and are you well, and are all your loved ones well? I'm living in the country here and enjoying far niente [doing nothing] and hunting. The only bad thing is that the hunting for scant fowl is middling and the weather is miserable. I finished reading your memoirs in the second part of the *Polar Star*.[3] They are marvellous—I only regret that the language is uneven. But you must continue these stories: there is a courageous and unaffected truth in them—and as if involuntarily, merriness and freshness break through their sad sounds. I liked them all extraordinarily—and I repeat my request—you must continue them without being afraid of anything. It's a strange thing! In Russia I've been trying to persuade the old man Aksakov to continue his memoirs, and here—you. And that's not as contradictory as it seems at first glance. Both your memoirs and his are a truthful picture of Russian life, only at two different extremes and from two different points of view. But our land is not only great and wealthy—it is broad as well—and embraces many things that seem alien to each other.

Fet came here for a couple days—I gave him a book of his verses and your address—he'll forward it to you.

Write me, please, and when I get to Paris, I'll write you often and intelligently; but I've been seized by indescribable laziness here—here's my address: au château de Courtavenel, près de Rozoy-en-Brie (Seine-et-Marne).

I embrace your family and Ogaryov. Be well.

Your Ivan Turgenev.

Letter 74 (474). To M.N. Tolstaya.
September 11/23, 1856. Courtavenel.

Courtavenel.
(near Paris)
September 11/23, 1856.

Dear Countess,

I'm writing you from Madame Viardot's village, where I've been more than a month (I went to London for about ten days, though). I'm very happy here; I'm among people whom I love and who love me; there's only one bad thing: the weather is disgusting and there's absolutely no wild fowl. I'm certain that it can't be as bad at home. But I know absolutely nothing about what's happening at home: I still have not received a single line from my uncle;[1] only from your brother Lev have I received a letter, which I'm answering in your letter. Please convey my answer to him.[2] He is a great eccentric; we are fated to love each other from a distance—but to experience mutual constraint at close quarters. How is your other brother, Nikolay? Can he really still be in the Caucasus and not back in our "peaceful regions"?[3] Write me a few words about your life and doings. Are you continuing your music studies—and where are you planning to spend the winter—in the country or in Moscow? What are all your friends doing, your Adjutant, Olga Petrovna, Nastenka, and so on?[4] At times, in the midst of the French nature and French society that surround me, I recall your lovely little house on the bank of the Snezhed. By the way, can you really still be continuing your bathing? It's been so cold here for more than a month that Lord help you! Do you at least occasionally see your brother Lev—or is he still in Yasnaya with his aunts?[5] I'm showering you with questions, but you may think that I ought rather to tell than inquire, but tell. But there's nothing to tell; I live here in a place that is as isolated as yours; the only difference is that you aren't acquainted with any of the people here. I'll say a few words about my daughter, though. I like her; she's a little lazy—but very good and kind; she's tall and looks like me, only her eyes are almost black; she's completely forgotten Russian—and speaks with a Parisian accent. We spend a lot of time with music, reading, and acting out comedies. But I don't really do anything; I'm planning to work hard in Paris, though.

Read my povest "Faust" in the October issue of *The Contemporary* and tell me your opinion of it. Write me a letter mostly about whatever comes into your head; and I give you my word that I'll answer promptly. I hope that your arm is now completely back to normal. Do you see your uncle and his family?

Well, farewell, dear Maria Nikolayevna. I clasp your hand with a truly cordial feeling. And what is the Count doing?[6] Is he still angry at *The Russian Messenger?*[7] They say that *The Messenger* is planning to destroy me.[8]

I embrace the Count and all your children: may you all be well and happy.

Your Ivan Turgenev.

P.S. I'm not going to frank this letter; that way it will reach you more surely—you shouldn't frank your answer either.

Letter 75 (475). To L.N. Tolstoy.
September 13/25, 1856. Courtavenel.

Courtavenel (near Paris).
September 13/25, 1856.

Your letter reached me rather late, dear Lev Nikolayevich,—I had gone to England and found it here upon my return. I'll begin with the fact that I'm very grateful for what you wrote and for having sent it to me; I will never cease loving you and treasuring your friendship, although—and this is probably my fault—for a long time each of us will feel a certain awkwardness in the presence of the other. I'm certain that we'll see each other again and will see each other often; when I was leaving, I told your sister that I wouldn't have the time to visit you at Yasnaya,—but she understood my words quite differently. I think that you yourself understand the source of the awkwardness that I just mentioned. You are the only person with whom I have had such misunderstandings; that has happened precisely because I did not want to limit myself just to simple friendly relations with you—I wanted to go further and deeper; but I did that incautiously, I upset you, alarmed you, and when I noticed my mistake I backed away, perhaps too hurriedly; that's the reason that this "ravine" has formed between us. But this awkwardness is only a *physical* impression and nothing more; and if on meeting you I act upset again, it really won't be because I am a bad person. I assure you that there's no reason to think up a different explanation. Perhaps just to add that I am much older than you and have travelled a different road. Besides our own so-called literary interests—I am convinced of this—we have few points of contact; your whole life has been aimed at the future, all mine has been built on the past. For me to follow you is impossible; for you to follow me is just as impossible; you are too remote from me, besides which, you are too strong on your own feet to become anyone's follower. I can assure you that I never thought that you were malicious, and I never suspected literary envy in you. I assumed (excuse me for saying this) that there was a great deal of confusion in you, but never anything bad; and you yourself are too perspicacious not to know that if one of us should envy the other, then it won't be me. In a word, I doubt that we will ever be friends in the Rousseauan sense of the word; but each of us will love the other, rejoice at his successes, and when you calm down, I'm certain that we'll offer each other our hands just as gayly and freely as on that day when I first met you at Petersburg.

But enough about this. Better that you tell me what you've been doing. Have you written anything? What about *Youth?* What about the Caucasus povest?[1] And your brother's notes—have you published them and sent them to Petersburg?[2] And can he really be planning to remain in the Caucasus? If he returns to the Tula Province, give him my regards. Where do you intend to spend the winter? All of this interests me very much. As for myself, I won't get to Spasskoye before next June. I haven't yet done anything here; but when I move to Paris (in about three weeks), I'll get down to work. I'm very happy here; I'm with people whom I sincerely love—and who love me. My povest will be in the October issue of *The Contemporary;* tell me whether you like it.[3] My address for the time being is: Paris, poste restante. Fet is in Paris—he sends his regards—and I received a letter from Nekrasov in Berlin. *The Contemporary* will somehow manage without him.

Farewell, be well; I clasp your hand firmly.

Your Ivan Turgenev.

P.S. I'm writing to you in a letter to your sister. My regards to your aunt. By the way, if it's a matter of the 28th day of the month, I too was born on the 28th.

Letter 76 (491). To I.A. Goncharov.[1]
November 11/23, 1856. Paris.

... And as for your literary activity, I don't even want to think about the possibility of your laying your golden pen on the shelf; I'm ready to say to you, as Mirabeau did to Sieyès: le silence de Mr. Gontscharoff est une calamité publique [Mr. Goncharov's silence is a public calamity]! I'm certain that in spite of your many censorship duties you'll find it possible to work on your own things, and certain words of yours spoken to me before my departure give me reason to think that not all hopes have fallen through. I'll pester you with exclamations of "*Oblomov* and a second novel!" until you finish them, if only to be rid of me—I really will, you'll see.

Joking aside, I beg you to let me know what state those two novels are in: the passionate interest that I take in them gives me a certain right to ask you that immodest question.

I intend to make the acquaintance of the literati here and to try to penetrate French life a little more deeply.

... I think that in complaining about yourself, you purposely exaggerated, wishing to irritate and spur yourself (I know that feeling myself), but in your letter there is such genuine seriousness and sincerity that my hands sank. Can it really be, I thought, that we have to renounce Goncharov the writer? Can it really be that that marvellous novel, the sketch for which, worked out by him on a single winter evening in Petersburg (at Stepanov's house), filled Dudyshkin[2] and me with such merry emotion (You haven't forgotten that evening?), can it really be that that novel, which is already almost ready, which begs for the light of day, must disappear forever? ...

Letter 77 (492). To L.N. Tolstoy.
November 16/28, 1856. Paris.

Paris.
November 16/28, 1856

Dear Tolstoy, it took your letter of October 15th a month to crawl here—I didn't receive it until yesterday. I've thought seriously about what you wrote to me—and I think that you are wrong. I really can't be absolutely honest with you because I can't be absolutely frank; I think that we met in an awkward way and at the wrong moment—and when we see each other again things will go much more smoothly and easily. I feel that I love you as a person (and of course as an author); but much about you bothers me; and I finally found it more comfortable to keep my distance from you. When we see each other again let's try to go arm in arm again—perhaps we'll be more successful, and at a remove (although that sounds rather strange)—my heart feels for you what it would for a brother—and I even feel tenderness for you. In a word, I love you—that's for certain, perhaps because of that, with time everything will turn out all right.

I heard about your illness and was upset, but now cast memories of it out of your head. After all, you're a hypochondriac too—and you may be thinking of tuberculosis, but, honest to God, you don't have it. I feel very sorry for your sister;[1] who should be well if not she—that is, I mean that if anyone deserves to be healthy, it is she; but instead of that—she's ill all the time. It would be good if Moscow treatment could help her. Why don't you send for your brother?[2] Why does he want to stay in the Caucasus? Or does he want to become a great warrior? My uncle informed me that you'd all left for Moscow; and that's why I am addressing this letter to Moscow, care of Botkin.

French phrase mongering is just as disgusting to me as it is to you—and Paris has never seemed so prosaically plain. Satisfaction does not suit it; I've seen it at other moments—and I liked it more then. What keeps me here is an old, inseparable link with a certain family[3]—and my daughter, whom I like very much: she's a sweet, bright girl. If it weren't for that, I'd have left to see Nekrasov in Rome long ago. I've received two letters from him in Rome—he's a little lonely—but that's understandable—everything great in Rome merely surrounds him; he doesn't live with it—and one can't be long nourished by rare moments of involuntary sympathy and surprise. But all the same he's better off than in Petersburg—and his health is improving. Fet is now with him in Rome . . . Yes, my friend, he was in Paris, but a more unhappy, lost creature you can't imagine. He was so homesick that, scream as I did, he didn't see anyone except for his French servant. He came to visit me (i.e., at Mr. Viardot's) in the country—and (just between us) he left an unpleasant impression. An officer, endimanché [all got up], with rings on his fingers and an Annensky ribbon in his buttonhole, telling the dullest anecdotes in broken French—the humor disappeared completely, his eyes wide and round, his mouth wide and round, senseless amazement on his face—if he'd only stop! In my room he and I argued to the point where the whole household was moaning from the wild sounds of Slavic speech, in a word—things were bad. But he has written several lovely poems and detailed travel notes where there is a lot of childishness, but also many intelligent and sensible things—and a touchingly simple-hearted sincerity of impression. He really is a dear, as you call him.

Now about Chernyshevsky's articles.[4] I don't like their brash, dry tone, the expression of a stale soul, but I rejoice at the possibility of their being published. I rejoice at the remarks about Belinsky—the excerpts from his articles, I rejoice that that name is finally being pronounced with respect. But you can't appreciate my joy. Annenkov writes me that this has the effect on me that it does because I'm abroad—that this business is outmoded; it's not what is needed now.[5] That may be;—it's easier for him to see from where he is; but it still pleases me.

You've finished the first part of "Youth"—that's marvellous. How sorry I am that I can't hear it! If you don't slip off the path (and there seems to be no reason to suppose that you will) you'll go very far. I wish you health, activity—and freedom—spiritual freedom.

As for my "Faust," I don't think that you'll like it. You could only have liked my things—and perhaps they had a certain influence on you—until you became independent. Now there's no point in your studying me, you see only the difference in style, you see the failures and omissions: what's left for you is to study man, your own heart—and truly great writers. But I'm a writer of a transitional time—and only suitable for people in a transitional state.

Well, farewell and be healthy! Write me—my address now is Rue de Rivoli, No. 206. I thank your sister for the couple of words she appended, regards to her and her husband. Thanks to Varenka[6] for not forgetting me. I was going to talk to you about the literati here—but I'll wait till the next time. I clasp your hand firmly.

Your Ivan Turgenev.

Letter 78 (503). To L.N. Tolstoy.
December 16, 23/December 28, January 4, 1857. Paris.

Paris.
December 6/28, 1856.

Dear Tolstoy, I received your letter in which you reproach me for not answering you; but by now you have probably received my two letters and been persuaded that I'm not in debt to you.

On the basis of what you write I'm almost ready to conclude that you repent the formation of a union of allies.[1] If our ally were Druzhinin instead of Nekrasov, I think that you wouldn't even think of repenting. The unpleasantness that you've noted stuns me too;—but to withdraw now would be both dishonest and awkward—even funny. Chernyshevsky is least of all to your taste; but in this regard you exaggerate a little. Let's suppose that you find his "fetishism" revolting[2]—and you are displeased by his digging up old times which you think one ought not to touch; but remember that we're talking about the name of a person who all his life was—I won't say a martyr (you don't like pompous words), but the laborer, the servant of a speculator who raked in money with the former's hand and often ascribed his merits to himself.[3] (I myself was a witness to that on more than one occasion.) Remember that during his whole life poor Belinsky not only knew neither happiness nor peace—but not even the most ordinary pleasures and comforts; that for expressing thoughts that have become clichés by now he was attacked from all sides with mud, stones, epigrams, and denunciations; that by his death he avoided a fate that might have been very bitter—and can it really be that after all that, you find that two or three articles in his favor, written perhaps somewhat dithyrambically—are too great a reward, that this is too much to bear—that it is "rotten eggs?" In order for you to understand my feelings about these articles, I propose a date with you in ten years; at that time I'll see whether you enjoy it if you are forbidden to express a word of affection for a friend of your youth, a person who both rejoiced and suffered and lived by virtue of his convictions . . . It's just that I doubt that you'll find such a person among your recollections.

I gave a close reading to Druzhinin's article in the November issue of *Library for Reading*[4]—I know that you're delighted by it—but I frankly confess that I expected much more. It's intelligent and perhaps fair, but cold and in essence—useless. For instance: Druzhinin, by the way, says that if the critics of the time hadn't been so mercilessly severe in regard to Marlinsky[5] he might have improved and not vanished.[6] What a childish—or perhaps senile view! As if the point were the survival of Marlinsky's talent! The point was the rejection of a whole direction that was false and empty, the point was the destruction of an authority, illusory strength and grandeur. As long as that authority was recognized it was impossible to expect the correct and healthy development of our literature—and thanks to Belinsky's article about Marlinsky—and two or three similar ones— about Benediktov[7] and others—we moved forward. If you're going to hit a bull, then do it with a blunt object—but you'd like to strike it with a stick and even wet it with rose water to make it painless. But perhaps you find that we haven't moved ahead at all—and that this is all the same passion for general conclusions—and strong words. That angers you; but I still haven't lost hope of seeing you disillusioned with regard to the elegant and gentlemanly restraint which is perhaps very much at home in the *Revue des 2 Mondes* or *Revue Britannique*—but which doesn't look good on us.[8] By the way, do you know that I used *to kiss* Marlinsky's name on journal covers—cried in Granovsky's arms over a book of Benediktov's verses— and was horribly irritated on hearing of Belinsky's brazenness in raising his hand against them? You must be able to see that what he said back then seemed an unheard-of novelty. You missed all of this, since you're ten years younger than us; you already knew Gogol, and Marlinsky and tutti quanti [the like] were already long dead—and therefore you can't be a worthy judge of Belinsky's merits.

But enough about that. I'll get your story in *Library for Reading*—so don't send it—but please send the piece in *Notes of the Fatherland.*[9] I need it very much—I wish to follow your every step.

Don't forget to write me about your sister's health; I think of her often. I'm very happy about your intention to leave the service. Play my piano as much as you like. I'm leaving here in April and will definitely be in Russia in June. My bladder is still bothering me—but less so.

Farewell, until the next letter. This one has somehow turned out to be very polemical. But it was finished on January 4, New Style. Happy Russian New Year!

Your

Ivan Turgenev.

Letter 79 (505). To M.N. Tolstaya.
December 25, 1856/January 6, 1857. Paris.

Paris,
January 6, 1857, New Style.

How happy you made me with your letter, dear Countess! Rumors have reached me that you are very ill, and though I see from your husband's note and from your handwriting that you're not completely well— nonetheless things aren't as bad as I had thought. Please get well so that we can spend the summer more pleasantly; I'll definitely return to Spasskoye at the end of May—we'll invite your two brothers, Lev and Nikolay—and you'll see what a fine time we'll have. I'm very pleased that you liked "Faust," and your saying that there is a dualistic personage in me is altogether accurate—only you perhaps don't know the reason for that duality. I'll be frank with you too. You see, it was painful for me to grow old without having known complete happiness—and without having made a quiet nest for myself. The soul in me was still young, and it searched and grieved; but my mind, cooled by experience, rarely succumbing to its impulses, vented its own weakness on it with bitterness and irony; but when the soul in its turn asked what the *mind* had done, whether it had arranged my life correctly and reasonably, it was forced to lapse into a pained silence—and then both of them—mind and soul—began racing each other to depression. All of that has now changed ... When you saw me I was still dreaming of happiness, I didn't want to part with the hope; now I've given up on that forever. Everything has quieted down—the inner reproaches have been silenced—what's the point of fanning the ashes? You won't manage a flame no matter what. What caused all of this is a long story— besides which, the years have taken their course. When you see me you'll be amazed at my égalité d'humeur [spiritual equilibrium]. As for what grief is frozen underneath it—there's no point in digging down to that—there's no point in digging to the bottom of anyone. "Faust" was written at a breaking point, at a crucial turn in my life—my whole soul had flared up with the last fire of memories, hopes, and youth ... That won't be repeated. But it is in vain that you speak of my happiness: the grass is always greener on the other side. Enough about that. I repeat—let's try to get together this summer—and begin living as merry, kind old folks.

I've been corresponding with your brother Lev rather often. It seems to me that a change for the better is taking place in him. If God grant that he calm down and soften—he'll become a great writer (I'm not exaggerating) and an outstanding person. He and Druzhinin are now very close; I would wish him another comrade—but getting along with your brother is very difficult. Until a dish makes him throw up (please excuse the coarseness of the metaphor) he won't stop eating and praising it—and will continue to praise it even though he feels a pain at the pit of his stomach. Druzhinin is a very good person, but for all that, he's not for your brother. But that's the difference between grain and chaff: grind the former and you get flour— but all you'll get from the chaff is dust. Let him grind away!

And what do you hear of your other brother, that dear and undervalued Nikolay Nikolayevich? Can he really still be in the Caucasus? Does he wish to stay there forever? How happy I would be to see him!

I very much sympathize for you in your helpless, painful state. If you could write, I would advise you to put down on paper all the thoughts that come to and pass through your head. There's nothing you can do—be patient—happy days will come again—and you'll get well. 130 beats a minute shouldn't frighten you—that has happened with me as well. When it's not caused by an inflammation, it's not dangerous.

Give my regards to your husband. Will he by any chance subscribe to *The Library for Reading,* since they've announced for a future issue Ye. Ya. Kolbasin's povest "Academy Lane" by "Khi Kha Kho"?[1] By the way, did you receive the copy of *Povests and Stories* intended for you?

Farewell, dear Countess—get well, please. I clasp your husband's hand firmly—and yours, with your permission, I kiss.

Your sincerely devoted

Iv. Turgenev.

Letter 80 (506). To S.T. Aksakov.
December 27, 1856/January 8, 1857. Paris.

Paris.
January 8, 1857. New Style.

Dear and respected Sergey Timofeyevich, I received your letter a long time ago and I've long been planning to answer—and it's not that there was no time, rather I had to wait for that disposition of spirit in which one wants to converse with absent friends. The "whirlwind" of Parisian life is not the reason for that: I live here practically as a hermit—besides which, Paris with its glamor and glitter can turn a youth's head—or perhaps an old man's; but I'm not yet an old man—though Lord only knows how long ago I ceased being a youth. Since I last wrote you I've become acquainted with many of the writers here—not with the old glories, the former leaders (as with a goat, one gets neither wool nor milk from them) but with the young progressive ones. I have to confess that they're all extremely minor, prosaic, empty, and untalented. Lifeless fussiness, elegance, or flatness of debility, extreme lack of understanding of anything non-French, a lack of any sort of faith or conviction, even artistic conviction,—that's what meets you wherever you look. The best of them feel this themselves—and just moan and groan. There is no criticism—just trashy condescension toward everything and everyone; everyone sits on his own hobbyhorse, in his own manner and censes someone else so that he too will be censed—that's the whole picture. A certain poet will imagine that he needs to help realism along—and with an effort, with forced simplicity he sings of "Steam" and "Machines"[1]—another cries for a return to Zeus, Eros, and Pallas[2]—and sings of them, enjoying placing Greek names in his French verses, and in neither of them is there a drop of poetry. Through this second-rate din and noise penetrate, like the voices of antiquated singers, the rattling sounds of Hugo, Lamartine's sickly whining, Sand's nonsensical babble; Balzac is being raised up as an idol, and the new school of realists is crawling in the dust before him, slavishly venerating Accident, which they choose to call Reality and Truth; and the general level of morality declines with every day—that's France for you! If I live here, it's not for her or for Paris—but because of circumstances independent of my will. But spring will come—and I'll fly off to the homeland—where life is still young and rich in hopes. Oh, with what joy I'll see our semi-steppe areas! And in May I'll definitely be with you at Abramtsevo.

I'm very grieved by the news of your daughter's illness and your being upset over it. God grant that all of this correct itself and return to normal! An article about your *Chronicles* has been written by a certain Delaveau,[3] a writer from here who knows Russian well; I helped him and explained some things for him. The article should appear soon in *Revue des 2 Mondes*. Your idea of writing the story of a child for children is excellent—and I'm certain that you'll carry it out superbly, with that epic clarity and simplicity that distinguishes you among all our literary fraternity.[4] *The Russian Messenger* in which there is an excerpt from your *Chronicle* has been promised me by Prince Trubetskoy[5] (Konstantin Sergeyevich's[6] friend). I see him rather often—he is a very nice, kind person—and he loves all of you very much. He also receives *Russian Conversation*, but the fourth part has not been received here yet.

Give my regards to all your family, to your wife and Konstantin Sergeyevich and Ivan Sergeyevich in particular. Have Konstantin Sergeyevich write me a letter—I'll answer him right away—and what discussions we'll have this spring! I love arguing with him because in spite of our shouts and heat, the friendly smiles never leave our souls and can be felt in every word. But with other people you can agree about everything and have nothing to argue about—while between him and you there's an entire ravine.

I see Vasilchikov here, the brother of the General Vasilchikov under whom Ivan Sergeyevich worked.[7] As far as I can tell, nothing special has resulted from the investigation.

Well, farewell, dear and respected Sergey Timofeyevich. Be well—and God grant you the time and desire to write. For some reason or other I can't do anything—it's as if my hand were sprained. Maybe I'll get back to normal.

Until we see each other this spring.

Entirely yours,

Iv. Turgenev.

P.S. I can't even tell you how sorry I feel about both Kireyevskys.[8]

Letter 81 (510). L.N. Tolstoy.
January 3/15, 1857. Paris.

Paris.
January 3/15, 1857.

Dear Tolstoy,

I don't know whether my letters make you very happy, but yours comfort me. A change—a very good one—is obviously taking place in you. (Excuse me for seeming to pat you on the head: I'm a full ten years older than you—and in general I feel myself becoming an old prattler.) You are calming down, becoming serene and—most importantly—you're growing free, free of your own views and prejudices. To take a look to the left is just as nice as to the right—there are no impediments—there are "perspectives" everywhere (Botkin stole that word from me)—all you have to do is open your eyes wide. God grant that your horizons widen with every passing day! The only people who treasure systems are those whom the whole truth evades, who want to catch it by the tail; a system is just likes truth's tail, but the truth is like a lizard; it will leave the tail in your hand and escape: it knows that it will soon grow another tail. That comparison is somewhat bold, but the fact is that your letters comfort me. That's beyond doubt.

I received a very nice and rather lengthy letter from your sister.[1] It made me very happy; I'm sincerely attached to her—and the news of her illness saddened me greatly. She also like my "Faust." What a strange fate that piece has had! Some people find it not at all to their taste—by the way, and to my extreme regret—that includes Mme Viardot. Apropos, what

121

absurd rumors are being spread among you back home! Her husband is as healthy as can be, and I'm as far away from marriage as, for example, you are. But I love her more than ever, and more than anyone on earth. That's the truth.[2]

Your "Childhood and Adolescence" is creating a furor among the Russian ladies here; the copy that I had sent me is being read greedily—and I've already had to promise several people that I'd introduce them to you—they ask me for your autograph—in a word—you're in fashion—even more so than crinoline. I'm telling you this because no matter what you say—in your heart somewhere there's a little bump that such praise (moreover, any kind of praise) tickles pleasantly. And let it tickle—to your heart's content!

From the letters I receive from Petersburg I have to conclude that literary life there—and every other sort too—is on the move. Sometimes I'm greatly vexed that I'm not with all of you at this time—and I even think ("Man is egotistical") that I could be useful. But I can't even think of leaving here before April—and therefore I'm postponing all such fantasies until next winter. You write that you won't even sit out this winter in Petersburg. Why on earth do you have the idea of going to the Caucasus? It would be better for you to get your brother out of there.[3]

Don't forget to send me everything that appears in *The Contemporary*.

Your acquaintance with Shakespeare—or more accurately—your approaching it—makes me happy. He is like Nature; sometimes it has such a vile physiognomy (just recall any of our lachrymose, slimy, October days in the steppe)—but even then there is necessity and truth in her—and (prepare yourself: your hair will stand on end) purpose. Get to know *Hamlet, Julius Caesar, Coriolanus, Henry IV, Macbeth,* and *Othello* as well. Don't let superficial absurdities repel you; dig down to the center, to the heart of the work—and you'll be amazed at the harmony and profound truth in that great spirit. Even from here I can see you smiling as you read these lines; but just think—Turgenev *might* just be right. Stranger things happen.[4]

I haven't been telling you about my acquaintances here; I've only met one nice woman—and she's Russian; and one very intelligent man—and he's a Jew.[5] Frenchies don't attract me; they may be superb soldiers and administrators, but all they have in all their heads is the same little lane down which the same thoughts—always the same—scurry along. Anything that is not theirs seems wild and stupid to them. "Ah! le lecteur Français ne saurait admettre cela!" [Ah, the French reader wouldn't permit that!] And having pronounced those words, a Frenchman can't even imagine that you might object in some way. The devil can take them!

Well, farewell, dear Tolstoy. Grow as broad as you've been growing deep up to now—and in time we'll all sit under your shade and praise its beauty and coolness.

Your

Ivan Turgenev.

Letter 82 (520). To D. Ya. Kolbasin.
February 16/28, 1857. Paris.

Saturday.
February 16/28, 1857.
Paris.

Dear Kolbasin, I'm giving a brief answer to your very short letter. In the first place, I've sent the letter you attached to Nekrasov in Rome, where he ran off to last Sunday; in the second place—don't even ask me about my health: my damned bladder has murdered me, and I can hardly wait for the day I finally leave Paris (that will be in a month). And in the third place, it would be better for you, villain, not to mention gossip that's being spread about me—because you write that rumors are going around, you even add that they're quite vile—but, you don't tell me what they are... For Heaven's sake let me know what's going on, otherwise I'm going to think that they're accusing me of stealing handkerchiefs or of <————>. Please write me about this. I've sent Panayev the slightly amended *Hanger-On* (with the title changed)—we'll see whether the censors will pass it.[1] I sent the letter to Podlinsky in Constantinople a long time ago.[2] Tolstoy has been here about a week. He has gotten much better—but he still behaves eccentrically. But I'm very glad that he's come. Please tell me why on earth I haven't received the 12th or 1st issues of *The Library* or the 17th, 12th, or 1st issues of *The Contemporary?* It's very unpleasant. They were about to start sending them—and that's as far as they got. What's your relative up to? I'm waiting for my usual monthly letter from him—tell him that. Be sure to do that.[3] Has your "Lane" found a publisher yet?[4] They say my povests are selling poorly: is that true? Please don't hesitate to write me the truth: if you knew how indifferent I am to literature in general and especially to my junk...[5]

123

I would love to have seen you holding an icon at Feoktista's[6] wedding! Importance written all over your face, and those sideburns, the sideburns!

Expect me in May—unless I kick the bucket, which wouldn't be so bad. Be well and believe in the sincere, cordial attachment of

Your

Ivan Turgenev.

P.S. I kiss your "relative's" brow all furrowed with thought.

Letter 83 (521). To V.P. Botkin.
February 17/March 1, 1857. Paris.

Paris.
February 17/March 1, 1857.

Dear Botkin, I'm not exaggerating when I say that I've started to write you ten times, but not once could I write more than half a page; maybe this time I'll be more lucky. I won't bother to tell you about myself: I'm a bankrupt man—and that's that; there's no point in talking about it. I constantly feel like trash that someone forgot to sweep out—that's my Stimmung [mood]. Perhaps it will pass when I leave Paris. You know that Nekrasov was here and then suddenly took off for Rome; Tolstoy is here— he looks at everything in wide-eyed silence; he's gotten much smarter: but he still feels uncomfortable with himself—and that's why other people don't feel completely at ease around him. But I rejoice in seeing him: to tell the truth, he is our literature's single hope. As concerns me, I'll whisper this in your ear along with the request that you not spread it any further: besides the piece promised to Druzhinin, which I'm sending off only because I don't want a repeat of the Katkov[1] incident—not a single line of *mine* will be published (or even written) before the end of the world. The day before yesterday I didn't burn them (because I was afraid of imitating Gogol), but I tore up and threw down the watercloset all my beginnings, plans, and so on. It's all nonsense. I don't have the sort of talent that has its own special physiognomy and integrity; there were some poetic strains—but they've sounded and died away—I don't feel like repeating myself—so time to retire! This is no flash or vexation, believe me—it's the expression or fruit of slowly ripening convictions. The failure of my povests (a fact related to me by very reliable sources, Kolbasin, and others) came as nothing new to me. I'm removing myself from the scene; as a writer with tendencies Mr. Shchedrin[2] will replace me (the public now needs things that are piquant and coarse)—and full, poetic natures such as Tolstoy will finish and present clearly and fully that at which I could only hint. All this is rather strange after "the obligatory invitation,"[3] mais je m'en lave les mains [but I wash my hands of it]. Since I have a decent command of the Russian language, I'm planning to translate *Don Quixote*—if my health holds out.[4] You'll probably think this is all an exaggeration—and you won't believe me. You'll see, I hope, that I've never spoken more seriously or sincerely.

Thank you for sending the article about Fet;[5] the main idea is correct and sensible, and there are subtle and intelligent remarks generously sprinkled throughout. If I discover a talent for it, I wouldn't mind writing articles of that sort—and maybe I'll try myself. But as for writing fiction— no more! You know that I stopped writing poetry just as soon as I became convinced that I wasn't a poet; and my present conviction is that I'm as much a teller of tales as I was a poet.

I've met a lot of people, including Mérimée! I could be spending time very, very pleasantly if I weren't so miserable. When we see each other I'll have lots of things to tell you—but I don't feel like writing them.

Farewell, dear Botkin. I don't know whether you're in Petersburg or Moscow—and that's why I'm sending you this letter via Annenkov. Be healthy. I embrace you.

Your

Ivan Turgenev.

Letter 84 (522). To A.I. Herzen.
February 21/March 5, 1857. Paris.

A Detailed Historical Account of a Battle that Took Place in the
Capital City of Moscow Between Count Bobrinsky[1] and Shevyrov,[2] the
Professor of Elocution.

The former Marshal of the Nobility Chertkov,[3] who was removed
from office for appointing as militia officers people taken from taverns or
from under the Iverskaya,[4] was hosting an evening for members of the
Society of Art Lovers. Present at the event, among others, were the above-
indicated Professor and Count. Arguments arose (as is the custom in
Moscow) over Slavophiles, over Aksakov's article on folk warrior heroes,[5]
and finally, over Robert Peel's speech,[6] which the aforementioned Count
took it into his head to defend. "In that case you are not a patriot,"
remarked the Professor. The Count took issue with these words and with
remarkable resourcefulness and quite à propos remarked: "And you, you
son of a bitch, are married to the spawn of a whore."[7] "And you yourself
were born of the spawn of a whore,"[8] remarked the Professor in turn and
punched the Count in the face. At that point the Count lost all patience and
having knocked the Professor off his feet, he began to stomp on him and
strike him with a chair. The guests, seeing such a spectacle and realizing
that the Count, a large and powerful man, would certainly kill the old and
weak professor, scattered as quickly as possible; only the host retained his
presence of mind—and he also ran out, but straight to Zakrevsky,[9] to
whom he immediately reported all. Zakrevsky, well known for his good
sense and his good administrative head, immediately figured out what to
do: he let Petersburg know via telegraph that so-and-so and so-and-so were
fighting—and what should be done?[10] All the while Bobrinsky continued
beating Shevyrov and would probably have killed him, were it not for Mrs.
Chertkova, who, left alone in the theater of battle, managed, partly with her
own weak arms, partly with admonitions and tears, to stop the enraged
Count, so that he only broke one of Shevyrov's ribs. Shevyrov was taken
away unconscious—and he's still recovering in bed. The matter ended
there—as yet there have been no further consequences.

There you have it, dear Herzen—a detailed and exact description of
the famous brawl that had all Moscow talking of nothing else.

I gave your regards to Tolstoy; they made him very happy and he asks
me to tell you that he's wanted to make your acquaintance for a long time—
and that he loves you beforehand, just as he loved your works (though N.B.
he is hardly a red).

126

We'll see each other in a month, and my bladder continues to torment me.

Farewell for now. Be well. Regards to all your family and to Ogaryov.

(I haven't read the introduction to Dashkova because I only have an excerpt of it. But the phrase is superb.)[11]

Your

Iv. Turgenev

Paris.
March 5, 1857.

Letter 85 (524). To V.N. Kashperov.[1]
February 23/March 7, 1857. Paris.

Paris.
March 7, 1857

Dear Kashperov, I kept planning to reply to your letter, and then suddenly the grievous news of Glinka's[2] death came. Although one could no longer expect a great deal from him, I still feel very, very sad for him, especially when you think how much the man could have accomplished and how little he left behind. But even for that little we will be grateful. His name will not be forgotten in Russian music—and if our music is ever fated to develop—it will find its starting point in him.

Will you stay in Berlin after this death? Won't it seem empty and depressing for you there? If Gribovsky[3] were still here, I'd know what you plan to do with yourself; but as you know, Nekrasov attracted him away to Rome. Write me about yourself—and also include some details about Glinka's death. I took Madame Viardot the romanza you sent and she praised it.

Tolstoy (L.N.T.) is here, and I see him daily. Unfortunately, I can't boast about my health. My bladder is torturing me—and I think it will continue to do so as long as I'm in Paris. I'm planning to leave here at the beginning of April. In June I'll already be in Russia.

Where and when will we see each other? God only knows. But I hope you don't doubt that no matter where we meet, I'll clasp your hand with sincere joy. Give my regards to Stolevsky,[4] whom I really liked very much. Be healthy and cheerful.

Your devoted

Iv. Turgenev.

P.S. My address is: Rue de l'Arcade, No. 11. I am writing you at your old Berlin address in the hopes that they'll forward the letter to you.

Letter 86 (533). To P.V. Annenkov.
March 9/21, 1857. Paris.

Paris.
March 9/21, 1857

Dear Annenkov, although recently my letters have been falling on you like hail, nonetheless, since I received a charming billet-doux from you in which I found the majestic word "publishable,"[1] I can't restrain myself from having a chat with you, the more so as my illness hasn't been gnawing at me so strongly today. A propos of my illness—I recall once saying that a sign of old age was when one's comrades are appointed generals; but there's a sign that's even more reliable and therefore worse—when comrades begin to creak and crack like rotting timber—one has cancer of the lip,[2] another passes <...> instead of urine—things are bad. Our grandchildren are beginning to crowd us out of the world.[3] You alone (I have yet to spoil anyone's luck through praises[4]) still hold yourself up high, like an oak in the middle of a flat valley, on a smooth height.[5] But, o strong oak!—beware the dangerous, boring woodpecker by the name of apoplexy! And that woodpecker lives in the kitchen at the English Club.

That my "narrowed eye," as you say, read your article about Gogol with great pleasure, about that you already received suitable notice in my previous letter—and I am really anxiously awaiting your article on Stankevich.[6] But I absolutely cannot read Mr. Shchedrin. (We've received the first two issues of *The Russian Messenger* here.)[7] That vulgar sarcasm,

128

that heavy humor, the language that reeks of bureaucratic sourness... No! Better to retire—if *that* is what is to reign. Now Pisemsky—that's a master for you. How well that man draws! His "Old Gentry Woman" amazed me with its firmness and accuracy of contours! Pisemsky is a professor of the literary portrait!

As for my own daubings, I'm glad that Druzhinin accepted that unfortunate product; a second "day" has already been sent off to you; and if I feel better this summer, I may squeeze out a third "day" as well; but it seems as though two are more than enough.[8] Whether the desire to write and faith in my own ability will return to me—I don't know; but right now I feel exploded, like those white mushrooms with a green filling that you keep stepping on while taking a walk in Russia. You hear a sound: p-s-s-t...and all that's left is a certain stench in the air—and that's it. I liked N.N. Tolstoy's "Hunting in the Caucasus" very much.

What ought I to tell you of events here? I was at a home where Hume,[9] the well-known magician, about whom you've probably heard—was supposed to produce his miracles; but nothing happened; only once upon my demand did something knock three times under the bottom of my right foot. I don't understand at all how that was done. But Paris is doing nothing but speaking of him; during a single week he was at the Tuillerie Palace three times—and they say that amazing things occurred there: a table rose up in the air, some hands appeared, concertinas played by themselves, bells threw themselves on the floor... We, sinners that we are, didn't see any of that.

Do you know what idea I've conceived? Let's go to Italy next spring—true, let's go after we've spent the winter in Petersburg. And now here is what my plans are: on April 15 I'm going to London, I'll stay there a month—then I'll set off somewhere to take the waters—and in the fall I'll head home. And we'll make our trip to Italy as old bachelor roosters; perhaps for a last time the feeling of youth and beauty will waft over us. Just imagine that and don't go saying "sure! sure! sure!"... don't slap your thighs—instead, get the necessary means ready ahead of time.

No! In spite of all my efforts, I can't really draw close to Tolstoy. He and I are of too different a make-up. He doesn't like anything that I do—and vice versa. I feel uncomfortable around him—and he probably feels the same about me. He lacks, on the one hand, tranquility—and on the other hand, he lacks the ardor of youth—and it turns out que je ne sais pas où le prendre [that I don't know how to approach him]. But he will end up a remarkable man—and I'll be the first to admire and applaud—from a distance.

Why is it you've not written anything about Olga Alexandrovna?[10] Yes, I'll send you—that is, care of you (in a few days)—a letter for Countess

Lambert—please seek her out. I think she lives on Furshtadt Street. She's the wife of a Wing-Adjutant. You won't have any trouble finding her. Farewell, my dear little hippopotamus; may the Lord take care of you!

Your loving

Iv. Turgenev.

P.S. You can still write me in Paris—but why are you thinking of leaving for the country so early?

Letter 87 (534). To V.N. Kashperov.
March 13/25, 1857. Paris.

Paris.
March 25, 1857.

Dear Kashperov,

Thank you, thank you very much for your letter and the details of Glinka's last moments;[1] although there is little to rejoice at there, on the other hand there is much that is instructive. Can it really be that if a person isn't religious, then he has to be cynical? Or that while dying, only a religious person remains a human being? The trouble was that Glinka had neither religion nor faith, i.e., no sort of faith either in Beauty or in Art or in Human Dignity. He had a great talent, but he landed in the swamp of Petersburg life, picked up the poisons of friends in high places—and by the way, that was when his inborn laziness, parasitical friends, wine, whims and caprices appeared—and everything went to the devil!

Oh, when you think of it, how many more decent people will have to perish and fertilize the soil before that soil brings forth abundant and wholesome fruit!

I'm very glad that you are not despondent and that you're working in Berlin. God grant you patience and health!

I can't send you the books you want; I don't have them, and I don't think that Shchedrin's *Sketches* have been issued in a separate edition.

Melgunov[2] promises to pay at least part of the money owed to

Gribovsky by the end of this month; I'm afraid he'll make it an April 1st payment.[3]

My health continues to be unsatisfactory; my bladder is torturing me. I'm staying here until the 15th, leaving that day for London, where I'll stay until mid-May; at the end of May I'll be in Berlin to consult with Schönlein;[4] we'll see each other then, if you're still in Berlin.

Farewell; I press your hand cordially—give my regards to dear Stolevsky.

Your devoted

Iv. Turgenev.

Letter 88 (548). To A.I. Herzen.
July 10/22, 1857. Sinzig.

Sinzig.
July 22, 1857.

I have to admit, dear friend, that in spite of my sheeplike nature, your letter made me angry at Nekrasov. He accuses me of not having explained to you and so on. But did I ever enter into his financial affairs or relations? They were always such that there was no point in an outsider's looking into them. He says that I'll pay you out of the money that I owe him. But do you know what sort of a debt that is? I sold him the second edition of *Notes of a Hunter* for 1000 silver rubles—and he immediately resold it to Bazunov the bookseller for 2500 (I was very happy about that, because the reason I sold him *Notes of a Hunter* was so that he could make a profit); the second edition has not yet been passed by the censor—but not only did he never offer to return to me the rights he'd bought, but even now, as he was leaving for Petersburg, he was planning to get that permission.[1] I wrote him a letter today in which, citing your words, or better to say, Nekrasov's words as relayed by you, I ask him either immediately to send me a document according to which I transfer to him the rights to an edition of *Notes of a Hunter*—and then I'll be prepared to pay you the 1000 rubles—or if he wants to keep the rights himself, then not to consider me in *debt,* since I do not recognize the *debt.*[2]

131

All this is really unpleasant, and though it reveals nothing new to me, it still has and will have its effect. No, things are quite impossible without honesty—just as without bread.

I'll deliver your letter at the earliest opportunity (I can't send it through the mail),[3] but that opportunity probably won't present itself earlier than the departure of Druzhinin, who wrote me from Paris and with whom I agreed to meet at the Rhine. But I assure that the letter will be delivered, and I ask you not to print anything in *The Bell* from that point of view from which I dissuaded you of speaking about Konstantin Nikolaye-vich.[4] Although Nekrasov is not at all *your sort* of person, you still have to agree that it would mean beating one's own people.[5]

I'm very grateful to you for Delaveau and Lang;[6] yesterday I received money from the country and I can send you the 250 francs and 3 1/2 pounds tomorrow or the day after, i.e., on my first trip into Bonn.

My health is still unsatisfactory; my bladder aches almost continually, and the Sinzig waters don't seem to be helping me at all. They work miracles for friends; my English neighbor arrived here without the use of his legs, entirely immobile—and now he goes mountain climbing. Good fortune is not granted to all in equal measure.

Farewell, my friend. Regards to the Ogaryovs and all your family. What's the news of his illness? A few days ago I received a pile of magazines from Orlov *(The Conversation, The Messenger, The Library,* and so on). As soon as I read them I'll send them to you sous bande [parcel post]. Be well and don't forget

Your devoted

Iv. Turgenev.

**Letter 89 (551). To V.P. Botkin.
July 17/29, 1857. Sinzig.**

Sinzig.
July 29, 1857.

My dear friend Vasily Petrovich—I allowed myself to unseal your letter to Tolstoy addressed to here; in a moment you'll see why I did that—and I hope you'll think me justified. I should tell you that the waters here, instead of helping me, have positively harmed me, and I'm planning to leave here tomorrow and go to the seashore as well; Druzhinin, who just left here yesterday after spending three days visiting, told me that you too are planning to bathe in the sea—and therefore, I would very much like to know where you're going, so that we could bathe together; but that alone wouldn't have made me unseal your letter if I hadn't received from Baden today a letter from Tolstoy in which he informs me that he lost all his money at roulette, asks me to send him 500 francs immediately, and so on. He was on his way here, stopped off in Baden—and perished. So here's what I'm planning to do now—I'll go to Baden tomorrow, get him out of there and try to persuade him to come with me to Fécamp via Strassbourg and Paris—I think it wouldn't be a bad idea for him to take sea baths too.[1] I don't have an extra 500 francs, but 200 will be enough to pay his travel expenses. Now here's what I'd like to do: when you get this letter write me immediately poste restante in Paris and tell me where you'll be—I'm afraid that it will be disgusting at Fécamp—I was thinking of going to Dieppe; in any event, write me immediately in Paris. I'll write you from Baden post restante at Fécamp and Paris and tell you what I find there and whether I'll be coming alone or with Tolstoy.

And so, until we see each other soon—be well. I embrace you.

Your

Iv. Turgenev.

Letter 90 (553). To V.P. Botkin.
July 23/August 4, 1857. Boulogne.

Boulogne.
August 4, 1857.

Dear Vasily Petrovich, you'll probably be surprised and perhaps angry at me when you find out that instead of heading off to see you in Fécamp, I came here to take the sea waters.[1] But I had the following reason for that: sometime during this week I absolutely must go to London for a day—when exactly, I don't know: but it would be difficult to do that from Fécamp. And so I decided to come here for the meanwhile and write you to ask whether you'll be staying at Fécamp or moving on to some other place. After I receive your answer and make my run to London, I'll immediately set off to see you via Paris. I terribly want to see you and have a talk with you; we haven't seen each other for more than a year—and at our age, a year is not a year, but a good ten years. I don't know whether you received the letter I sent you from Sinzig; in it I asked you to write me in Paris, poste restante. While I was passing through I stopped off at the post office, but there wasn't anything there. I won't relate all my adventures—that's for when we see each other in person—but I'll tell you about Tolstoy. I wrote you that I intended to take him away from Baden and come to see you together with him. But things turned out quite differently—I found him broke from gambling and with a strong. . . .[2] He was sitting in Baden as though in a whirlpool, and he was at a complete loss. I suggested that he come with me, and he agreed—when suddenly he received a letter from home which informed him that his sister,[3] no longer in any condition to live with a husband who has four mistresses, etc., has moved in with her brother Nikolay Nikolayevich (the one you saw at Spasskoye). One of the mistresses, out of jealousy, had brought the Countess a letter in which her husband deliberates with another mistress about what he'll do after his wife's death, etc. After reading that letter, Tolstoy decided to go to Russia immediately (they want him to come back). I approved his plan—and since I had no money of my own—I addressed myself to Smirnov (the husband of Alexandra Osipovna, who—just between the two of us—is a *bitch*)— and he gave us the needed money.[4] The doctor, on his part, gave instructions and pills—and Tolstoy sails for Petersburg from Stettin this very Saturday. He's thinking of moving his sister to Moscow or Petersburg for the winter.

I read a short piece that he wrote in Switzerland—I didn't like it: it's a mixture of Rousseau, Thackeray and the Short Orthodox Catechism.[5] Like Hercules, he's at a crossroads; God grant that he'll take the good road.

I won't write any more for the time being—but I'll be waiting impatiently for your reply: write me à Boulogne, Hôtel du pavillon Impérial—chambre No. 62. Be sure to write *Impérial,* because there's another Hôtel du pavillon.

Give my regards to Delaveau. I embrace you with all my heart and say: until we see each other soon.

Your

Iv. Turgenev.

P.S. Send your exact address and answer me right away.

Letter 91 (559). To N.A. Nekrasov.
August 12/24, 1857. Courtavenel.

Courtavenel.
August 12/24, 1857.

I've been here since yesterday, dear friend, and I left Boulogne (where I bathed in the sea) three days ago and spent a day-and-a-half in Paris with Botkin and Fet. In Paris I found your two (or three) letters waiting for me and I hasten to answer you. First of all I'll tell you that there was no reason for you to have been so upset by my letter[1]; it never occurred to me to be suspicious of you—and I attributed this whole misunderstanding[2] (which somewhat bothered me, I must admit) to your carelessness; the same thing forced me to write my uncle[3] to ask him to send you the money I owe you; wherever these damned accounts are involved sooner or later misunderstandings will be involved too; but I don't want them to exist between us. I assure you that this "incident," as you call it, hadn't the slightest effect on me; I love you just as I did before—and there's no point even in thinking about this business any more.

Let's move on to other questions.

You see that I'm here, i.e., I committed that very folly which you tried to dissuade me from. . . . But it was impossible for me to act otherwise. However, the result of this folly will likely be that I'll arrive in Petersburg earlier than I had planned. No, it's absolutely true: "One can't live like this." I had enough of sitting on the edge of someone else's nest. If you don't have your own—then you don't need any at all.[4]

Your rifle is ready and I have it with me. It's a marvellous rifle!

Fet's wedding will take place September 2nd—and I've promised to be his best man. He's terribly cheerful, talkative, and happy. God grant him happiness! He's good and deserves it. We spent a few hours with Botkin in the most cordial conversation. He's really falling apart; but his spirit is vital, he's in a superb mood and so on.

Fet's stories about you made me very happy. According to him, you're being terrific and not feeling depressed. That's fine. In Boulogne I made great progress on my povest,[5] and now if I can get two or three painless mornings, I'll get down to making a fresh copy of it. I very much want to do something for the poor *Contemporary*—otherwise people really will be pointing fingers at us.[6] But if my illness abandons me when I return to Petersburg—that's when I'll get down to work! You'll see! Lord, how I want to get to Russia as soon as possible. I've had enough, enough!

Until we see each other soon, dear friend. I repeat—don't have doubts

135

about me, just as I have no doubts about you. Well, sometimes we can complain about each other—with whom doesn't that happen? Regards to all our friends and acquaintances—I embrace you.

Iv. Turgenev

P.S. My address is au château de Courtavenel, près de Rozoy-en-Brie—Seine-et-Marne. Confirm for the Kolbasin brothers what I asked Druzhinin to convey to them—that is that I definitely wish to have an apartment *from October 15th on—a warm one.*

Letter 92 (570). To P.V. Annenkov.
September 23/October 5, 1857. Courtavenel.

Courtavenel. Oct. 5/Sept. 23, 1857.

Dear Annenkov, a few days ago I received a letter from Nekrasov with an attached announcement of the publication of an almanac for the Belinsky family, but since I wrote him recently, I prefer to have a talk with you. First of all—tell Nekrasov that I promise him two pieces—a povest or a story and recollections of Belinsky. I can't believe my eyes—can it really be that they've finally allowed an almanac with Belinsky's name on the title page and remarks about him![1] Whatever the case, I'll be delighted to harness myself to that cart and I'll pull with all my might.

As for my sudden journey to Rome, I hope that when you've had a chance to think it over a little, you'll be convinced that after all my anxieties and spiritual torments, after a horrible winter in Paris—a quiet winter in Rome filled with calm work among that majestic and dying environment is simply salvation for my soul. It would be fine to be in Petersburg with all of you, my friends—but it would be pointless even to think about work; and now, after such lengthy inactivity, I'm faced with the choice of either giving up literature once and for all or of making an attempt to regenerate my spirit once more. I was first amazed at the proposal (V.P. Botkin's), then seized on it greedily, and now every night I dream of myself in Rome. I'll tell you very frankly: for my complete satisfaction I'd need your presence in Rome, then I think there would be nothing left to desire... As far as I remember, you were planning to go to Rome, what would you think of

136

fulfilling that intention just now? Really do think about it. We'd have a marvellous time living together! If you don't come, I'll write you and Nekrasov often. I hope that my illness doesn't grab me by the neck again; in such an event, of course, I'll be silent, but I hope it won't come back. Farewell, my friend Pavel Vasilievich. Send me the seventh volume of Pushkin[2] in Rome. I embrace you!

Letter 93 (577). To P.V. Annenkov.
October 31/November 12, 1857. Rome.

Rome, Oct. 31 (Nov. 12), 1857.

Dear Annenkov, I was very happy to receive your letter, and I hope that our correspondence will come alive again. You and I absolutely must write to each other, even if only occasionally. I'll soon have been in Rome for two weeks; the weather is superb; but my illness has begun gnawing at me again. That depresses me very much, because if it weren't for that, I'd be working. I sense that, and even in spite of my illness I've been able to do a little bit. I'm not going to tell you about Rome—it's not worth saying too little, and it's impossible to say too much. I'm getting acquainted with it gradually—there's no point in rushing; I went to your apartment on the Via Felice; but everything has already changed since then, and there's a new landlord—there was no one to ask. I'll try to carry out your wish and write a letter for Korsh, that is to say—two or three letters, but I don't know whether they'll be interesting.[1] *The Contemporary* has a right to be angry with me; but really, I'm not guilty. They say Nekrasov has started grumbling again... You imagine that people are writing to me "from all over." No one is writing me. So please give me as much news as possible.

I've made the acquaintance of the painter Ivanov here and I've seen his picture.[2] In profundity of thought, strength of expression, truth and honest strictness of execution it is a first-class work. Not in vain has he put 25 years of his life into it. But there are flaws, too. The coloration is altogether too dry and sharp, there is no unity, there is no air in the foreplane (the landscape in the distance is remarkable), everything is somehow motley and yellow. But when all is said and done, I'm certain that the picture will make a great impression (there will be fanatics, though not many), and more importantly: one ought to hope that it will signal opposition to

Bryullovian Marlinskyism.[3] On the other hand, Prince Gagarin's Byzantine school ...[4] Art is still in a bad way in Russia. The other Russian artists here are bad. Sorokin screams that Raphael is trash and that "everything" is trash, but he himself paints junk; we know that vile Russian habit.[5] Ignorance is ruining all of them. Ivanov, on the contrary, is a remarkable person; he's original, intelligent, righteous and a thinker, but I think he's a little touched: 25 years of solitude have affected him. I can't forget how (but this is strictly between the two of us) during our trip to Albano he suddenly began to try to persuade Botkin and me—he was completely pale and his laughter was forced—that he was being slowly poisoned, that he rarely ate and so on.[6] We see him often, he seems to be well inclined to us.

You praise me for my intention to spend the winter in Rome. I too feel that the idea wasn't a bad one—but I can't tell you what a hard, bitter time I'm having of it. Work is the only thing that can save me, but if I turn out to be incapable of it, things will be bad! I've joked my way through life—but now it's too late for regrets. But enough about that. In any event, I feel better here than in Paris or Petersburg.

I don't know whether I wrote you that I met Olga Alexandrovna[7] in Paris. She's not quite well and will be spending the winter in Nice. There aren't any of the Russians here yet: the Cherkasskys are expected.[8]

God help you if you don't send me the 7th volume of Pushkin, Stankevich's correspondence, and your letter about Gogol.[9] Find out from Nekrasov and the Kolbasins how they had books sent here—and act accordingly.

A tramontano has been blowing since yesterday—before that it was so hot that words fail me. The day before yesterday Botkin and I spent a remarkable day at the Villa Pamfili. Nature here is enchantingly majestic—and gentle and feminine at the same time. I'm in love with the eternally green oaks, the umbrella-shaped pines, and the distant, pale-blue hills. Alas! I can only empathize with the beauty of life—I can no longer live it myself. A dark cover has fallen on me and enveloped me; I can't shake it from my shoulders. I try, however, not to let this soot into what I do; who needs it? And even I would find it revolting.

Botkin is well; I see him daily, but I'm not living with him. There's a sort of old-age irritability in his character—the epicure in him constantly squeaks and creaks; he's become terribly infected with art.

Write me everything that you find out or hear about Tolstoy and his sister.[10] I don't think you'll like his last work,[11] but he has other, good things. He likes you very much.

Have you met Countess Lambert? She wished for that, and I recommend it. I'll write her another letter with you as go-between. This time go to see her.

Well, here it is—our correspondence has been successfully revived; be careful that it doesn't break off. Regards to all our friends, and I clasp your hand firmly. Have you read Mommsen's *History of Rome?*[12] I'm enjoying reading it here.

Your I.T.

P.S. Write me the details of whether Bazunov lost money on my povests.[13] If not, my self-esteem would be somewhat reassured.

Letter 94 (578). To Ye. Ye. Lambert.
November 3/15, 1857. Rome.

Rome.
November 3/15, 1857.

Dear Countess,

I consider myself still in debt to you for the long and kind letter that I received from you in April; therefore I cannot possibly count my short note to you a serious reply. I was then planning to return to Russia for the winter—and therefore, since I hoped to see you soon, I didn't consider it necessary to dilate on paper; but instead of Petersburg, I wound up in Rome and I won't arrive in Russia before May. In part this happened by accident: a good friend of mine[1] was going to Rome and invited me to come along; but there was another reason for my agreeing so quickly. Lately, as the result of various circumstances, I haven't done anything and haven't been able to do anything;[2] I now feel the desire to get down to work—but that would be impossible in Petersburg; there I would be surrounded by friends, whom it would be a real joy to see, but who would prevent me (and I'd prevent myself as well) from being alone; and without being alone there can be no work. Rome is just the sort of city where it's easiest to be by oneself; and if you feel like taking a look around—it's not empty pleasures that await you, but the great traces of a great life, which don't oppress you with a feeling of your own insignificance before them, as one might expect, but which—on the contrary—lift you and give your soul a mood that is somewhat sad, but elevated and vigorous. If I can't accomplish anything

139

even in Rome, then the only thing left to do will be to wash my hands of everything.

In a man's life there are turning points, moments in which the past dies and something new is born; woe unto him who is unable to sense them—and either clings stubbornly to the dead past or prematurely wants to call to life that which hasn't yet matured. I have often been guilty of impatience or stubbornness; I'd like to be a little wiser now. I'll soon be 40 years old: not only my first and second youths have passed, but my third as well—and it's time for me to become if not a competent and reliable person, then at least a person who knows where he's going and what he wants to attain. The only thing I can be is a man of letters—but up to now I've been more a dilettante than anything else. There will be no more of that in the future.

For the time being I'm enjoying Rome and its beautiful environs. The weather is superb; you can hardly believe your eyes when you see roses in bloom in November. But these unusual things don't strike me as much as the whole character of winter nature here. Such clear, gentle, and elevated beauty is bestowed everywhere!

There aren't many Russians here—at least I'm acquainted with only a few. And to heck with them! Out of 50 Russians abroad it's better not to make the acquaintance of 49 of them. Their all consumed by ennui, that special ennui of Russians abroad about which I'll write an article some day.[3] Of the artists here the most remarkable is Ivanov—and in his picture (which he showed me in secrecy) there is first-class beauty.

And what's happening back in Russia? We hear the most contradictory rumors here.[4] If it weren't for literature, I would have returned to Russia long since; everyone needs to be in his own nest now. I hope to arrive at my country place in May—and I won't leave there until I arrange things with my peasants. By next winter, if God grants it, I'll be a landowner, but no longer a master.[5]

This letter will be brought to you by Annenkov. Get to know him: you'll like him. He's a wonderful, intelligent, and kind person.

Write me a few words (in French, of course) about yourself, about your husband, and about your son. Do you still live on Furshtatskaya, and what is your friend Mme Veriguine doing?[6] I would be very grateful if you would tell me where Yevreinov's widow is and what her extraordinary daughter Lydia is doing.[7]

Farewell; I wish you all manner of good things and clasp your hand firmly. My address is Rome, poste restante. That's the most reliable.

Your devoted

Iv. Turgenev

P.S. Send me your address.

140

Letter 95 (581). To Pauline Turgeneva.[1]
November 22/December 4, 1857. Rome.

Rome.
December 4, 1857.

My little one,

I thank you for thinking of me from time to time. Your two letters gave me great pleasure—and they would have made me even happier had the handwriting been more readable and the spelling less chaotic. You know my old refrain: reflection and attention! Don't be in such a rush in everything you do—you have plenty of time ahead of you.

Princess Trubetskaya[2] will soon be returning to Paris and she may send for you some Sunday: tell Mme Harang that I authorize her to entrust you to the person whom that woman sends. That will allow you to amuse yourself a bit during Mme Viardot's absence.[3] Only I advise you not to be a savage. What is the advice you wished to ask me in your first letter? There needn't be any reticence with me.

Do well at your piano and English lessons if you wish to give me pleasure.

Write me if you need anything.

Give my regards to Mme Harang—I kiss you on both cheeks.

Your father,

I. Turgenev,

P.S. My brother[4] was in Paris, but he has already returned to Russia.

Letter 96 (588). To A.I. Herzen.
December 26, 1857/January 7, 1858. Rome.

Rome.
January 7, 1858.

Dear Herzen,

I am replying to your pun-filled, friendly letter. Thank you for sending excerpts from *The Bell*—but yesterday I received the complete second issue from one of your most ardent admirers (their name is legion). In the future please send me *The Bell sous bande* [parcel post]—and *The Polar Star idem* [also] and the book about Korf[1] *idem*. That is the fastest and most reliable method of delivery. The sixth issue of *The Bell* is fine, but I think it resembles *Charivari*[2] a little—and there is a great difference between *The Bell* and *Charivari*. I know that you can't write a piece like your letter to the Emperor for every issue, but "playfulness" is unnecessary, especially now when very serious things are underway in Russia.[3] The two rescripts and the third one to Ignatiev about the same thing produced unheard-of alarm in our gentry;[4] beneath surface readiness is concealed the most obtuse stubbornness—and terror and stingy covetousness; but it's too late to turn back—le vin est tiré—il faut le boire [the wine has been drawn—it must be drunk]. It's also too bad that you printed the news of Bering's victorious tenure[5] just as he was replaced by Akhmatov. That gentleman is of quite another type: he's sweet, polite, prayerful—and at inquests he flogs peasants without raising his voice or removing his gloves. Under Nikolay Pavlovich he was aiming for General Procurator of the Holy Synod; now he's ended up as General Procurator of the Police—the positions, however, are quite similar.[6] By the way, I hope that you'll publish "Zaltsman" in *The Bell* rather than in *The Polar Star*.[7] It will be 1000 times more effective in *The Bell*. Again by the way—here's an anecdote for you, but *don't publicize it*. Actors in Moscow had the squeeze put on them and there were attempts to take their own money away from them; the actors decided to send the old man Shchepkin to seek justice from Geodonov (milk from a ram).[8] It goes without saying that the latter didn't even want to hear about it; "Then," said Shchepkin, "we'll have to complain to the Minister." "Don't you dare!" "In that case," countered Shchepkin, "our only option is to complain to *The Bell*." Geodonov erupted and ended up by returning the actors their money. That's the sort of tricks your *Bell* performs, my friend.

I'm very happy that you both liked my little piece;[9] I wrote it mit schwerem Herzen [with a heavy heart]. I'll hope for your kind offices in the future.

Botkin, whom I see every day, approves of your activity completely and asks me to tell you that in his opinion you and your publications comprise a whole epoch in the life of Russia.

I was very pleased to hear that after such a ghastly operation Ogaryov has recovered completely; I'll write him in a few days. My bladder continues to bother me; I'll see whether your puns don't have a positive effect on it.

You write that you recommend a book for Ivanov,[10] but you forgot to say which one.

Please don't scold Alexander Nikolayevich[11]—because as it is, he's being scolded by all the reactionaries in Petersburg—so why pound him from two sides?—he might lose his spirit that way.

Well, farewell, be healthy, and send me *sous bande* everything you have ready. My portrait is being sold absolutely without my knowledge. God knows by whom and what it looks like! I myself have yet to reach the point of thinking that my face could be of interest au gros du public [to the public at large].

Your

I. Turgenev.

Letter 97 (623). To A.I. Herzen.
May 18/30, 1858. Paris.

Paris.
May 30, 1858.

My dear friend, please don't be angry at me for my silence; I had to gather exact information about the matter at hand. Here's what I found out:

The source of the difficulties is not the local Embassy or Frank's[1] intrigues; they had their origin in certain Northern *German* governments which addressed themselves to the local police and pointed out the alleged danger of your publications. The result of this instruction was that booksellers were prohibited from selling any of your publications at all; for 14 days they indeed were not available for sale;[2] but now they've been allowed again, i.e., the ruling isn't enforced—and I myself saw *The Bell*, etc.

143

at Frank's and on the Rue de Rivoli; only certain issues of *The Bell* (for some reasons numbers 8 and 12) and *Letters from Italy*[3] have been permanently forbidden. All of this was conveyed to me in secret and with a request not to divulge it; and therefore I ask you too not to speak about this, the more so as things are back to normal—for the time being. Foreign booksellers in Paris are completely in the hands of the police; one word—and they'll throw them out of here. But here's what unfortunately seems to have gone astray: our domestic affairs.[4] Reaction has finally raised its head. Titov has been replaced by some idiot named Grimm, Kavelin has been removed, Shcherbatov has retired from service; a few days ago Kovalevsky gathered together all the editors and delivered them a very depressing speech: "I'm too old," he said, "and I can't fight with obstacles; they'll just throw me out—but the consequences could be worse for you, gentlemen; I implore you to be extremely careful."[5] After that speech he went to Moscow *to put a prohibition on everything.* One should have expected these revirements [revolutions], but there's no need for exaggerated fear; no matter what they do, the stone has already started rolling downhill—and it's impossible to restrain it. But I still have faith in Alexander Nikolayevich,[6] though, unfortunately, he's probably surrounded in an even worse way than we had assumed.

I send my regards to all our friends and embrace you. I'm heading for Russia on Wednesday; I'll write you from Berlin. Addio [farewell]. I have difficult moments awaiting me in our dear fatherland.[7]

Your

I. Turgenev.

Letter 98 (646). To A.N. Apukhtin.[1]
September 29/October 11, 1858. Spasskoye.

Village of Spasskoye.
September 29, 1858.

What a gloomy letter you wrote me, dear Alexey Nikolayevich! I sympathize with you very much—because, as you correctly observed, I myself ran along the same path; but I have less sympathy for your

144

melancholy; that melancholy is the inevitable companion of youth, which exerts itself so precisely because it is in no condition to master its own wealth. That's in the nature of things; but to give in to that melancholy too much is harmful; and the voice of a forty-year-old person may be helpful in this situation. Why are you so depressed? Is it because you don't know whether you have talent? Give it time to mature; and even if it turns out not to be there, is it really essential for a person to have precisely a *poetic* talent in order to live and function? The surrounding *milieu* weighs upon you? But, in the first place, it seems to me that you dwell on the surface of phenomena, and in the second place, if you are depressed and in despair now, in 1858, what would you have done if you had been 18 years old in 1838, when everything ahead was so dark—and has remained so? There is neither time nor reason for you to grieve now; you are faced with a great obligation to yourself: you must make *yourself*, make a person out of yourself—and as for what will come of you, where your life will lead you— you should leave that to your nature: you will be justified before your own conscience. Think less about your personality and about your sufferings and joys; look at your personality as a form that needs to be filled with good and sensible content; work, study, sow seeds: they will grow up in their time and place. Remember that many people like you all over the face of Russia are laboring and striving; you are not alone—what more do you need? Why despair and sit idly? If others do the same thing, what will be the results? You have a moral obligation to your comrades (many of whom you don't know) not to sit idly.

As regards the two poems that you sent me, they could just as easily be the youthful works of a genuine poet as youthful ones by a skillful dilettante. As of yet they have no physiognomy, and without it there can be no poetry—especially lyric poetry. But don't worry about that or be distressed by it. Allow me to offer myself as an example: my physiognomy made itself felt when I was just under thirty—but, unfortunately, I didn't start writing at thirty![2]

And so, Corraggio, Santo Padre! Corraggio Signore Alexis! [Take heart, holy father! Take heart, signore Alexey!] Work steadily, calmly, without impatience: any land gives only that fruit of which it is capable. Continue to write poetry. Who knows?—perhaps your calling is to be a poet—but don't publish it and don't succumb to the *torpor of melancholy:* it's onanism, and just as harmful as the physical kind.

I don't know whether you'll be pleased by this letter—but it is dictated by my sincere concern for you. I'll be in Petersburg around the 10th of

November and I hope to see you often in the winter. Until then be well. I clasp your hand cordially and remain

Your devoted

Iv. Turgenev.

**Letter 99 (21*). To Alexander II.
March 5/17, 1859. Petersburg.**

All-gracious Sovereign!

I hesitated for several days before making up my mind to write to Your Majesty; I am well aware that such an action may strike You as unseemly; but as a Russian, as Your subject, as a person for whom You once saw fit to intervene and who remembers kind deeds,[1] I consider it my sacred duty to address myself to You, Sovereign. I am certain of the purity of my intentions; I beg Your Majesty's pardon if their expression seems out of place.

I have no need to speak of the feelings that I nourish for Your Person; I share them with all Russians: a monarch who has wisely begun and resolutely furthers the great cause of the liberation of the serfs has by that alone already assured himself both posterity's blessing and his subjects' eternal love; but my conscience commands me to bring to Your attention, Sovereign, the fact that precisely those of Your subjects to whom Your renown is more precious than anything else fail to recognize in the government's latest action that spirit which, to Russia's great fortune, has marked Your reign up until now. The incarceration of a person who is innocent before the essence of the law if not before its letter, the closing of a journal which had as its aim the independent, i.e., the only sensible unification and reconciliation of two nationalities[2]—these measures and others like them have saddened all people sincerely devoted to Your Majesty, they have done away with the confidence that had arisen, shaken the sense of legality which is unfortunately still so weak in our national consciousness, and they have postponed the era of the ultimate merging of state and personal interests—that merging in which Authority finds its most reliable source of support. Never, Sovereign, in the course of the last four years has public opinion expressed itself so unanimously against a governmental measure. Without allowing myself to judge to what extent a farsighted government ought to take such expressions into account, I consider it my responsibility to submit this fact for Your Majesty's consideration.

I know that my solitary voice means nothing, though fortunate are the times when even a solitary voice reaches the Throne; but I have definite reason to think that I am expressing common convictions—including the convictions of people whom Your Majesty may consider suspect—but who, I dare to assure You, Sovereign, yield to no one in devotion to You and who place all their hopes exclusively on You. That well-being, that development of Russia, for which they are prepared to make every sort of sacrifice, is linked in their eyes with the success of the government. Allow them, Sovereign, to continue to nourish their faith in our Fatherland's glorious future, that faith which rests on reliance on Your Majesty.[3]

All-gracious Sovereign!

> Your Imperial Majesty's
> Loyal Subject,
>
> Ivan Turgenev

March 5, 1859.
My place of residence in
St. Petersburg, the Greater Konyushennaya,
Veber's Building.

Letter 100 (689). To K.S. Aksakov.
March 12/24, 1859. Petersburg.

Dear Konstantin Sergeyevich,

I'm taking advantage of N.A. Osnovsky's[1] departure and sending with him a few words to you. I'll begin by apologizing for not answering your letter, but the situation was such that I didn't have a single free, or at least calm minute. *The Contemporary*'s review of your father's works[2] upset me at least as much as it did you; I've expressed my displeasure to them—and, just between the two of us—I'll never publish another line in *The Contemporary*;[3] but the method you propose (a review) seems awkward and useless to me. Things are going badly here, as you know: everyone is especially upset over the business with *The Word* and Ohrysko's incarceration.[4] I must say that public opinion has expressed itself quite unanimously in this regard; the Emperor has received several letters—among them one from me, a copy of which Osnovsky has taken and which you may read if you're interested. But I'll talk over all of this with you in person in a few days: I'll be in Moscow on Wednesday of next week—and I'll be staying until Saturday.

I expect to see you soon and clasp your hand cordially—give my regards to your father and to the rest of your family, about whom I have the freshest possible news from Mr. Kartashevsky.[5]

Your devoted

Iv. Turgenev.

St. Petersburg
March 12, 1859.

Letter 101 (694). To Pauline Turgéneva.[1]
February 16/28, Petersburg, and March 23/April 4, 1859, Moscow.

St. Petersburg. February 16/28, 1859.

My dear little girl,

Thank you very much for your long letter. It was a little disorderly—but that doesn't make any difference. I don't mean to be a lazy-bones this time and I'm replying to you right away. You'll find enclosed a note for Mme Turgeneva[2]—and you'll deliver it to her. I'm glad to know that you're in good health. But since I ought to speak frankly with you, I must admit that I'm not very pleased with a certain frivolousness that I seem to observe in you. I don't want to be a pedant or reproach you for enjoying yourself; it's just that I worry that these balls, these toilettes may interfere with your studies. My child, you will yet have time to amuse yourself; be afraid of

wasting it when you can still work. Dancing doesn't go well with spelling—
and your spelling still limps a little. In a word, think about the fact that you
really must finish your studies in September in order for me to decide to
allow you to leave the boarding school; you must work hard from now until
then.

Moscow
March 23/April 4, 1859.

You may give me a bawling out any time you wish, my dear little girl.
My letter wasn't sent to you—and there's no letter for Mme Turgeneva. I
left Petersburg two days ago—and in an hour I'm leaving for the country,
where I'll stay about a month. I'll be in Paris May 8/20, if the Lord extends
my life. I hope that this news will make you happy. Expect me; but I'll write
again from the country anyway.

Good-bye. I embrace you. Give my regards to Mme Turgeneva.

Your father,

Iv. Turgenev.

Letter 102 (695). To Ye. Ye. Lambert
March 27/April 8, 1859. Spasskoye.

Village of Spasskoye.
March 27, 1859.

I arrived here yesterday, and today I'm writing to you, dear Countess.
I'm not saying that in order to boast, but to prove to you that thoughts of
you come to my mind before anything else. I found everything here as it had
been: only to my genuine grief, in my absence death has carried off almost
our only neighbor, a very nice, kind young man by the name of
Karateyev... My former attendant, an old man of about 65, also died...[1]
Death isn't selective when it takes people. We're all in its debt, and debtors
can't tell a creditor with whom he should begin to collect...

But let's leave these sad meditations aside. I found winter here (that's
sad, too, but what can be done about it?). Five days or so ago there was such

an enormous snowfall that I had trouble making it home—but let's hope that all this will soon change. In a few days I'm going to Oryol—to be present, if possible, at the committee's meetings,[2] but by April 5th, i.e., by the time the woodcocks arrive, I'll be home again. On the 23rd, you remember, you're having tea at my place in Petersburg.

I'm now busy with formulating the plan and so on for a new povest:[3] it's rather exhausting—all the more so as it doesn't leave any *visible* traces: you lie on the couch or pace around the room while turning over in your head some character or situation—you look, and three or four hours have passed—but you seem to have made little headway. Frankly speaking, there is rather little pleasure in our craft—but that's as things should be: everyone, even artists, even wealthy people, ought to live by the sweat of his brow...and so much the worse for anyone whose brow isn't sweaty: his heart is either ill or withering up. During all these days I've often been recalling the little room on Furshtatskaya Street and the evenings that I spent there...These recollections turn out to be the best thing that I brought away from Petersburg life. I'm very glad that I didn't yield to the desire to take advantage of my novel's success and didn't make forays all over the place: besides tiredness and perhaps the sinful pleasure of the petty and worthless feeling of vanity—it wouldn't have provided me with anything.[4] I have become convinced that every person should treat himself strictly and even rudely and distrustfully; it's difficult to tame the beast in oneself. It sometimes happens that you don't yield to coarse, stupid flattery and think "What a fine person I am!", but if they served you the same flattery with tastier seasoning—you'd begin to swallow it like oysters.—I don't know why I'm indulging in these thoughts; since I left I haven't succumbed to the slightest temptation of flattery; obviously something was sitting inside me that needed to find its way out.

Please write me at the following address: Oryol Province, City of Mtsensk. Give my regards to your husband and all the residents and guests of your home on Furshtatskaya. By the way, I forgot to give you the 75 rubles (do you remember for what use?). Please use that sum of money as you see fit and I'll return it to you in Petersburg.[5]

Be well and don't be depressed—that's the main thing—and don't forget me: that's the main thing for me. I wish you all the best and kiss your hands. You remember our agreement: write me in French.

Your sincerely devoted

Iv. Turgenev.

Letter 103 (702). To I.A. Goncharov.
April 7/19, 1859. Spasskoye.

April 7, 1859.

I cannot conceal the fact, dear Ivan Alexandrovich, that contrary to usual, this time it is with little pleasure that I take pen in hand to reply to you, because what pleasure is there in writing to a person who considers you the appropriator of others' ideas (plagiare), a liar (you suspect that there is craftiness again in my new povest, that I only intend to divert your attention), and a chatterbox (you suppose that I told Annenkov about our conversation).[1] You have to agree that whatever my "diplomacy," it's difficult to smile and be diffident when you receive such bitter pills. You must also agree that in response to half—what am I saying!—the tenth part of similar accusations you would have grown completely furious. But I—call this in me what you please, weakness or dissimulation—I only wondered "Does he have a good opinion of me?" and was only surprised that you still found something in me that you could like. Thanks even for that! It's without any false humility that I tell you that I agree completely with what "the teacher" said about my *Nest of Gentlefolk*.[2] But what would you have me do? I can't repeat *The Notes of a Hunter* ad infinitum! Nor do I feel like giving up writing either. All I can do is compose the sort of povest in which, without making any claims to integrity or strength of the characters, or to a profound, multi-faceted penetration into life, I might express what comes into my head. There will be torn spots sewn up with white thread and so on. But what can I do about that? Whoever needs a novel in the epic meaning of that word has no need of me; but I think of writing a novel as much as I do about walking on my head: no matter what I write, the result is a series of sketches. E sempre bene! [And that's fine!] But even in this confession you'll see diplomacy: Tolstoy thinks that I sneeze, drink, and sleep—all for the sake of a phrase. Take me as I am or don't take me at all; but don't demand that I remake myself, and most importantly, don't consider me such a Talleyrand! But enough about that. All this fuss leads to nothing: we'll all die and stink after death. Spring has arrived here, almost all the snow has melted, but it's rather ugly and lifeless. The days are wet, cold, and gray; the fields are naked and deathly yellow. The grass is already coming up in the woods, though. There is little wild fowl. I hope to finish up everything here by the 20th; I'll be in Petersburg on the 24th (on the 29th, you know, I'm leaving for abroad). We'll see each other in Petersburg and perhaps abroad as well, although they'll probably recommend different waters for me than for you. I hope that your stay in

Marienbad will be as beneficial in all respects as it was in '57.[3] Give my regards to all our good acquaintances and to dear Maykova.[4] I learned of Bosio's death today and felt very bad for her. I saw her on the day of her last performance: she was playing *"Traviata"*; she had no idea then, while she was playing a dying person, that she would soon have to perform that role in real life. Everything earthly is dust and decay and falsehood. Good-bye, unjust person! I clasp your hand.

I forgot the most important thing: the letter to Count Kushelev[5] about Solyanikov's[6] translation; I'll write to him tomorrow, but to tell the truth, I haven't the least bit of faith in that Mitrofanushka-Maecenas.[7]

Letter 104 (734). To Ye. Ye. Lambert.
Mid-July (O.S.), 1859. Courtavenel.

Dear Countess, you write such nice letters that a conceited person would find it hard to answer you—but it's easy for me—not because there's no conceit in me—but because I don't try to show you a superficial side. Though we haven't been long acquainted, we've already felt much and thought over many things together and—I dare to think—we've become attached to each other not because of our hopes, but because of our recollections and common experiences; consequently, we can put vanity aside and be with each other the people that God made us. I'm very glad that you tell me straight out everything that you have in your heart; I just feel sorry for you when there's darkness in your heart, and I'd like to be with you in order to help you a little and dispel that gloom. I hope that your stay at the seashore will help you, and I think with joy of those evenings that I'll spend in your lovely room this winter. You just watch how well we'll behave ourselves—quietly and calmly—like children during Holy Week. I answer for myself. You may perhaps find that last sentence impudent; all I meant was that you are younger than I am.

I'm writing you from Madame Viardot's castle (château); its name is Courtavenel—it is located about fifty versts from Paris. I recently returned from Vichy, where I drank the waters with great success. My health is good; but my soul is sad. All around is a correct family life ... what am I here for, and why, having abandoned everything dear to me, why should I cast backward glances? You'll easily understand both what I mean and my situation.[1] But I don't feel any alarm; they say that a person dies several times before his death . . . I know what has died in me; but why stand and look at a closed coffin? It's not feeling that has died . . . but the chance for its realization. I look at *my* happiness—the same way I look at *my* youth, at another's youth and happiness; I'm here—and that's all over there; and between that *here* and the *there* is an abyss which nothing could ever, ever fill in. There's only one thing left to do: stay afloat on life's waves for the time being and think about a wharf—and having found a dear, kind friend like you, a comrade in feelings, thoughts—and most important—in *situation* (neither you nor I expects much for himself), to hold his hand and float along together, until . . . Here's the confession for you of a man who is not a "siren," unfortunately! . . . nor a "tiger," nor a "polar bear,"[2] but simply an old man who has not yet forgotten how to love—and loves you very much.

I've seen my daughter quite a bit lately—and gotten to know her. In spite of the great similarity to me, hers is a completely different nature from mine: there isn't the slightest trace of an artistic bent in her; she's very positive, gifted with character, calm, common sense: she will be a good wife, a good mother, and a marvellous housewife—everything romantic and dreamy is alien to her; she has a great deal of perspicacity and is silently observant: she will be religious, a woman with rules . . . She'll probably be happy. I was at our church with her and introduced her to our priest, who gives her lessons and is very pleased with her. She loves me passionately—but she will love very few. Will she have the chance to get to know you?

I'm now busy with a large povest into which I intend to put everything that's still left in my soul . . .[3] Lord only knows whether I'll be successful. I'm constantly playing around with my characters—I even see them in my dreams. If I'm satisfied with my work I'll dedicate it to you.

Well, farewell for now. Be well—that's the main thing. Give my regards to your husband and all our Petersburg friends, Madame Verigina, too. Write me at the following address: au château de Courtavenel, près de Rozoy-en-Brie (Seine-et-Marne).

I kiss your hands and remain

Your loving

Iv. Turgenev.

Letter 105 (752). To A.I. Herzen.
September 4/16, 1859. Paris.

Paris.
Friday. September 16, 1859.

Dear Alexander Ivanich,

I'm going back to Russia tomorrow, and you'll add: "And only now does it occur to him to write me." It really is a little late—but that can't be helped. Frankly, I'm writing you to find out whether it's true that Chernyshevsky visited you, and what was the reason for the visit, and how did you like him?[1] Send all the details, but not to me—your letter won't reach me—besides which I'll find out everything in Petersburg—so write to Kolbasin or Shenshin, who are very interested in this. You know Kolbasin's address: Asnières, près de Paris, 4, Boulevard de la Comète (Lehotville—Asnières). You'll oblige them very much by that. In a couple of weeks a man will turn up at your place whom you'll surely greet warmly—the Decembrist Vegelin,[2] who wants to make your acquaintance. He'll bring you two important manuscripts which were delivered to me for *The Polar Star* while I was in Vichy. I've met another Decembrist, Volkonsky,[3] a very nice and good old man who also likes you and appreciates you. Have you seen the young Rostovtsev?[4]

Be well. My regards to Ogaryov, his wife,[5] and all your family. I press your hand firmly.

Your

Iv. Turgenev.

P.S. For the sake of security you can write about Chernyshevsky allegorically. Kolbasin's no fool—he'll understand.

Letter 106 (754). To M.A. Markovich.[1]
September 6-8/18-20, 1859. Paris.

Beat me, curse me, stomp on me, dear Maria Alexandrovna: I'm a hideous person—I won't be coming to Ostend, instead I'll gallop straight to Berlin, and from there to Stettin to the steamship (which leaves on Thursday)—and then to Petersburg, to Moscow, and to the country—where I absolutely must be by September 20, our style! I've already lost count of how many times I've deceived you—I'm red as a lobster from shame at this moment, I don't even dare to beg your pardon. But I hope you'll nevertheless be magnanimous and write me: Oryol Province, City of Mtsensk—and tell me where you're planning to spend the winter. I'll be in Petersburg.

I'm sending you the ticket for your fur coat that was left in Koenigsberg.

I'll deliver the translation of "The Institute Student" to Krayevsky, and I'll pass on the original to Belozersky.[2] Two letters are supposed to be delivered to me at the Hôtel de l'Agneau in Ostend. Please do me the favor of forwarding them to me at my Oryol address.

I'm ashamed, ashamed—and vexed—but it can't be helped. I scarcely dare to clasp your hand, kiss Bogdan, and give my regards to Afanasy Vasilievich.[3] Come to Petersburg for the winter. We'll be able to arrange things better than last year.

Oh, how ashamed I am! Good-bye.

Your

Iv. Turgenev.

Letter 107 (763). To D.I. Yazdovskaya.[1]
October 10/22, 1859. Spasskoye.

Dear Darya! My angel, I thank YOU from the bottom of my heart for carrying out my assignment—and as a reward, I'm giving YOU another one—and it is—to go to Ruzanov's[2] and buy the tooth water called "Eau de Botot" (it's Parisian)—and send it here right and with wildly ecstatic

155

gratitude I'll repay YOU all the money I owe you when I arrive in Petersburg. Yes, and by the way, pull the divinely handsome Kolbasin's ears (1) for having refuted my words; I may have made everything up—but where is his respect?—and (2) for not having written me immediately after his arrival in Russia. Farewell, *Little Angel,* be well and give my regards to everyone. I've lost my voice again, just like last year. Your seducer, Ivan Turgenev. Spasskoye, October 10, 1859.

Letter 108 (764). To Ye. Ye. Lambert.
October 14/26, 1859. Spasskoye.

Village of Spasskoye.
October 14, 1859.

Why do you tell me sweet things, dear Countess? After all, I don't tell you sweet things. However, I console myself with the thought that in sending me the excerpt from the letter you wrote about me, you were moved not so much by the desire to say sweet things to me as by the intention to reproach me indirectly for the insignificance and paleness of my last letters. But a person who, like me, wrote you a few days ago what was practically an eclogue, can calmly cross his arms on his chest and await the sentence of dispassionate fate or your sentence—which aren't quite the same things.

But all the same, don't write me sweet things. Man is so made that he's always ready to stuff himself with fruit preserves, even if he knows that they're bad for him and that the preserves, properly speaking, don't even belong to him. But women love to stroke your head, especially after they've scratched you—and they call *that* kindness.

But I'm nevertheless happy that your skeptical and mistrustful mood has been replaced by a melancholy and sad one. A skeptic is dissatisfied with others and with himself, but a melancholic only with himself, which is much easier and better.

I'm sitting here like a crayfish on the riverbottom—I don't even show my nose outside the room—I can't speak—I cough, but I'm working hard. The weather here is warm—I passionately adore such autumn days, but I'm forced to admire them through double windows. It's not fun: but as I was

156

once asked by Count Bludov[1] (the secretary to the Ambassador in London), who was amazed to see me hurrying to the train station: "Can there really be anything on earth for which it is worth hurrying?" That's just the way I sometimes think: isn't it all the same where one is? Can there really by anything worth desiring?

As soon as I wrote these words, I realized that I'd written nonsense. Too bad! I know many things that I passionately desire—and that will probably never be granted to me. In your letter you already commented on one of my wishes and used a terrible phrase which I don't want to repeat and which made me shudder. But besides *that* single, main wish, I have many others whose realization would make me very glad: for instance, I'd like to be healthy and sitting with you in your little room on Furshtatskaya; I'd like my novel to be a success; I'd like . . . but I can't even list them all. There's a Russian saying: "Even as a man dies, he jerks his foot."

It recently occurred to me that there's something tragic in the fate of almost every person—it's just that the tragic is often concealed from a person by the banal surface of life. One who remains on the surface (and there are many of them) often fails even to suspect that he's the hero of a tragedy. A woman will complain of indigestion and not even know that what she means is that her whole life has been shattered. For example: all around me here are peaceful, quiet existences, yet if you take a close look— you see something tragic in each of them—something either their own, or imposed on them by history, by the development of the nation. And besides that, we're all fated to die . . . What more tragic thing could one want?

I don't know what brought on this attack of philosophizing. But when I write you I never know what I'll end up saying, nor do I want to know. I do know that I'll never under any circumstances write that I don't love you. Farewell, dear Countess, be cheerful, give my regards to your husband and all our friends. I kiss your hands.

Your Iv. Turgenev.

P.S. Why do you send your letters registered? As a result they take an extra day to reach me.

157

Letter 109 (767). To I.S. Aksakov.
October 22/November 3, 1859. Spasskoye.

Village of Spasskoye.
October 22, 1859.

I passed through Moscow so quickly, dear Ivan Sergeyevich, that I didn't have time to see anyone—I was in a hurry to get here to hunt and work—but now I'd like to give you word of myself—but mainly—to hear what you and yours are doing. I have very little to tell: after visiting you in the spring (a few days before your father's death; the news of it reached me abroad—and saddened me greatly, though I was expecting it)[1]—after that visit I was in France, in England, took the waters in Vichy—and that was all; and when I arrived here, I first went hunting—with a very bad showing due to the lack of game; and then I fell sick with a stupid and very unpleasant illness that was tormenting me even in Petersburg: I caught cold—and it has especially affected my chest and throat: I've become completely mute, I can't even whisper, I'm racked by coughing—and this has been going on now for three weeks. Of course I'm not seeing anyone, nor, for that matter, is there anyone to see. I've been working very hard and have written a long povest for *The Russian Messenger;* I very much hope that you'll approve of it.[2] I haven't read anything here—and therefore I'm behind the times in literature—but I've heard much praise for your journal.[3] I've divvied up the land with peasants almost everywhere (I left the same amount of land, of course), I've resettled them (with their agreement)—and beginning this winter they'll all be on quitrent, at 3 silver rubles per desyatina; I've been saying *"I,"* but I should have said my uncle,[4] who doesn't care for *the new ways,* but who realizes that *the old ways* can't return. Before parting with their "masters" the peasants turn into Cossacks—and extort everything from the masters that they can: wheat, woods, cattle, and so on. I understand that completely—but for a while the woods, which everyone now is selling like mad, will disappear in our region. That's all right: the woods will grow back—and not here and there and haphazardly—but in accordance with the directions of science. We have no sobriety—such a drunken region. And so the peasants will stay on quitrent based on *land* instead of the desyatina or per capita until instructions arrive from above. No one in our area even wants to hear of the *mir,* the *commune,* or communal responsibility. I'm almost certain that that will have to be *forced* upon the peasants as an administrative and financial measure: they will never agree to it on their own—i.e., they value the mir only from a judicial point of view, as *self-adjudication,* if there is such a term, but in no other way.[5]

158

That's all that I have to tell you—will you tell me anything? Write me a couple of lines if you feel like it. (My address is Oryol Province, City of Mtsensk.) Because of my illness I definitely cannot give a date when I'll leave here; I had wanted to arrive in Moscow by November 15 for three days or so—and then come back for about 20 days (beginning with Christmas) to supervise the printing of my povest; but I can't guarantee anything now, though I still hope to fulfill my intentions. Please give my regards to your mother,[6] Konstantin Sergeyevich, and your whole family— as well as to Khomyakov,[7] the Yelagins,[8] and other good friends. Be well— that's the main thing—and good-bye. I clasp your hand firmly.

Your devoted

Iv. Turgenev.

Letter 110 (773). To Pauline Turgeneva.[1]
November 10/22, 1859. Spasskoye.

Spasskoye.
November 10/22, 1859.

My darling little girl,

I must nevertheless write you this *long* letter, which I've been promising you for a long time and which you have probably been awaiting with rather great impatience. Yes, unfortunately, my child, if I have hesitated until now, it's because I've nothing pleasant to tell you: but pleasant things aren't always wholesome—and I beg you to read this letter just as I'm going to write it—that is to say with the conviction that truth must be above all other considerations.

I must tell you frankly that I was not very pleased with you during my last stay in France. I discovered several rather grave faults in you that were less pronounced a year ago. You are touchy, vain, obstinate and secretive. You don't like it when people tell you the truth and as soon as they cease spoiling you, you quickly turn away from those people whom you ought to love most. You are jealous: do you suppose that I didn't understand why you tried to avoid my presence during the last days of my stay at

159

Courtavenel? As soon as you realized that I wasn't occupying myself exclusively with you, I didn't see you anymore: you disappeared. You lack trust; how many times did you refuse to finish telling me something that you yourself had begun? You don't like to associate with anyone except those you consider below you; your amour-propre is acquiring a savage aspect, and if it continues like this, your mind, by not associating with other, superior minds, will not develop. You are touchy even in regards to me, who has certainly done nothing that could have wounded you; do you think that you're behaving like a good daughter when you haven't written me a single time in the two months since we saw each other? You'll say that I've only written once to you, that you've been waiting for my letters: you would be right if you were a lawyer pleading his case against a stranger: but such considerations are quite inappropriate between a father and daughter. You have many good qualities—and if I don't speak of them it's because I find it as out of place as if I were to compliment myself for the good qualities I may have: you are too close to me, I love you too much not to see you as part of myself. I prefer to point out your faults to you with what may be exaggerated severity; I am certain that you couldn't attribute to my words anything but the desire to see you as perfect as possible—and that even if there is a certain exaggeration in my reproaches, you must not take offense—you should not see anything in them but new proof of my affection for you.

My dear little girl, I want to love you even more than I love you now; all that requires is that you remove the obstacles that stand in the way. Think about what I've said—and you'll see that it's not difficult. At your age I also had the capricious touchiness that wants nothing better than to isolate oneself within oneself and that believes it can get along without affection. Ah, my child—affection is such a rare and precious thing that it is madness to repulse it no matter where it comes from—all the more so— when it's an old simpleminded father who asks nothing more than to cherish his daughter. Well, that's all. This letter will be painful for you to read—it's been distressing for me to write—and I hasten to kiss you, very hard, as Didie says,[2] to reward myself for this anguish.

I'm leaving Spasskoye—God willing—in a week. Write me in Petersburg, Grande rue des Écuries, maison Weber.

I kiss you again.

Your loving father,

I. Turgenev.

Letter 111 (790). To P.V. Annenkov.
December 3/15, 1859. Petersburg.

Thursday evening.

Dear Pavel Vasilievich. A most unusual situation has just developed. Countess Lambert and her husband were just here, and she (after reading my novel[1]) so irrefutably demonstrated to me that it is worthless, counterfeit, and mendacious from A to Z that I'm seriously thinking of throwing it into the fire. Please don't laugh, but come to see me at about three o'clock—and I'll show you her written comments and convey her conclusions as well. I tell you without the slightest exaggeration that she has inspired in me revulsion for my own product—and quite seriously, it was only out of respect for you and because I believe in your taste that I didn't destroy my work immediately. Come see me, we'll have a discussion, and maybe you'll be persuaded of the judiciousness of her words. It's better to destroy now than to reproach oneself later. I'm writing all of this not without vexation, but absolutely without bile, honest to God. I'll be waiting for you and will keep a fire in the fireplace. Until I see you. Your I.T.

Letter 112 (800). To Ye. Ye. Lambert.
December 12/24, 1859. Petersburg.

Ah, dear Countess, what a lovely letter you write me! I read it several times and found myself deeply touched. It's always good to disclose one's soul to another: it's good for oneself and for the other. But you are wrong in accusing me of authorial coquettishness: if I couldn't write more than ten lines for you, then for the public I wouldn't write even two words—in my present psychic state. I have work to do, but I'm in no condition to work.[1] It's not that I feel ennui or grief, but here's what I'm feeling now: the passionate, insuperable desire for my own nest, my own *home*—together with the awareness of the impossibility of realizing my dream—and at the same time—the presence of constant thoughts about the transitoriness of all earthly things, about the closeness of *something* that I cannot name. The word "death" does not alone completely express that *something,* and hence the appeal to God—along with impulsive urges toward beloved green meadows. But the lamp must be flaring up one last time just before the end. So much for it!

I find that man is altogether too much inclined to complain on his own account. I'm sitting with a full stomach in a warm, smoke-filled room and whining...and there are so many poor people...I'm ashamed even to finish the thought.

And therefore I inform you not at all from the point of view of a complaint—but as a fact, that my throat hurts worse than before and that the doctor has absolutely forbidden me to leave the house—jusqu'à nouvel ordre [until a new order]—which I find very unpleasant—most of all because this prohibition deprives me of the chance to visit you.

And do you know that you write marvellous Russian? Your cute little grammatical mistakes (*ya bredu* instead of *ya brozhu*)[2] only give added charm to your speech. If it's not difficult for you to write in that language—do so: you'll see that although it doesn't have the *spineless* flexibility of French—yet by virtue of its honest simplicity and free strength it is amazingly good for expressing many and the best thoughts—Strange! Those four qualities—honesty, simplicity, freedom, and strength—are missing in the people, but the language has them...That means that the people will too.

You shouldn't say that it would be better for you and me not to see each other often...What does it matter that sometimes in these contacts, especially if other people are there, the conversation takes on a light and frivolous direction...All that counts is that there not be frivolity in the heart, otherwise that is also a kind of haughtiness. I remember that in my youth I wanted every moment of my life to be significant...An impudent, and probably sinful wish! Let the brook babble along until it merges with the sea!

Farewell and good-bye. I kiss your hands and thank you for chatting with me.

Your

Iv. Turgenev.

P.S. Do you by any chance have the newest issue of *Revue des 2 mondes* in which there's an article about *Orfeo?*[3]

Letter 113 (863). To K.N. Leontiev.
February 16/28, 1860. Petersburg.

St. Petersburg.
February 16, 1860.

Dear Konstantin Nikolayevich, I haven't answered you until now because I wanted to say something positive about your povest,[1] both from the point of view of inner virtues and its external (journal) evaluation. I can tell you that your povest isn't bad; it reads easily, but no more than that: it was cleverly conceived, with a striving for simplicity and clarity, the characters are truthful, but there's little vitality, beauty, or movement; all those things have been replaced by a sort of playful and often affected authorial cunning; the author, while obviously portraying things, mocks them himself, and the result is something cold, bloodless, and pale. Your mind has worked a great deal: you have obviously passed through a rather complex spiritual development, you have matured, but are you an artist? Putting my hand on my heart and weighing my words, I can answer neither yes nor no to that question. I would be very sorry if my words prevented you from writing; I wouldn't be able to forgive myself for that: continue working; maybe you'll finally become master of yourself and of your energies and you'll clearly comprehend your calling; but until then you won't produce living images; subtleties and clever remarks and hints are of no help in the matter. Why don't you try uniting critical and esthetic studies? I'm certain that you have all the essentials for that.[2]

The Library for Reading offers you 50 silver rubles per printer's sheet; having received your answer, it can send you the money in advance. However, I'll have *The Contemporary* and *Notes of the Fatherland* read your povest; if anyone will give more, I'll give instructions accordingly.

Any reader who starts your povest will definitely read it to the end and think, "Why, this is interesting and well-written," but that will be the limit of his impressions. That's too little for you; I know that perhaps with time you'll be capable of more.

Dear Konstantin Nikolayevich, please don't be grieved by my letter; the opinion expressed is probably harsher than it should be, but you're not a little boy, and you stand firmly on your own two feet: that's obvious from everything. Keep going forward—and you'll get there.

My address is: Greater Konyushennaya, Weber's Building, Apartment No. 34. I'll be waiting for your reply. Give my regards to your kind and good Baron Rozen[3] and his spouse, whom I love though I haven't the honor of knowing her. I press your hand cordially and remain

Your devoted

Iv. Turgenev.

Letter 114 (865). To N.A. Nekrasov.
Around February 19/March 2, 1860. Petersburg.

I earnestly beg you, dear Nekrasov, *not to publish that article:* all it can do is cause me trouble; it is inaccurate and shrill—I won't know what to do if it's published. Please respect my request.—I'll drop by to see you.[1]

Your

Iv. Turgenev

Letter 115 (887). To A.A. Fet.
March 13-16/25-28, 1860. Petersburg.

St. Petersburg
March 13, 1860

I'm in debt to you, Fethie carissime [dearest Fet], but I can partially justify myself with the fact that I used the past week to finish a povest which has already been turned in to *Library for Reading* and will appear in the March issue. (By the way, all the rumors about the shakiness of *Library for Reading* turn out to be false—and Pechatkin's bookshop is only closed on Sundays.) My povest is called "First Love." I think you know the subject matter. I read it a few days ago to an Areopagus composed of Ostrovsky,

Pisemsky, Annenkov, Druzhinin and Maykov; Goncharov, who was invited, came five minutes after I'd finished my reading. The Areopagus was satisfied and only had a few minor criticisms; all that's left is to find out what the *public,* whom you so dislike, will say. The only person whom I despair of ever satisfying is Lev Tolstoy. But that can't be helped! It's obvious that such is my fate. Rumors are circulating here to the effect that he's started working again—and we're all glad.

Well, my dear friends Afanasy Afanasievich and Ivan Petrovich,[1] you'll see me soon—not in person, but in a photograph that I've ordered specially for you, from Denier.[2] As regards my person, I'm sincerely unhappy to say that I won't be going to the country; instead I'm going abroad in the spring for treatment. No matter what you say about my hypochondria, I feel plainly that something's wrong with my throat and chest; my cough doesn't go away—blood turns up a couple of times a week—and I can't show my nose outside without a muzzle (i.e., a respirator). How could I even think about hunting in the spring and so on and so forth. I need to drink the waters and take baths—and take care of my vile body! That distresses me—and I make bold to think that it will distress both of you too. But it can't be helped! "What will be, will be." Remember me when you're hunting... Judging by the news from the country, Bubulka[3] seems not far from dead...

Your dog's bad health is not good, dear Afanasy Afanasievich. You need to treat her; I'm a little afraid that she might turn out weak in the chase. Oh, what a time we'd have hunting... Ugh, it's better not to talk about it!

But don't abandon your idea about *Kalna;*[4] talk about it on the spot and in a sensible way with my uncle: I'm ready for anything in order to have you as a neighbor.

Don't be angry—just consider that I'm not happy either. I embrace both of you heartily and remain

Your ever-devoted

Iv. Turgenev.

Letter 116 (916). To Ye. Ye. Lambert.
April 29/May 11, 1860. Koenigsberg.

Koenigsberg.
Friday, April 29/May 11, 1860.

Dear Countess, I'm writing to you from this city, where I arrived last night after a torturous journey. Two reasons caused me to take pen in hand: the first is that the last evening I spent with you wasn't so friendly and pleasant—we argued and so on—and I want to tell you that I love you very much and that I treasure your friendship (by the way, how glad I am that you'll be in Ems! I'll definitely come to see you); and the second reason is the following:

Copy:

Titular Councilor Dmitry Kolbasin earnestly requests that his nine-year-old niece, Olga Zgurskaya, the daughter of the deceased Captain Andrey Zgursky, who served for 30 years and did not leave his wife and two children any estate, be accepted in one of the Petersburg or Moscow institutes. The necessary documents will be presented immediately upon request.

Now I'll say a few words for myself. I don't apologize for turning to you with incessant requests: the source of spring water is valued precisely because each person goes to drink from it. But I would very much like to do something for Kolbasin. He's a splendid, noble, and self-sacrificing person, who, in a far from glittering position (he's not wealthy and he serves as the assistant to the manager of the Land Office in *Novgorod*), thinks only of helping others. That is his constant concern and only passion. Couldn't you do something special for him, though I know how hard that is. I would be greatly obliged.[1]

I bow at your feet and kiss your hand. I'll write you from Paris, where I ask you to write me a few lines c/o *poste restante*. Goodbye until Ems. Regards to your husband and your whole household.

Your devoted

Iv. Turgenev

166

Letter 117 (944). To P.V. Annenkov.
June 26/July 3, 1860. Soden.

Soden. July 8, 1860.

Dear Pavel Vasilievich, I just received your letter and am answering it. The details that you sent are very interesting. What would happen to us if you had not been shot, although you probably wouldn't even have tried to defend yourself![1] But a bullet is a fool. We'll have to spend a long time talking about everything that you've séen—we'll talk on the Isle of Wight: we won't see each other before that. My plans have undergone a slight change about which I count it my duty to inform you. I'm staying here until the 16th, and then I go straight to Courtavenel, to Mme Viardot's, where I'll stay until August 1st, i.e., until the era of sea baths on Wight. Mme Viardot wishes this, and for me her will is law. Her son nearly died, and she has been through a great deal. She wants to relax in the tranquil society of friends. Speaking of death, imagine what woeful news I received from Pisemsky. Polonsky's sweet, pretty little wife died![2] I can't tell you how sorry I am for her and for him—and you too surely share my sorrow. Why couldn't she have lived? Didn't Polonsky deserve a little reward for all his past woes? Where is justice?

We're leading an extraordinarily quiet life here in Soden. My health is excellent; unfortunately, the weather is cold and foul: continual rains. You write of hot weather—and I've never been so frozen in my life as the day before yesterday, when I rode in an open carriage from Ems, where I'd visited Countess Lambert, to Schwalbach, where M.A. Markovich has taken up lodging. She is a very nice, intelligent, good woman with a poetic disposition of soul. She will be on Wight, and I'm certain that the two of you will get along well... Watch out that you don't fall in love! Which is quite possible, in spite of the fact that she's not very beautiful. But you and I are over-smoked herrings that no one will take. Kartashevskaya[3] whirled through here with her brother[4] and is living for the time being in Bonn, in the Hôtel Belle-Vue under Kilian's guidance.[5] She'll spend a month there; I sent her your address. You can drop in on her when you're sailing on the green waters of the Rhein.

Here I've been seeing Lev Tolstoy's brother Nikolay more often than anyone else. He's a wonderful fellow, but his situation is a sad one: he has hopeless consumption. He's waiting for his brother Lev and his sister to come here; but God only knows whether they'll come. I've been receiving letters from Rostovtsev: he's on Wight, in Ventnor. There are no words in any human language to describe the extent to which I haven't been doing anything here. My fingers ache when I hold a pen. Can literature really be my occupation?

Well, farewell. Perhaps after all my postponed meetings we'll see each other in Ventnor or Wight. For some reason I imagine that it will be very nice there. Be well and try to keep your nice round chin above the water. Your I.T.

Letter 118 (947). To Pauline Turgeneva.[1]
June 26/July 8, 1860. Soden.

Soden.
July 8, 1860.

My dear Paulinette, an absence of several days has prevented me from responding to your letter as soon as I would have liked. I sympathize with your difficulties, although you've brought them on yourself: I confess that I didn't understand a thing about the story with the pastries, etc., that resulted in a debt of 84 francs; all I see is that such intimacy with Mme Julie is worthless and I hope that there will be no more question of it. As for this debt, that lady can certainly wait until I return, which will be in a dozen days. This is a lesson for the future: it's not because of your "generosity" or your "great-heartedness" that you're in trouble—it's simply because of your amour propre and because of a tendency that I seem to observe in you—to avoid any budgetary limitations—I'm certain that you've thought over everything that just happened—and I beg you to give me the exact sum of all your little debts—so that this may no longer be a question. There's no danger that you will ruin me—but I'll be in despair if I see you adopt the habit of spending money thoughtlessly: that habit is bad even if one has a large fortune. It is a sort of negligence against which one must keep onself on guard.

The news of little Anna's death has greatly saddened me.[2] If you see Mr. Turgenev,[3] tell him that I offer my condolences for the misfortune that has just stricken him.

I'm very happy to see M. Delioux[4] making you work—but I don't like the word "discouraged" that appears in your letter. That's a little premature at your age.

My health is very good and I'm satisfied with my stay in Soden. Expect me in ten days—and in the meantime accept several good kisses from your father, who would scold you less if he didn't love you so much.

J. Tourguéneff

Letter 119 (955). To A.A. Fet.
July 16/28, 1860. Courtavenel.

Courtavenel.
July 16/28, 1860.

Dear Afanasy Afanasievich, I've already written you from here, but yesterday I received the letter that you mailed from Mtsensk on July 2/14 (our mail is like a capricious woman—it always surprises us with the unexpected)—and I make haste to reply. To a certain extent I'm even obligated to reply—since you are in a depression caused by reflection,[1] which in your words, *I brought on you* by having mentioned it. A likely story! In the first place, as I recall, even before becoming acquainted with me you were infected by that epidemic, as you call it—and in the second place, in our arguments I always protested against your rectilinearly mathematical abstractions—and was amazed that they could even live in harmony with your poetic nature. But that's not the issue. I want to dispel an error of yours. You call yourself a retired officer, poet, and man (but who isn't a retiree, say I—Sire, qui est-ce qui a des dents? [Sire, who *does* have any teeth?])[2]—and you attribute your *withering up*, your depressions to the absence of proper activity...Ah, my friend, it's all wrong!... Youth has passed, but old age hasn't arrived—that's why you're down in the dumps. I myself am suffering through that difficult twilight age, an age of impulses made all the stronger by the fact that they aren't justified by anything—an age of tranquility without rest, hopes that resemble regrets, and regrets that resemble hopes.[3] We just need to be patient a little longer, wait a bit, dear Afanasy Afanasievich, and we'll enter the quiet haven of old age at long last, and then we'll have the opportunity for the activity of old age and even those joys of old age about which Marcus Tullius Cicero speaks so eloquently in his treatise "De senectute." Just a few more gray hairs in the beard— and a missing tooth or two, and a touch of rheumatism

169

in the small of the back or the legs—and everything will be fine! But for the meantime, so that the time not seem too long, let's do some shooting:

Speaking of grouse, I was hoping to receive a description of your first hunts in the woodland, but you're still only getting ready! That's bad. I'm certain that by now you've already seen the error of your ways and have hunted to your heart's content. God only knows when the hunting season will arrive in France! It's absolutely wintry here, your teeth chatter, it rains daily—disgusting! No one can say when harvesting will begin or end. But what sort of hunting is it anyway! The same old partridges and hares! As for the time of my return home, for the time being I can't say anything definite. In a few days the question of whether I'll have to spend the winter in Paris or whether I'll return to my woodcocks at Spasskoye will be resolved.[4]

And as for the purchase of land, the use of your capital, and so on— allow me to give you one piece of advice: don't let that thought gnaw at you and upset you—don't let it take on the form d'une idée fixe [of an obsession]. "Don't fuss," said the wise man Tyutchev, "madness searches."[5] The moment will come or an opportunity will come—and fine! But to rush out to meet the moment or to meet the opportunity is madness. "Tout vient à point à qui sait attendre" [Everything comes in the nick of time to him who knows how to wait]. You shouldn't buy an estate on the basis of "nothing to do!"

I presume that the Tolstoys are all in Soden: one of them has probably written to me in Paris, poste restante. I'm leaving here in a few days for England, for the Isle of Wight, for sea baths, if only the sea hasn't frozen over.

I send 10,000 greetings to your wife[6] and Borisov, I clasp your hand firmly and remain

Innocent of having infected you
with reflection,

Iv. Turgenev.

Letter 120 (963). To Ye. Ye. Lambert
August 6/18, 1860. Ventnor.

Ventnor.
August 18, 1860.

Honestly, you are so kind and so good, dear Countess, that I really don't know how to thank you. I received your letter from my daughter, who is absolutely delighted with you and told me everything in great detail. I'm afraid that you'll spoil her: she's very affectionate—but she also likes people to be affectionate to her and pat her on the head. I know, for example, why she no longer loves Mme Viardot: because the latter has recently been paying less attention to her. Young people love other people not for their qualities, not even for the favors or benefits received, but for the caresses that those people grant them: that egoism of youth is more pardonable than the egoism of the elderly—but it's still egoism. At the same time she has a good heart; she was born under a lucky star—and if one judges by probabilities, her life will be good and correct. May God grant that!

Just between us—Mme Verigina is wrong to upset her with reproaches for her lack of knowledge of Russian, with suggestions that she return to Russia, where, in her words, she'll find a good husband and so on. My daughter unfortunately cannot return to Russia—and therefore it's pointless to incite these thoughts in her.[1]

Pauline writes me about a marvellous gift you made her: I kiss your hands and thank you. I find it so pleasant thanking you that I'm certain you won't reproach me for it.

There are quite a few Russians here—and good ones, among them N. Ya. Rostovtsev (the son of the well-known Yakov Ivanovich[2])—a wonder-

171

ful person. I'd be very glad if you could meet him sometime. The weather just keeps on being bad—and today there's such a storm that it's impossible to bathe. The sea through my windows is all dark and white from foam. The wind is horrible.

I hope that the difficulties which you mentioned at the end of your letter have already been dispelled. The sun ought to shine on you!

I've begun working a little; I'm planning a new long *povest*—will anything come of it?[3]

I'll see you in two weeks. Watch out—don't leave Paris without me. Give my regards to all your household—I love you with all my heart.

Iv. Turgenev

Letter 121 (969). To P.V. Annenkov.
August 19/31. 1860. Ventnor.

Ventnor. Friday, August 31.

Dear friend Pavel Vasilievich, here's a copy of the plan and a copy of one of the circulars.[1] From the enclosure you'll notice that the draft has undergone minor abridgements, and in one place a proviso has been added as a safeguard against future objections. I'm just afraid that this letter may find you in Aachen already, since according to the mysterious Maria Alexandrovna's[2] letter, Makarov has *galloped off* to break up Shevchenko's *wedding*![3]

I wrote on the address that in case you had already left, the letter should be sent to Petersburg. There's no need to ask you to disseminate our plan as widely as possible. Even without that you'll do everything in your power—I'm sure of that. Following your copy 10 others are being sent to Petersburg and Moscow. Strike while the iron is hot! Here's a copy of the circular: "Dear So-and-so! From the attached draft plan for a Society for the Dissemination of Literacy and Primary Education you see the point of my letter to you. This program was prepared with the encouragement and assent of several Russians who came together by chance in a foreign city, and it represents only the primary features of the society. I hope that you will approve the idea that lies at its basis and that you will want to devote your own thoughts and conversations with friends to it. I would consider

172

myself fortunate if, by the time of my return to Russia (spring, 1861), the proposed idea had been worked out enough to allow it to be brought to fruition. In turning to you for help, I don't need grandiloquent words: I'm certain as it is that you will very much want to participate actively in a matter of such importance or that you will at least express your views. I'm also certain that you won't refuse to circulate copies of our plan. This undertaking concerns all Russia: we need to know, as far as possible, all Russia's opinion about it. I would be genuinely grateful to receive any objections or comments from you. My address is Paris, poste restante. Respectfully, your devoted I.T."[4]

I think that there's nothing either superfluous or inappropriate. On each copy there will be an additional notation (and you take care of that) that any and all comments and objections will be gratefully accepted in Turgenev's name—poste restante in Paris, and in P.V. Annenkov's name in St. Petersburg.

I hope you arrive safely and find everything in order. Give my regards to everyone and we'll keep in touch. My address in Paris is poste restante or rue Lafitte, Hôtel Byron.

Sollte Herr Pavel Annenkow durchgereist sein, so wird gebeten diesen Brief nach Russland, S. Petersburg, Demidoff Pereulok. Haus Wisconti, zu schicken. [If Mr. Pavel Annenkov has passed through, please forward this letter to Russia, St. Petersburg, Demidov Lane, the Visconti Building.]

Letter 122 (974). To A.A. Fet.
August 27, 31/September 8, 12, 1860. Paris, Courtavenel.

Paris.
Saturday, Sept. 8 N.S.

I too exclaim hurrah! And even Hosanna! And even Eljen [hurrah], which means something good in Hungarian. I'm very happy for you that you really made a good purchase[1] and have calmed down and acquired a new field of action. It's too bad that it's a little far from Spasskoye—but with replacement horses one can get there speedily—and it's a good spot for hunting. I can already forewarn you that you'll be seeing me often as a guest—with Flambeau (who has turned out to be a superb dog) or some other canine comrade. We'll live a few peaceful years more before the end— and then may

"Indifferent nature
Shimmer with its eternal beauty."[2]

I'll give you a brief account of the news that concerns me personally. (N.B. Beginning on this page I'm writing from Courtavenel, September 12 [August 31 O.S.]. I arrived here yesterday and found this whole old nest in order—though very dilapidated. Mme Viardot and her daughter are gone: they're both in Ireland. Old man Viardot and I aren't starting hunting until the day after tomorrow; the hunting season is terribly late because of the rains.)

I haven't found a husband for my daughter yet—and up till now there hasn't even been anyone in sight, but during the winter someone will probably turn up—the thought of it makes me tremble. She came here with me. As you already know, I'll be spending the winter in Paris.

The latest news about the Tolstoys is that they planned to go to the Isles of Hyères; I invited them to come to Paris on their way—but they didn't come...Poor Nikolay's consumption is already in his throat: he doesn't have long to live. There's still no news of Lev; and I have to confess that I'm not terribly interested in knowing about a person who isn't himself interested in anyone.

For the time being I'm not undertaking any literary work: and to judge from the comments of the so-called young critics, it's time for me, too, to retire from literature. So you and I have wound up among the Podolinskys, Trilunnys, and other venerable retired majors! What's to be done, old man? It's time to make way for the young. But where are they, where are our heirs?[3]

During our stay on the Isle of Wight, Annenkov and I thought up a plan for a "Society for the Dissemination of Literacy and Primary Education." I've sent several copies of that plan to Russia—and will continue to do so.[4] I'll send one to you too. Read it and give me your opinion.[5] It seems to be a worthwhile cause—and conceived in a practical manner. I'm now putting this idea into circulation, and I'd be very happy if it could be realized at least by next winter. Write me your opinion—and should it be the case, your objections.

Well—let me congratulate you once more, new landowner! I expect a detailed description of your land from the point of view of hunting. As for Snobs, because of his hind legs I was already certain that he'd be weak, but I didn't want to distress you. Next year, if Flambeau survives, you'll hunt with Spring. Write me for the time being in Paris, poste restante.

Good-bye, dear Afanasy Afanasievich. Regards to your wife, Borisov, and all our good acquaintances.

Your devoted

Iv. Turgenev.

Letter 123 (982). To Ye. Ye. Lambert.
September 21/October 3, 1860. Courtavenel.

Courtavenel.
Oct. 3 N.S., 1860

Here I am writing to you in Petersburg again, dear Countess—and you'll be reading this letter in your nice little room where, unfortunately, I won't be able to be this winter! Instead of Petersburg I'll be staying in Paris—and I'm not looking forward to that stay. I can't stand Parisians, my daughter and I (I have to admit this—though she's a wonderful girl) have too little in common, and a sort of sad fog has settled, over the other relationships that you know about.[1] But there's no point in complaining and whining: a carefree, satisfying life has long since ceased to exist for me—and now I need to accustom myself to *real* self-sacrifice—not the sort about which we speak so much in youth and which we imagine in the form of love, i.e., enjoyment, nonetheless—but the sort that gives the personality nothing, except perhaps a feeling of duty fulfilled, and note—it's an alien, cold feeling without the slightest admixture of exaltation or enthusiasm. All this is familiar to you: we're berries from the same field—and I'm telling you this for reinforcement of myself and you in these thoughts.

I wasn't especially satisfied with our last meeting in Paris: you were continually occupied with some troublesome worry (préoccupation)—I felt cold and dull—besides which, we didn't see each other much. Sometimes letters give you relief; write me what you're feeling in your heart: I need not tell you with what a warm and friendly feeling I take everything that comes from you.—By the way, I've rented an apartment—rue Rivoli, 210—write me there; the apartment is rather decent, a little expensive—but I'll have a separate study for work. I'll probably stay at home a lot; I've started a rather large piece and I'd be very glad if I managed to finish it over the winter.[2]

I want to explain to you just why it is that my daughter and I have so little in common: she loves neither music, nor poetry, nor nature—nor dogs—and those are the only things I love. It's from this point of view that it's difficult for me to live in France—where the poetry is petty and insignificant, nature is absolutely ugly, music smacks of vaudeville or a joke, and the hunting is disgusting. Frankly, this is all fine for my daughter—and she makes up for qualities she lacks with other, more positive and useful ones: but for me—just between us—she is the same as Insarov.[3] I respect her, but that's not enough.

Please don't forget to put in a good word for our plan where possible.[4] Annenkov will see that you get a precise, accurate copy.

I've received another letter from my acquaintance N.R. Tsebrikov,[5] about whom I asked you and whom I recommended as a wonderfully honest and competent person for managing an estate; he still hasn't found a place (and he's looking for a position at 1200 silver rubles). If you have a chance, don't forget him either, and I personally stand behind him.

His address is: The Corner of Gorokhovaya and Meschanskaya Streets, Ossov's Building, Kilgast's apartment, No. 13.

Be well, dear Countess—and don't lose heart—that's the main thing. Give my regards to your household—and I clasp your hand very, very firmly.

Your devoted

Iv. Turgenev.

Letter 124 (983). To K.N. Leontiev.
September 21/October 3, 1860. Courtavenel.

Courtavenel.
October 3 N.S., 1860

I'm writing to you, dear Konstantin Nikolayevich, from a village located 50 versts from Paris, or more accurately, from a chateau that belongs to good friends of mine. I received your kind letter two weeks ago and I thank you for remembering me and for your interest. Unfortunately, I can't return to Russia this year; I say unfortunately, because, due to family obligations,[1] I'll have to spend the winter in Paris, which I find loathsome. If the case were otherwise, I'd definitely come to see you and take a look at how you live. I've rented an apartment in Paris on Rue de Rivoli, 210; write me at that address and tell me which capital you settle in; I'd like it to be Petersburg. God grant that you move on firm legs down the literary road which you haven't yet properly set foot on; but that shouldn't depress you; talents, like fruits, don't mature at the same time or in the same season of the year. Fall fruits are sometimes sweeter than summer ones. Your weakness lies (as is always the case) just where your strength is: your devices are too subtle and exquisitely clever, often to the point of obscurity. A poet must be a psychologist, but a secret one: he should know and feel the roots of phenomena, but he presents only the phenomena themselves—in their full blossom or withering away.[2] I took the liberty of eliminating several superfluous psychological bits from your povest that was published in *Library for Reading*,[3] and I hope that you weren't irritated with me for that. And I expect many good things from your *Podlipki*, just finish it soon: don't spend too long on it. You read it to Dudyshkin, and he sang its praises to me; and he's a good judge. It's obvious from what he said, however, that your novel ought to be shortened.

Everything you write about Baron Rozen's family interests me very much. I don't know whether I'll ever manage to meet his wife in person; life brings some people into constant contact with each other and seems to keep others apart; God only knows, for instance, when you and I will see each other. Give my regards to both of them if you write them or see them.

I enjoyed reading your opinion of "First Love." For people like me, a veteran on the eve of full retirement, it's hard to change: what we did badly can't be corrected; what was successful can't be repeated. We have only one thing left that we should think about: being able to fall silent in time. For the meantime work isn't yet over; and now I've planned a rather long piece.[4] And there's nothing suprising in the fact that, as you say, I've recently grown sad: I'll soon be 42, and I haven't made a nest for myself or secured any place for myself on earth: there's little cause for merriment in that.

While awaiting a reply from you, I wish you all the best and clasp your hand cordially. Mrs. Markovich (Marko Vovchok), about whom you want to write an article, is here in Paris: she's a wonderful woman. But do you really like "The King of Hearts"? It strikes me that that particular story is the least successful of all her stories, though the basic idea in it is true-to-life, as is always the case with Marko Vovchok.

Your devoted

Iv. Turgenev.

P.S. To insure more accurate delivery, I don't frank my letters.

Letter 125 (984). To P.V. Annenkov.[1]
September 30/October 12, 1860. Paris.

Paris, October 12, N.S., 1860.

... I'll tell you a few words about myself. I've rented an apartment on Rue de Rivoli, 210, and have settled in there with my daughter and a wonderful old English lady[2] whom God helped me find. I intend to work as hard as possible. The plan for my new povest is ready down to the slightest details—and I'm anxious to get to work on it. I don't know whether it will turn out to be any good, but Botkin, who is here... greatly approves the idea at its basis. I'd like to finish this thing by spring, by April, and bring it to Russia myself.[3] *The Age* ought to consider me among its most serious permanent collaborators.[4] Please send me your statement of purpose, and in my spare hours from my major work I'll write little pieces that I'll try to make as interesting as possible.

Thanks for the books, old boy... And thanks for the forty rubles that you gave to my dissolute cousin.[5] For everything, I thank you.[6] That crazy no-good bum, who got the nickname Shamil in our province, spent his way through a very respectable estate in an instant, has been a monk, a gypsy, and an army officer, and now seems to have devoted himself to the craft of drunkard and wheedler. I wrote my uncle and told him to take care of the dissolute clown at Spasskoye. As for the 100 rubles, have the publishers of *The Age* pay you—I'll earn that from them within a month.

Pass the enclosed note on to Ivan Ivanovich Panayev.[7] If he would like to know the real reason for my not wanting to be a collaborator on *The Contemporary* anymore—ask him to read in the June issue of this year, in "Contemporary Survey," p. 240, the 3rd line from the top, the passage where Mr. Dobrolyubov accuses me of having deliberately made a caricature of Rudin in order to ingratiate myself with my *wealthy* literary friends, in whose eyes any poor person is a scoundrel.[8] That's just a little too much—and a decent person ought not to contribute to such a journal.

Arrange a position for, i.e., help arrange a position for Markovich via Yegor Kovalevsky (to whom I send my cordial regards).

His wife is here; she's not quite well and she's depressed. But that will pass and she'll recover. But the main thing is that she doesn't have a farthing. Though her husband won't be sending her any money, if he has a decent salary then he at least won't rob her. Makarov is still here, but will soon return.

Poor, noble Nikolay Tolstoy died at Hyères.[9] His sister is wintering there, and Lev Nikolaevich is still here.

Well, farewell. I kiss your sugary lips and await a reply. Give my regards to all our friends . . . What is poor Polonsky doing?[10] Your devoted I.T.

Letter 126 (987). To I.I. Panayev.
October 1/13, 1860. Paris.

October 1/13, 1860.

Dear Ivan Ivanovich, although as far as I remember, you have already ceased to announce your collaborators in *The Contemporary*, judging by your references to me, I have to assume that you no longer need me,[1] however, to make certain, I ask you not to list my name among your collaborators, the more so as I have nothing ready and the long work which I have just now started on and which I will not finish earlier than next May, is already destined for *The Russian Messenger*.[2]

As you know, I am staying in Paris for the winter. I hope that you're well and cheerful, and I press your hand. Your devoted Iv. Turgenev.

Paris. Rue de Rivoli, 210.

Letter 127 (988). To A.A. Fet.
October 3/15, 1860. Paris.

Paris.
Oct. 3/15, 1860.

Beatus ille, amice Fethie [Blessed is he, my friend Fet]—and so on—see your translation of Horace.[1] With both my hands I bless your little nest[2] and those people dear to my heart who are sitting in it. Have no regrets about anything: neither about any extra kopecks paid nor about any fuss and bother: that's all trifles, and der Hauptgriff ist gethan [the main thing is done]! The heavens themselves smile on you—those heavens which have wafted nastiness and cold for six months here have spat (and are spitting) rain at us, and have approximated the look of dirty linen; I hear that you have warmth, beatitude, and sunshine! I await with genuine impatience that happy moment next spring when, to the accompaniment of songs of the nightingale, I'll turn off the Kursk road into your farm. Then we'll ignore our age for a last time and drink from the goblet of youth—and from another goblet of Röderer[3]—but *that* won't be for the last time. Yes, here you and I are still planning to live; but for Nikolay Tolstoy there no longer exists either spring or the songs of nightingales—nothing! He died, poor man, on the Isles of Hyères, where he had just arrived. I received that news from his sister. You can imagine how it grieved me—though I had long since lost hope for his recovery—and though his life was worse than death—if only there is anything worse than death. Lev Nikolayevich was with him—and is still in Hyères (Nikolay Nikolayevich passed away in Hyères—not on the islands). Die Guten sterben jung [the good die young]. I know that you and Borisov will recall him often: he was a golden man—intelligent and simple and kind. I'd like to talk with Lev Nikolayevich about his last days—but God only knows when and where I'll see him.

I've settled in for the winter with my daughter and her English governess—on Rue de Rivoli, 210—and I may be forced to move, because the room that I intended to make into my study is infected with a stench. They're promising to correct that—but all the same you'd better write me poste restante. This is all the more irritating in that the plan for my new povest is ready down to all the details[4]—and though I've fallen to the level of the Trilunnys, I wouldn't mind working a little. I recommend that you too—though you too are a Trilunny[5]—not disdain conversation with the Muses; but that's the farthest thing from your mind now; but when you've calmed down and dug your pond, take advantage of the last days of autumn, in which there is concealed an especially "poignant, mysterious charm,"[6] and try to tune the strings of your lyre—and send me the results. Because it's very prosaic and dry (in the figurative sense) here. You'll have a dog, I swear to you by Castor and Pollux (for some reason I'm stressing Classical metaphors today)—and a good dog... In the spring you and I'll go hunting—definitely! definitely!! definitely!!!

The news of your sister's recovery[7] cheered me greatly. Give my regards to Borisov and congratulate him.

Well, be healthy and vigorous in spirit. I cordially clasp your hand and your wife's. Let's write more often.

Your devoted

Iv. Turgenev

Letter 128 (993). To A.I. Herzen.
October 23/November 4, 1860. Paris.

Paris.

Nov. 4, 1860.

"Dear to my heart and eyes" (even the strongest friendship doesn't allow me, however, to add the line that follows: "Like a spring flower just opened")[1] Alexander Ivanovich! I received your note with the enclosures. Mrs. Shenshina's address is: Passage Sandrié, 5.[2] I doubt that you'll accomplish anything: she has fits of hysteria, curses, lies, weeps, faints—in a word, she's putting on a show. "Out of respect to the memory of Alexander," who made some sort of avowal to her before his death, she doesn't want to recognize the child as his son—and she only gave the mother 2000 francs—as alms. We want to prevent the child from dying of starvation—and are planning to set up a pension for him: couldn't you give at least a hundred francs a year? Let me know about this.

The translation of your message to the Serbs[3] is written in rather aventuré [risky] French, but for the Serbs—that's fine.

I can swear to you that Maria Alexandrovna Markovich is not at all a Circe—and she hasn't the slightest intention of seducing the young Passek.[4] Whether *he's* in love with her—that I don't know, but she does not at all deserve to be the object of maternal despair and so on and so forth.—It would seem that the city of Heidelberg is noted for making up gossip: it is said of me there that I keep a serf mistress by force and that Mrs. Beecher Stowe (!) publicly reproached me for that, and that I swore at her.[5] That's also eine schöne Gegend [a beautiful spot].

Thanks for *The Bell*. Please don't forget me in the future.

I press your hand firmly and remain

Your devoted

Iv. Turgenev.

Letter 129 (1004). To Ye. Ya. Kolbasin.
November 12/14, 1860. Paris.

Paris.
November 12/24, 1860.

I have the honor of congratulating you, dear Yelisey Yakovlevich, on the occasion of your entering government service![1] Seriously, I was very happy to hear the news: you have fine and honest activity ahead of you— and you can do a lot of good. It's more trustworthy than literature, which there's no reason for you to abandon, however. Next April I'll definitely stop off to see you when I take the train back to Spasskoye.

Unfortunately, I'm not at Spasskoye now, but in repugnant Paris. I'm getting down to work gradually and sluggishly. The thing that I've started is a rather large one.[2] I've also had a lot of fuss and bother with the repugnant Mrs. Viktorina Shenshina (you must have received a letter from her). You probably know that Shenshin died of a stroke at his mistress's without leaving any document, without making any provisions for her or the son, whom he was holding in his arms when the stroke felled him. Several friends, and I among them, tried to persuade Mrs. Shenshina to do something, and then the fun began. She immediately surrounded herself with that vile French household with which you are familiar—and what nonsense didn't she pull! A woman who was not an emancipée would simply have said: "The money is mine, there are no papers—and I won't give up anything"; but Mrs. Shenshina, as an emancipée, announced that she doesn't recognize any conjugal obligations—and that she'd give up everything to the child if only the child were her husband's; but, to quote her, this husband, just before his death, tearfully kissing her feet (I'd love to have seen that scene), swore to her that it was all slander, that the child wasn't his at all, that he so despised his mistress that he lent her out to his friends, and that the only one he adored and loved was her, her, Mrs. Shenshina, and that he'd just been boasting to his friends.

To that she added that Shenshin couldn't even have children, since he had <---> and that she didn't want to debase the sacred memory of her husband, *with whom she intends to live* (?!), by recognizing an unknown child as his son. All this was accompanied by hysterics, oaths, inability to speak, and affectations... I've never seen anything more outrageous. It ended with her sending some blackguard to threaten me with *tribunals* if I don't drop this child. I threw him out, of course, and recalling my more than cold relations with Shenshin, was amazed at my own unselfishness. But what scenes there were here!! In connection with them I met Cupid

Shenshin and so on and so forth. It was incredible!

Have you written to her? I hope that you gave her a good piece of your mind.

You write that *Grandpa* is on a business trip[3]—that must mean he's well. Why is he so bored and indifferent to everything on earth?

Your position in Novgorod has an added advantage in that it breaks off your ties to *The Contemporary*. That journal is growing better and better. In one issue it directly hints that if I presented *Rudin* from a critical point of view, then it was because I'd been paid to do that—or something like that. (See the July issue, "Contemporary Survey," p. 240.)[4] What's important here is not the fact that I am criticized, but the ease with which they allow themselves conscious slander.

I often see M.A. Markovich (Marko Vovchok) here. She's very nice and intelligent. Among the rest of the Russians there isn't a single pleasant one... Rostovtsev is in Florence and Botkin's there too. You know that dear N.N. Tolstoy died. His brother is in Hyères (in southern France).

Be well and don't forget

Your loving

Iv. Turgenev.

Letter 130 (1033). To A.I. Herzen.
February 10-12/22-24, 1861 (?). Paris.

Dear Alexander Ivanovich—here's the information that I was able to gather: Prince N.P. Trubetskoy, the former adjutant of the Duke of Meklenburg (the husband of Grand Duchess Yelena Pavlovna's daughter)—is by all accounts a good and noble person.[1] Prince Dolgorukov[2] speaks very well of him: he doesn't know him personally, but he knows the family in which he was raised and so on. Nobody knows anything about Dubrovin.[3] But there's a person here (a colonel of Headquarters whom you name)[4] from whom I can collect information both about Dubrovin and about the arrests of officers in St. Petersburg, which apparently remained a secret, if in fact they occurred.[5] I'll see him and let you know the outcome of our conversations. Sleptsov didn't tell me anything about a deacon.[6]

I think I wrote you about Botkin's arrival here: he's very ill, poor man;

his brain and sight are affected. We want to put him in the same boarding house where M.A. Markovich is: she's so good—and will look after him. L. Tolstoy has arrived in Paris, but I haven't seen him yet.

I've been receiving *ecstatic* letters from Annenkov: I'm happy for his happiness.[7] I can also tell you—*based on a very reliable source*—that the emancipation ukase will come out *soon:*[8] don't believe any other rumors; and who do you suppose are the ukase's main opponents?—(not counting Gagarin, which goes without saying)—Muraviov, Knyazhevich and... Prince *A.M. Gorchakov!!*[9] My uncle writes that fierce cold and snowstorms are causing great damage: communications have been cut off, cattle are dying, and so on.

P.S. I'll write you again soon; until then, be well. I embrace you and send my regards to your family.

Your I.T.

Letter 131 (1034). To P.V. Annenkov.
February 15/27, 1861. Paris.

February 15/27, 1861. Paris.

Dear friend Pavel Vasilievich, I'm ashamed to trouble you with any request whatsoever at the present time, when your head is probably spinning—but in spite of your "préoccupations," you're nonetheless the most reliable commissionaire, and my commission is the following: please send me sous bande [parcel post] the volumes of my edition[1] that have come out so that I might have some idea of how it looks—that will cost 5 or 6 rubles—and I'll gladly pay it. Please take care of this, old fellow, without putting it in the back of the drawer.

When my letter reaches you it's likely that the great ukase—the ukase that places the Tsar on such a high, marvellous step—will probably already have come out.[2] Oh, if only you have the good sense to notify me of that by telegram. But in any event, I sincerely hope that you'll find the time to use your encyclopaedic, panoramic pen to describe for me the state of the city of Petersburg on the eve of that great day and on the day itself. I'm terribly vexed at myself for not having asked you to send a telegram earlier. But I still console myself with the hope that you'll think to do it yourself.

There isn't really anything new happening in my Paris life: work is moving ahead a bit at a time; the piece for *The Age* will soon be finished.[3] (I haven't yet received the journal itself; on the other hand, *Russian Speech* arrives with revolting regularity.)[4] Well, and there are outrageous scandals occurring in Parisian public life: the Mirès affair is growing not by the day, but by the hour; guilty bankers (Richemont, Solar) are shooting themselves and hanging themselves; the sons of ministers (Baroche, Fould, Magne) see Toulon and striped galley clothes just beyond the horizon.[5] Mirès, who is being held in secret in Mazas, howls à la lettre [literally] like a wild animal throughout the whole prison. Major financial tremors are expected, and the Italian ship is being launched gradually and successfully.

A few days ago Tolstoy arrived from Italy, not without eccentricities, but pacified and softened. His brother's death[6] had a very strong effect on him. He read me some excerpts from his latest literary works, on the basis of which one may conclude that his talent is far from drying up and that he still has a great future.[7] By the way, who is Mr. Potanin,[8] whose praises *The Contemporary* is trumpeting? Is he really a remarkable writer? God grant it, but I fear for him when I recall Nekrasov's ecstatic remarks about Messrs. Bervi, Nadezhdin, Ip. Panayev[9] e tutti quanti[and the like]... And I read Goncharov's excerpt in *Notes of the Fatherland* and was won over again. It's charming![10]

Botkin is a little better, and there is hope for his final recovery. But if you knew how outrageously crudely and...[11] the egoist in him has come forth. It's shocking even! Oh, Pavel Vasilievich, in every person there sits a beast who is tamed by love alone. I'll write you again soon. Until then, be well and cheerful and give my most cordial regards to your fiancée.[12] Your I.T.

Letter 132 (1036). To Ye. Ye. Lambert.
February 16, 18/February 28, March 2, 1861. Paris.

Paris.
February 16/28, 1861.

Dear Countess, I owe you several letters; I've been either too unwell or depressed or lazy, and the time just went by. I'm finally taking pen in hand, though I foresee that my letter will be dull and short. (By the way, I don't remember at all what "wonderful" letters I wrote you . . . Your friendliness towards me probably disclosed virtues where there were none—ou j'ai fait de la prose sans le savoir [or I made prose without knowing it].)[1] An interruption in correspondence is especially bad in that it makes it impossible to respond to the contents of the last letter; for instance, you complain of terribly cold weather—but it has probably already passed. There are, however, less transitory questions than that of the weather: all of us Russians here are anxiously awaiting news of the emancipation proclamation. They say that the ukase will be issued February 19 O.S., i.e., in three days . . . [2] How sorry I am that I'm not in Petersburg now!

I'm continuing my letter of February 18/March 2.—Six years ago today (six years already!) Nikolay Pavlovich died . . . [3] That means that tomorrow is a great day. Meanwhile, in *Galignani*[4] there's a dispatch that alleges that the Governor-General of St. Petersburg has announced that there will be no publication on February 19; there's a rumor in Paris that a revolt has erupted in Warsaw.[5] God save us from such a disaster! A revolt in the Tsardom, like any revolt and any conspiracy, can only bring harm both to Poland and Russia. It's not by such means that we ought to move ahead. I hope that this rumor turns out to be false.—We live in a strange, troubled time. Take a close look at what's happening everywhere . . . The disintegration of the old has never occurred so quickly. But whether the new will be better—God only knows!

Enough about politics, though. I'm returning Mr. G's letter to you.[6] He's probably right (my friend Viardot is of exactly the same opinion about "First Love") and it's no excuse that I did not at all imagine the subject I'd chosen to be immoral. It is, rather, une circonstance aggravante [an aggravating circumstance]. I will allow myself to protest against one thing, however: specifically—I wasn't at all writing with the desire to achieve a shock effect, as they say; I didn't invent this povest; it was given to me in its entirety by life itself. I hasten to add that this doesn't justify me; I probably shouldn't have touched on all of this. I say "probably," because I don't want to lie. If anyone were to ask me whether I would agree to the destruction of that povest, so that not a trace of it remained . . . I would shake my head no. But I gladly agree never to speak of it or bring it up again.

Lev Tolstoy, the writer, was through here. I hadn't seen him for a long time—and found in him a change for the better. He seems to be beginning to settle down and stop wandering about. I think that in view of his undoubted talent, he can still accomplish a great deal.

My daughter is correcting some of the bad things in herself—but the distance between us is nonetheless great. There is still no marriage in sight.

I had dinner again with your beau-frère [brother-in-law],[7] but I haven't seen him for a long time.

Farewell, dear Countess; give my regards to your husband and son. Write me about your health; mine is en somme [in general] decent.

I kiss your hands and remain

Your loving

Iv. Turgenev.

Letter 133 (1045). To L.N. Tolstoy.
March 10/22, 1861. Paris.

Paris.

I'll tell you frankly, dear Tolstoy, that your letter made me very happy; in it was expressed an end to the, if not hostile, than at least cold relations that existed between us.[1] Our last meeting in Paris already indicated that—and I even wrote your sister about it yesterday; but what we each recognized for himself has now been stated—and past misunderstandings laid to rest. I'm certain that we'll meet in Russia as good friends and will remain such for as long as God grants us life. Spoiling it (life, that is) is permissible only for little boys, and you and I are no longer little. I thank you again for its occurring to you to write that letter, which set right the former rift once and for all.

The long-awaited and nonetheless sudden news from Russia[2] has aroused in me an even stronger desire to return home.

There's no likelihood of soon arranging a marriage for my daughter—and therefore I'm leaving here in five weeks, but will come back in the fall—and I'll spend all that time, i.e., spring and summer, in the country putting my relations with the serfs in order. I'm very glad that last year already I persuaded my uncle to establish a farm at Spasskoye and put the remaining estates on quitrent; now the difficulties will be fewer. The thought of the approaching trip and the stay in Russia occupies me almost constantly; in my mind's eye I can already see myself with Fet, Borisov—and now you, in our fields and groves and wooden houses; I imagine hunting trips and so on and so on. The one sad thing is that your good, unforgettable brother Nikolay won't be with us.[3]

Write and tell me when you're planning to arrive at Yasnaya Polyana; as I recall, you wanted to make some stops along the way—in addition to which the phrase "I'm waiting for money at Brussels" has a thoroughly vague meaning. I hope to be at Spasskoye by the beginning of May.

You didn't like the English... I somewhat expected that. I think that you had neither the time nor the chance to penetrate to that spiritual current that throbs in many of Dickens' characters, for instance, and that flows rather deeply in general in the English soil and in each individual Englishman. You shouldn't forget that they're just as bashful as they are haughty, and they neither know how to say what they feel nor display their virtues. And you're right—Herzen has aged greatly, poor man. There is a certain acerbic Moscow quality in Ogaryov that's not completely to my liking, although I know him as a wonderful and soft-hearted person.

I'll tell you a little about the Russians here: Botkin's health is improving very slowly; he's lapsed into a sort of soft flaccidity and tenderness of manner; but his mind is lively and subtle, and capricious as before. Chicherin[4] takes in the whole Parisian world, as before; Dolgorukov[5]—but it's better not to speak of that.

It's too bad that you didn't near either *Orfeo* (which they're giving again) or excerpts from *Alceste* at the conservatory.[6]

I press your hand and say goodbye.

Your devoted

Iv. Turgenev.

Letter 134 (1047). To A.I. Herzen.
March 14/26, 1861. Paris.

Dear Alexander Ivanovich,

I'm sending you a copy of Annenkov's letter written on the day after the great day, i.e., March 6th.[1] You'll see that it's interesting. Up until now telegrams (published and private) have been speaking unanimously of the absolute quiet with which the manifesto has been received all over Russia. Will anything happen later? The manifesto itself was obviously written in French and translated into awkward Russian by some German. There are phrases such as "to beneficially establish... good patriarchal conditions" which not a single Russian muzhik will understand. But he'll get to know the operation itself—and the operation has been set up as decently as possible.

Those of us here had a service of thanksgiving at church the day before yesterday—and the priest delivered a short, but intelligent and touching speech that reduced me to tears—and Nikolay Ivanych Turgenev was nearly sobbing. The old Prince Volkonsky (the Decembrist) was there too. Many people had left the church before that.

Thanks for *The Polar Star*, which I've been enjoying reading.[2] Your little excerpts are marvellous, as usual,[3] Bestuzhev's notes on Ryleyev are very interesting,[4]—Lunin's letters I already knew,[5] Pecherin's poems seemed to me au dessous de leur réputation [less good than their reputation],[6] I haven't yet had time to read about Owen.[7] But who was it that passed off a hoax on you by giving you the translation of a sermon by the very well-known Father Bridaine of the time of Louis XIV and calling it a contemporary work by some Nestor and so on, and how is it that you fell for it?[8]

Say a couple of words in *The Bell* about Shevchenko's death.[9] The poor fellow killed himself with the immoderate use of vodka. Not long before his death a remarkable thing happened to him: a police captain (in the Chernigov Province) arrested him and sent him in wooden fetters to the main city in the province for Shevchenko's *refusing to paint his portrait in oil, full size. That is a fact.*

I'm going to Russia, to the country, in a month—and on the way I'll stop off for a day in London to see you.

Farewell. I embrace you and send regards to all your family. Thank Kruze[10] for his letter; I'll be answering him.

Your

Iv. Turgenev.

P.S. The local Russians had their noses out of kilter: but they've already been mollified. And *The Times* talks of haughty and factious *noblesse!* <--->—that *noblesse* and thank God![11]

P.P.S. I recommend Mukhanov for the April *Bell;* give that vile, bloodthirsty, depraved old man a going-over.[12]

Letter 135 (1081). To Ye. Ye. Lambert.
May 21/June 2, 1861. Spasskoye.

Village of Spasskoye.
May 29, 1861.

Dear Countess,

I received your two letters almost coup sur coup [one after the other]. First of all, let me congratulate you, Tsebrikov, and myself on his appointment as your estate manager; I'm certain that you'll be pleased with him—and that your peasants will find in him a person both indulgent and firm—at one and the same time. God grant that my words come true![1]

You paint a rather gloomy picture of contemporary life in Russia and of the Russian character in general: unfortunately, a conscientious person is obliged to subscribe to every one of your statements. Whether history has made us the way we are, or whether in our very nature are to be found the guarantees of everything we see around us—we really just continue sitting up to our ears in filth—in plain view of heaven and striving to reach it. Some astronomers say that comets become planets by metamorphosis from a gaseous state into a solid one; Russia's all-round *gaseousness* disconcerts me—and makes me think that we're still far from a *planetary* state. There's nothing strong or firm anywhere—nowhere is there a seed; I don't mean the social estates—the people[2] themselves lack these things.

Rumors have probably reached you about the people's *unwillingness* to transfer from *statute labor to quitrent.* This significant fact—which, I confess, no one foresaw—proves that our people are ready to reject obvious advantage (statute-labor days are appraised at at least 80 silver rubles—and the very highest quitrent doesn't even reach 30 rubles) in the hope that—"just wait a bit—perhaps yet another ukase will be issued—and they'll give us the land for free—or the Tsar will give it to us in two years— and the quitrent peasants have already *tied themselves down,* i.e., entered into certain arrangements." Some quitrent peasants complained in my presence that the statute-labor peasants got a special favor—three days instead of six—while they didn't get anything. By the way, this proves how well the laws that have been in effect since the time of Peter the Great that forbid the taking of more than three days have been observed. Our government acted on the supposition that laws have their own force and are observed—it was difficult for the government to act otherwise—and it turned out that it seems to have performed an injustice: it rewarded some, and left others in their former position . . . There's no point in even thinking about participation in redemption on the part of the peasants; not just in 36 or 40 years—but if you tell one of our peasants that by paying an extra ruble for five years he'll acquire land for his son, he won't agree to it; in the first place—he thinks only of today, and in the second—he lacks faith in the authorities: "I'll pay five years," he thinks, "and then they'll issue a new order telling me to pay five more." And he's not completely wrong about that. We're now reaping the bitter fruits of the last 36 or 40 years.— Recently a friend of mine hired a free laborer and concluded a contract with him that was quite advantageous (for the laborer); in a few days the laborer's father came to him and with a crushed look said: "Oh, sir, sir! Why did you trick the little one with a contrack! He's still stupid, doesn't know how to think—and you . . . "

"But are the conditions really disadvantageous?" my friend interrupted him . . . "No, you couldn't say that, that they're disadvantageous," answered the muzhik, scratching the back of his head, then lower, "but still, why did you trick him with a *contrack* . . . "[3]

And so just try talking about legality, responsibility, division of authority, and so on and so on . . .

Fortunately, I'd already managed to transfer at least some of my peasants to quitrent.

You don't write anything about when you plan to go from Petersburg to Little Russia. You'll probably stay a few days in Tula, where your husband is. If I knew when that was to be I'd drive out to meet you. A visit by you to my modest Spasskoye would be a holiday for me. But that's perhaps more than I ought to dare hope for. The only pretty thing here is a garden—especially now, when everything is green, fresh, and luxuriant.

In any event, be well. Thank you for not forgetting me. I send my regards to all your household and kiss your hand firmly.

Your devoted

Iv. Turgenev.

Letter 136 (1088). To L.N. Tolstoy.
May 27/June 8, 1861. Spasskoye.

My dear sir, Lev Nikolayevich!

In reply to your letter[1] I can only repeat what I myself considered it my responsibility to tell you at Fet's: carried away by a feeling of involuntary hostility, the reasons for which I need not go into now, I insulted you without any definite cause on your part—and I begged your pardon. I'm prepared to repeat the same thing now in written form—and I beg your pardon for a second time.—This morning's incident has proved clearly that any attempts at closeness between two natures as opposite as yours and mine cannot lead to anything good; and therefore I all the more gladly fulfill my obligation to you, since the present letter is probably the last manifestation of any relations between us whatsoever. I hope with all my heart that it has satisfied you—and I announce in advance my consent to any use that you may see fit to make of it.

With absolute respect, I have the honor of remaining, dear sir, your humble servant,

Iv. Turgenev.

Village of Spasskoye.
May 27, 1861.

10:30 p.m.

Ivan Petrovich[2] just brought me the letter which my man sent by mistake to *Novoselki* instead of *Bogoslav*.

I most humbly beg your pardon for this involuntary unpleasant blunder. I hope that my messenger will catch you in Bogoslav.

Letter 137 (1089). To L.N. Tolstoy.
May 28/June 9, 1861. Spasskoye.

Your man says that you desire an answer to your letter:[1] but I do not see what I could add to what I've already written.

Perhaps just that I recognize your perfect right to demand satisfaction with hand weapons: you preferred the satisfaction of my stated and repeated apology—that was in your power. I'll tell you frankly that I would willingly have withstood your fire in order by so doing to make amends for my words. That I uttered them is so at odds with the habits of my whole life that I cannot attribute them to anything other than irritation produced by the extreme and constant antagonism of our views. That is not an excuse, I mean to say—not a justification, rather an explanation. And therefore, in parting with you forever—such incidents are inexpiable and irreparable—I consider it my duty to repeat once more that you are right in this affair, and I am at fault. I add that the question is not one of *courage*—that I want or don't want to demonstrate—but of the recognition that just as you have the right to call me up to a duel, in the accepted manner, of course (with seconds), so you also have the right to forgive me. You chose what you pleased—and all I can do is submit to your decision.[2]

I again beg you to accept the assurance of my complete respect.

Iv. Turgenev.

Letter 138 (1093). To A.A. Fet.
June 5/17, 1861. Spasskoye.

Village of Spasskoye.
June 5, 1861.

Dear Afanasy Afanasievich,

Allow me to write you what is, I hope, the final word in the unpleasant matter with which you are familiar.[1] It turns out that Count Tolstoy is offended by the formality of my apologies. He may be right; but since I want more than anything else to be sincere—I couldn't apologize any other way. My duty was to make these formal apologies as full, indubitable, and open as possible—and that's what I did. Count Tolstoy could have chosen not to accept that sort of apology; but to demand another—or, after having accepted it, to insult me—was going beyond the boundaries of what I recognize as his right. However, since to issue a challenge would have been funny and strange on my part—besides which, I feel that there is a legitimate aspect to his irritation—then there's nothing else for me to do but consign this affair to oblivion—and allow Count Tolstoy to judge of me as he pleases.

I remain your loving

Iv. Turgenev.

Letter 139 (1095). To P.V. Annenkov.
June 7/19, 1861. Spasskoye.

I didn't expect, carissimo mio Annenkovio [my dearest Annenkov], that you would pass through Moscow without favoring me with your pattes de mouches [flies legs],[1] in spite of the greetings that I sent you through that laziest of Ukrainians, Ivan Ilich (Maslov)![2] But Moscow evidently debilitated you, and I'm sending this billet doux of mine to Simbirsk Province, to the land of four-cornered mushrooms, thick roots, and so on.[3] I hope that in the isolation and quiet of the country you'll find more time to respond to my voice.

Since I'm awaiting details from you about your life and doings, I make bold to presume that you await the same sorts of details from me, and therefore I set out to transmit them. (Do you notice me imitating your style!)

I'm well—that's the most important thing; I'm working a little bit at a time—that's not so good; I take walks in expectation of the hunting season; I see some of my neighbors. The peasants and I are in the midst of mutual explanations, and they have shown me their good will: my concessions nearly approach vileness. But you know yourself (and in the country you'll get to know even better) what the Russian muzhik is all about: to rely on him in the matter of redemption [payments] is insanity. They aren't even going over to quitrent, in the first place, so as not "to get tied down," and in the second, so as not to deprive themselves of the chance to celebrate the three-day tribute-labor in the nastiest way imaginable. All arguments are powerless. You can prove to them a hundred times that on tribute labor they lose tremendously; they'll still answer that "we won't agree to that." The peasants on quitrent even envy those on tribute-labor because "look, they got a reduction—and we didn't." Fortunately, here at Spasskoye the peasants have been on quitrent since last year.[4]

I saw Fet and even visited him. For a fabulous sum he has acquired 200 desyatinas of bare, woodless, waterless land at a distance of 70 versts from here, together with a small house that can be seen for 5 versts around, near which he dug a pond that evaporated and planted birch trees that didn't take... I don't know how he'll stand that life (it's just as if he'd baked himself in a pie) and, more importantly, how his wife will keep from losing her mind out of boredom. He is, as ever, a wonderful, kind amusing fellow—and in his own way very intelligent.

An unpleasant incident occurred in that very place... I had a decisive quarrel with L.N. Tolstoy (entre nous [between us], the affair came to within a hair's breadth of a duel... and even now the hair could break).[5] *I was at fault,* but, to use scientific language, the explosion was caused by our long-standing hostility and the antipathy of our two natures. I sensed that he hated me and I didn't understand why he occasionally came back to me. I ought to have kept my distance, as before; I tried to be friends—and very nearly ended up at the barrier. And *I never liked him*—why couldn't this all have been understood a long time ago?

I'll try to send you the first (recopied) half of my novel.[6] It goes without saying that you should tell me the whole truth. But first write me... As I recall, the mail used to take nearly half a year from Simbirsk to Oryol, i.e., to Mtsensk. Perhaps at the present time when, etc.,[7] there will be an improvement.

Give my most heartful regards to your wife. They say she was the toast of Moscow. There's nothing surprising in that, but it makes me happy nonetheless.

Don't forget that next spring I'll be godfather at your son Ivan's christening.[8] Well, farewell, dear old boy. I await a reply from you and press your hand cordially and firmly. Your I.T.

Letter 140 (1117). To Ye. Ye. Lambert.
August 6/18, 1861. Spasskoye.

Village of Spasskoye.
August 6, 1861.

First of all, dear Countess, I beg your pardon. I did not at all expect to offend you—but that is no justification: I sinned through stupidity—and I'm nonetheless at fault. The phrase that you quote from my letter really is absurd: but I swear to you that I intended to say "to everything on account of which people in general grow alarmed and worry."[1] I meant to say something flattering to you, and I ended up offending you. Once more I beg your pardon—and hope that you won't deny me it.—But knowing me to be a *realist,* how could you think that I was upset with the *real* (i.e., domestic) direction of your letter? I took it into my head to calm your quite justifiable alarm with jokes, but there apparently was an unlucky star over me while I was writing the last letter to you. What can I do but submit and "encoger los hombros," as the Spanish say, i.e., *draw in the shoulders,* as children who have been punished do.

I'll be waiting for the povest from Mrs. Patkul and I'll try to say something like the truth about it, although I foresee that that will be difficult.[2] And why on earth would that wonderful woman want to engage in an activity for which she is so unsuited!

A propos of povests, I can report that I finished mine a few days ago[3]—and am now busy finishing copying it. Together with me, it will appear at your court in about *three* weeks, no later than that.

Don't be angry at me for the brevity of this letter—and be assured that I'm attached to you sincerely and forever—and thus don't take offense at some awkward word—and don't attribute a negative meaning to it, because in regard to you not *a single word of mine can have* a negative meaning.—Give me your hand—and I'll kiss it with gratitude and tenderness.

Your

Iv. Turgenev

Letter 141 (1135). To P.V. Annenkov.
September 26/October 8, 1861. Paris.

Paris. October 8 N.S., 1861.

How is it, dear Pavel Vasilievich, that you deign to keep such a stubborn silence—when you know that I await your letters at all times, and especially now. I assume that you have already arrived in Petersburg, and I'm writing you in care of the Tyutchevs, who (as they've probably already told you) condemned my povest[1] to the flame or at least to the back of the desk drawer. I wish to make an end to uncertainty—and if your opinion and the opinion of other Moscow friends confirm that of the Tyutchevs, *Fathers and Sons* will go to the...Please write me without delay. My address is Rue de Rivoli, 210.

I found eveything in order here: the weather is summery, you can't wear anything but summer breeches. There are hardly any Russians except V.P. Botkin, who—entre nous soit dit [just between us]—has turned permanently into a hideously egotistical, cynical, and coarse old man. His good taste hasn't dried up, however, and since he isn't personally well-disposed toward me, one will be able to believe his judgment about the child of my labors. I start reading it to him today.

Let me know, for Heaven's sake, how things are with you. When I left the weather was strange. Is everyone well?

Send me your address. My regards to your wife, all your household, and all our friends. Your I.T.

Letter 142 (1139). To P.V. Annenkov.
October 1/13, 1861. Paris.

Paris. October 1/13, 1861. Rue de Rivoli, 210.

Dear Pavel Vasilievich, please accept my sincere gratitude for the letter in which you express your views about my povest.[1] It made me very happy, all the more so as my confidence in my own work had been seriously shaken. I agree completely with all your comments (all the more so as V.P. Botkin finds them justified) and starting tomorrow I'll set to work on the corrections and revisions, which will probably take on major proportions, about which I've already written to Katkov.[2] I still have a lot of time ahead. Botkin, who is apparently getting better, also made several sensible comments and disagrees with you only on one point: he doesn't much care for the figure of Anna Sergeyevna. But I think that I see how and what needs to be done in order to give the whole thing the appropriate balance. When I finish the work I'll send it to you, and you can deliver it to Katkov. But enough about this and once again my sincere and ardent thanks.

The other news conveyed by you is unpleasant.[3] It can't be helped! God grant that nothing worse happen! Please, tenez moi au courant [keep me informed]. That is very important, and I again rely on your habitual and ancient kindness.

Here (that is, where I am) everything is going well and my health is not bad ... Only I too have a rather unpleasant piece of news to convey to you: after a long struggle with myself I sent Tolstoy a challenge and conveyed it to Ketcher[4] so that he could counteract the rumors being spread in Moscow.[5] In this affair, except for *the beginning, where I was at fault,* I've done everything to avoid this stupid denouement; but Tolstoy saw fit to put me au pied du mur [against the wall] (the Tyutchevs can tell you all the details)—and I could not have acted otherwise. We'll face each other this spring in Tula. By the way, here's a copy of my letter to him:

Dear Sir. Just before my departure from Petersburg I learned that in Moscow you circulated a copy of your last letter to me, in addition to which you call me a coward who refused to duel with you and so on. It would have been impossible for me to return to Tula Province, and I continued my journey. But since, *after everything that I have done to atone for the word that I let escape,* I consider such an action on your part both insulting and dishonorable, I am advising you that this time I will not let it pass unnoticed, and when I return to Russia next spring I shall demand satisfaction from you. I consider it necessary to inform you that I have made known my intention to my friends in Moscow so that they might counteract the rumors spread by you. I.T.

And so it will turn out that I mocked the gentry habit of duelling (in Pavel Petrovich)[6] and I myself act just like him. But apparently it was already so decreed in the book of Fate.

Well, farewell, my dear Pavel Vasilievich. Give my regards to your wife and all our friends and accept my firmest shakehand.[7] Your I.T.

P.S. Arapetov is here ... What a dinner he and I had with Botkin yesterday!

Letter 143 (1140). To M.N. Katkov.
October 1/13, 1861. Paris.

Paris. 1/13 Oct. 1861.

Dear Mikhail Nikiforovich—excuse me for bombarding you with letters, but I wanted to warn you that as a result of a letter that I received from Annenkov and comments from Botkin, to whom I read my povest here,[1] the revisions in *Fathers and Sons* will be more significant than I had supposed—and will take about two weeks of my time, after which you will receive a precise list of all the cuts and additions. And therefore I repeat my request *not to print an excerpt*—and also to keep the manuscript with you, i.e., not let others read it. I hope that as a consequence of my corrections the figure of Bazarov will become comprehensible to you and won't give you the impression of an apotheosis,[2] which I did not intend. I assume the other characters will gain from this as well. In a word, consider my work not completely finished, and since I have expended a great deal of labor on it, I would like to publish it in the best possible form.

I send my cordial regards and clasp your hand.

Your devoted

Iv. Turgenev.

Rue de Rivoli, 210.

Letter 144 (1143). To F.M. Dostoevsky.
October 16/28, 1861. Paris.

Paris.
Oct. 16/28, 1861.

Dear Fyodor Mikhailovich, allow me to ask you to send me—if possible—and at my expense, of course, the issues of your journal[1] from September on—here, at the following address: Rue de Rivoli, 210. (Please make them separate from the issues that are sent to me in the country.) I would be very much obliged.

Let me know about your health, too, and about what our acquaintances are up to ... I'm living here quietly—and of course I often think of Petersburg.

A few days ago I set to work on a povest[2] that ought to find a place in your journal. If nothing gets in the way, I hope to finish it by New Year's. But internal and external difficulties could arise—let's hope that everything goes well.

I clasp your hand cordially and remain

Your devoted

Iv. Turgenev.

Letter 145 (1149). To M.N. Katkov.
October 30/November 11, 1861. Paris.

Paris. Oct. 30/Nov. 11, 1861.

Dear Mikhail Nikiforovich, I recently wrote to you, but after receiving your letter yesterday,[1] I consider it necessary to reply to you briefly. I agree with your remarks—with almost all of them—especially regarding *Pavel Petrovich* and Bazarov himself. As for Odintsova, the vague impression produced by that character shows me that I still need to work a little on her too. (By the way, the *argument* between P.P. and Bazarov has been completely redone and shortened.) It's obvious that the povest, by reason of present circumstances, and as a result of it's internal lack of finish—must be put aside—*for the time being*[2]—with which you too will agree. I'm very sorry that things have turned out this way, but with such a subject one must appear before the reader as fully armed as possible. I want to look over all of it at leisure and replow it. I presume that all the difficulties—internal and external—that *now* exist will disappear by the time I return to Russia, i.e., by spring (by April)—and will finally succeed in letting this child out into the world.

There's one thing with which I can't agree:

Neither should Odintsova be mocking, nor should the peasant stand above Bazarov, even if he himself is empty and sterile ...[3] Perhaps my view of Russia is more misanthropic than you suppose: he—in my eyes—is really a hero of our time. "What a hero and what a time," you'll say ... But that's the way it is.

I repeat my request about keeping my work under lock and key, I clasp your hand firmly and remain

Your devoted

Iv. Turgenev.

Letter 146 (1157). To Ye. Ye. Lambert.
December 10 (22), 1861. Paris.

Paris.
December 10/22, 1861.

Dear Countess, I have read your touching letter several times and I feel an absolute conviction that God will help you endure the great sorrow that has befallen you. While taking all the charm out of life, grief also deprives it of falsehood and alarm—and that is what the real misfortune consists of. "This sorrow's sacred, it strikes where it does love,"[1] Shakespeare said somewhere, and in the Gospels the same idea is expressed even more simply. Grief purges us, and thus calms; but not everyone can bear that sort of tranquility; I repeat: I hope that God helps you.

I saw your poor brother not long before his death:[2] his wasted face, yellow as wax, showed all the signs of imminent demise—but he beat his head against the pillow and twice said to me, "I don't want to die." At that moment life was already an impossibility for him, and death a necessity, natural and inevitable. The naturalness of death is much more terrifying that its suddenness or unusualness. Religion alone can conquer that terror ... But religion itself has to become a natural need in man, and he who lacks it can only turn his eyes away with light-mindedness or with stoicism (in essence it's all the same). A few days ago Mansurova[3] died (she was the wife of our emissary in Holland and Prince N.I. Trubetskoy's sister); an acquaintance of mine, in whose arms she died, was struck by the ease with which a person dies: an open door closes—and that's all ... But can that really be the end? Can it really be that death is nothing more than life's final departure? I definitely don't know what to think—and can only repeat that "happy are those who believe!"

201

I'll tell you a little about my life here. My family relations haven't changed; my daughter's manner is becoming more sedate and quiet—but the essential foundations are the same; there is no suitor in sight. I've been working very little and in general I'm leading a rather idle life; I've met two or three new people, but rather superficially. My former relationships have grown somewhat coarse—but on the other hand they've grown stronger, like the bark on an aging tree: it seems that nothing can change them now.—I play chess, listen to good music—and float along with the current of a river that grows more and more calm and shallow. The news from Russia depresses me. I can't help but place a great deal of blame on my friends—but neither can I exonerate the government; an absence of people and a profound lack of knowledge about Russia can be felt at every step of the way. The news from the countryside is unpleasant: but that's a necessary, but transitory evil; I'm still convinced that things will work out well![4] In general I can feel myself growing over with bark: inside everything is still rather soft—but the fibers through which I make contact with the life around me have grown hard and insensitive... I'm preparing gradually for the unavoidable end. But enough about that.

If you have the time and inclination to read something—take a look at the povest "Molotov" by Mr. Pomyalovsky[5] in *The Contemporary* (October). I would like to know your opinion—it seems to me that there are signs of original thought and talent here.

Farewell, dear Countess. I kiss your hands and send my cordial regards to your husband. Write me about your beau-frère [brother-in-law][6] and give him my regards.

Your

Iv. Turgenev

**Letter 147 (1167). To A.I. Herzen.
January 13/25, 1862. Paris.**

Dear Alexander Ivanovich, Bakunin's brother[1] has probably informed you that he found me ill; and I still haven't been able to recover and don't yet dare to go out on the street. This has again put off the time of my London trip, which is really beginning to acquire a sort of mythical tinge; but I haven't lost hope.[2]

The inquiry about your son[3] has been passed on to Golovin[4] via Prince Orlov.[5] According to the latter, he foresees no obstacles to the fulfillment of your son's wish.

Arranging a *regular income* for Mikhail Alexandrovich[6] is fraught with difficulties. Soldatenkov[7] left for Egypt a long time ago—besides which, as far as I know, he's a swaggering beast who won't give a penny if he can't boast about it to everyone within earshot. Botkin will be giving small sums from time to time, but I don't think he'll agree to anything permanent. But I'll still have a discussion with him. There's no point in even talking about the other Russians here. As for me, I'll be very happy to take on the responsibility of giving Bakunin an annual sum of 1500 francs for an indefinite period—and I'll send the first 500 francs (reckoning from January 1) to your address immediately. Thus, one fourth of the desired sum is already guaranteed; we need to try to get the rest as well.

Rumors have reached me about the ovations given your son by the Russian youth in Heidelberg and Karlsruhe.[8] I rejoice for you, for your son, and mainly, for Russian youth. C'est un signe des temps! [It's a sign of the times!]

The first reports about Golovin are rather good; what will happen from here on in?[9] Did you read the article "La Russie sous Alexandre II" in *Revue des 2 Mondes?* You're surrounded by a halo, and that's as it should be.[10]

Give my regards to all our London friends, and I clasp your hand and say—au revoir—no matter what might happen.

Iv. Turgenev

25 Jan. 62.
Rue de Rivoli, 210.

Letter 148 (1171). To A.A. Fet.
January 23/February 4, 1862. Paris.

Paris. Feb. 4 N.S., 62.

It would be extremely ignoble of you, dear Fet, not to answer my cordial and numerous letters, and therefore I'm taking pen in hand and addressing this missive to blessed Stepanovka, where, according to you,

you'll be in a few days. First of all I welcome you upon your return to your peaceful rural retreat[1]—the only respectable retreat for middle-aged people like us! If I weren't so sincerely attached to you, I would envy you to the point of fury, I, who am forced to live in repugnant Paris—and awake every day with a desperate ennui[2] in my heart . . . But what's the point of talking about it—it's better to turn my thoughts to our native region and imagine myself sitting with you in an excellent carriage (thanks to you) and driving off to hunt grouse—we'll find them at last, damn it! This year I'll take other measures—and I hope they'll be crowned with success. If God grants, I'll be at Stepanovka at the end of April.

I was expecting your reactions to *Minin*[3]—but you sent me a whole diatribe about "Molotov."[4] You know what, my dear friend? Just as fear of the fine phrase has driven Tolstoy into the most desperate fine phrases, even so in you has the repulsion for *intellect* in art led you to the most refined cogitation and deprived you precisely of that naive feeling that you so strive for. Instead of realizing immediately that "Molotov" was written by a very young person who doesn't know himself which leg to dance on, you spotted in him "an educated Panayev!" You didn't notice the two or three marvellous and *naive* pages about Nadya or Nastya's[5] developing and growing; you didn't notice the other signs of a *young* talent—and became engrossed instead in the debris about which it wasn't even worth speaking. But that's been an unending argument between us: I say that art is such a gigantic matter that the whole person—with all his abilities, including intellect, by the way—is barely enough for it; you ostracize the intellect and in works of art you see only the unconscious babble of a sleeping person. I have to call that view Slavophile, since it bears the stamp of the school that says "everything here is black—and everything there white," "the truth is all on one side." But we, sinners that we are, suppose that by swinging the ax like that, you please only yourself . . . But that's easier, of course; otherwise, by admitting that truth is here and there, that keen definitions don't help define anything, you have to fuss around, weigh both sides, and so on. And that's boring. It's much better to blurt out orders in military fashion: "Ten-shun! Intellect—right face! March! Halt! Dress ranks! Art! Left-march! Halt! Dress ranks!" And it's marvellous! All you have to do is sign a report that everything is fine. But at this point one has to join Goethe (is he bright or stupid, what do you think?) in saying: "Ja! Wenn es wir nur nicht besser wüssten!" [Yes! If only we didn't know that better].[6] But your ideal is this:

Intellect.   Art.

I'm glad that you at least get along with Tolstoy—otherwise it would be too strange. As for the performance of my *Hanger-On,*[7] that's one of those misfortunes which might befall any decent person. I can just imagine how revolting it will be. The play and the performers are equally worthy of each other.

Good-bye. I clasp your hand firmly, send my regards to your wife, and remain

Your devoted Iv. Turgenev.

Letter 149 (1195). To F.M. Dostoevsky.
March 18/30, 1862. Paris.

Dear Fyodor Mikhailovich, I need hardly tell you how happy your reaction to *Fathers and Sons* made me.[1] It's not a question of satisfying one's vanity, but rather of convincing oneself that you didn't make a mistake and haven't completely blundered—and that your work didn't go for naught. That was all the more important for me inasmuch as people whom I trust very much (I don't mean Kolbasin[2]) seriously advised me to throw my work into the fire—and just a few days ago Pisemsky (just between us) wrote me that the character of Bazarov was a complete failure. How could I thus not have doubts and be puzzled? It's difficult for an author to sense *immediately* to what extent his idea has been embodied— and whether it's accurate—and whether he's mastered it—and so on. It's as though he were lost in the woods in his own work.

You have probably experienced this often yourself. And therefore thanks again. You grasped so completely and keenly what I wanted to express in Bazarov that I could only spread my arms in amazement—and pleasure. It's as if you had entered my soul and felt even those things that I didn't consider it necessary to say. May God grant that that shows not just the subtle perspicacity of a master, but the simple understanding of a reader as well—that is, God grant that everyone see at least a part of what you did! I'm now calm as regards the fate of my povest: it has done its work—and I have no reason to repent.

Here's one more proof for you of the extent to which you understood that character: in Arkady's meeting with Bazarov, where, as you say, there's something missing, Bazarov, in telling about the duel, made fun of *knights* and Arkady listened to him with secret horror and so on. I threw that out—and now I'm sorry that I did so.[3] In general I made many changes and redid a lot of things under the influence of unfavorable comments— and that may be the reason for the drawn-out quality which you remarked.

I received a nice letter from Maykov[4] and I'll answer him. People will be rebuking me strongly—but I just need to sit that out, as one does a summer rain.

I would be very sorry if I didn't find you in Petersburg. I'm leaving here at the end of this April, i.e., in a month. Now I can tell you *for certain* that I'll bring you my work in final form—it is not only going along well, but coming to an end. It will be about three signatures long. It's turning out to be a strange piece. It's the very same "Phantoms" as a result of which Katkov and I quarrelled several years ago[5]—I don't know whether you remember that. I was about to start on another piece[6]—but, suddenly latched onto this one and worked on it for several days with enthusiasm. Now all that's left is to finish off a few pages.

I'm happy for *Time*'s success. It's vexing that you can't arrange proper delivery of the journal.[7] I'm not saying this so much out of personal interest—after all, I'll soon be returning—but for your profit. *The Russian Messenger* is delivered here properly. (I haven't yet received the February issue, though.)

Again I clasp your hand very, very firmly and say thank you. Give my sincere regards to your wife[8] and be well.

Your devoted

Iv. Turgenev.

30/18 March 62.
    Paris.
Rue de Rivoli, 210.

Letter 150 (1197). To V. Ya. Kartashevskaya.
March 19/31, 1862. Paris.

Paris.

March 19/31, 62.

I'll begin by expressing my gratitude for the information that you sent, dear Varvara Yakovlevna. You are a truly indulgent being and you don't forget absent friends.

The news about your brother's marriage made me very happy—please convey to him my heartiest congratulations. I'm certain that he'll be happy—and there's no point in even talking about his future wife: your brother will be the best husband of the 19th century.[1]

Another excellent husband, your beau-frère [brother-in-law] and my friend, Pavel Vasilievich,[2] hasn't written me for a long time—and it's precisely now that I've been expecting a letter from him in which he would tell me about the fate of my latest offspring.[3] I've already received three letters from Petersburg from three different people about this matter—two of them laudatory, one negative. It would be nice to know what people are saying in general. And therefore, since in all the events of life it's better to rely on a woman, I'm addressing you with the humble request to write me absolutely impartially about what you hear. If *The Spark* calls me a retarded idiot, that's just what you should write to me. I expect cruel torments from the young generation—though it's more likely that given the present intellectual mood, the whole thing will pass unnoticed. And that's very understandable—Russia has no use for literature just now.

I also ask you to stick a needle (I'm speaking figuratively) in my friend Pavel Vasilievich's corpulent side and make him write me one of those marvellous encyclopedic missives of which he is such a master.

I think that I've already thanked you in writing for the labor to which you subjected yourself while copying my article about *Hamlet;* if I in fact let *that* opportunity slip, then I ask you now for permission to kiss your laboring hand.

You ask about Mrs. Markovich. She is still here and seems not to be in want. She is well paid for her works. And her spouse's salary is more significant than you assume. I see her very rarely though.

Please give my most cordial regards to all your family—and all the best to you. If God grants, we'll see each other in a month. I'll bring my portrait. Be well.

Your devoted

Iv. Turgenev

Rue de Rivoli, 210.

Letter 151 (1204). To N.N. Rashet.[1]
March O.S., 1862. Paris.

Note of Reminder.

1) Find out about the whereabouts and living conditions of Mikhail Alexandrovich *Bakunin's* wife.[2] She had been in Siberia and was supposed to arrive at the Bakunin's country place—Tver Province, Torzhov District, Village of Pryamukhino—when writing about her use the name Mrs. Meyer.

2) Find out about the two Bakunin brothers who were arrested in connection with the Tver Affair; one is named Nikolay, the other probably Ilya or Pavel.[3] Use the name the Nikolsky Brothers when writing about them.

Letter 152 (1206). To A.A. Fet.
April 6/18, 1862. Paris.

Paris.
April 6/18, 1862.

First of all, dear Afanasy Afanasievich, thanks for your letter[1]—and the thanks would be even larger if you hadn't felt it necessary to don your white gloves to thrash me. Believe me, I have borne and know how to bear the most painful truth from friends. And so—in spite of all your euphemisms—you don't like *Fathers and Sons*. I bow my head—since nothing can be done in the matter—but I want to say a few words in my defense, though I know how unsightly and useless that is. You attribute the whole misfortune to a *thesis, reflection,* in a word, to the intellect. But what you really ought to have said was that there was a lack of mastery. It turns out that I'm more naive than you suppose. Thesis! And what, may I ask, is the thesis in *Fathers and Sons?* Did I want to pour abuse on Bazarov or exalt him? *I don't know that myself,* since I don't know whether I love him or hate him! How's that for a thesis for you! Katkov gave me a dressing down for my having apotheosized Bazarov.[2] You go on to mention *parallelism,* but where is it, may I ask, and where are the believing and unbelieving *pairs?* Does Pavel Petrovich believe or not believe? I don't know, since through him I simply wanted to represent types like Stolypin,[3] the Rossets,[4] and other Russian ex-lions. It's a strange business: you reproach me for parallelism, and others write me and ask why Anna Sergeyevna isn't a higher nature so as to more fully emphasize the contrast with Bazarov. Why aren't Bazarov's folks completely patriarchal? Why is Arkady a little banal—and wouldn't it have been better to present him as an honest youth who was momentarily carried away? Why is Fenichka there—and what conclusion can you draw from her? The only thing I can say is that I drew all these characters just as I would draw mushrooms, leaves, and trees; I got fed up with looking at them and began to sketch them. And to free oneself from one's own impressions just because they resemble theses would be strange and laughable. I don't wish to conclude from all of this that I'm an admirable fellow; on the contrary, what can be concluded from what I said is even more offensive for me: it's not that I was too clever—but that I couldn't pull it off; but truth above all else. Omnia vanitas [all is vanity], however.

I definitely plan to leave here in three weeks;[5] as if to spite me grooms[6] are beginning to nibble at the hook just before my departure; and I know that nothing will come of it, but I have to fulfill my obligation to the end. We'll probably set off for Russia along with the great Vasily Petrovich.[7] I'm already looking forward to Stepanovka and our conversation and our hunting trips and so on and so forth. The trees here are in full bloom, but we still haven't had spring. Nothing but cold weather!

Give my best regards to your wife and our other friends. I clasp your hand cordially and remain

Your devoted

Iv. Turgenev.

P.S. How did you like the comedy *Gentry Elections* in the second issue of *The Contemporary*?[8] Isn't it just the Herculean Columns of banality? Nekrasov's jingles are good too—he, the foremost contemporary Russian bard!

Letter 153 (1210). To V.P. Botkin.
April 12/24, 1862. Paris.

Paris.
April 12/24, 1862.
Rue de Rivoli, 210.

My dear friend, Vasily Petrovich, the nocturnal pianist[1] has sent you the suitcase by vitesse accélérée [accelerated speed], as you wrote, and that probably means "grande vitesse" [great speed] so you'll receive it soon, if you haven't already. I sent you *Fathers and Sons* about a week ago. You write that you're planning to leave Rome at the end of April, i.e., soon. I

210

haven't lost hope that I'll leave here together with my ladies between May 10th and 15th, but here's what's happening right now (this is just between the two of us). A suitor that Khanykov[2] found has turned up—and he seems to have made a good impression on my daughter. Up till now, as you recall, all these gentlemen aroused revulsion in her. But this will in no event hinder our trip: on the contrary, I don't want to marry off my daughter in the French manner, i.e., without thinking—and subjecting young people to the ordeal of a short separation is even very useful: but I repeat that our departure may be delayed by a few days because of this—pour donner le temps à la position de se dessiner [to give us time for the situation to take shape], and anyway, you'll be notified about everything in good time.[3]

In Rome you're listening to the Papal Choir and to Liszt—while here Schumann is in vogue thanks to the arrival of his wife,[4] who is giving concerts. I have to admit that his music doesn't completely suit my taste. Sometimes it's marvellous, there's a great deal of imagination, mysterious perspectives—but there's no form, no outline—and an old man like me can't endure that à la longue [in the long run]. It really is music of the future: it lacks a present, it's all only Ahnungen, Sehnen [intimations, longing], and so on.

Goodbye, dear friend, be well: our ladies send their regards.

Your devoted I.T.

Letter 154 (1214). To K.K. Sluchevsky.[1]
April 14/26, 1862. Paris.

Paris.
April 14/26, 1862.

I hasten to reply to your letter, for which I am very grateful,[2] dear Sluchevsky. One can't help but value the opinion of young people; in any event I would very much like for there to be no misunderstandings about my intentions. I'll answer point by point.

(1) The first reproach reminds me of the accusation made to Gogol and others as to why *good* people weren't presented along with the others. Bazarov nevertheless overwhelms all the other characters in the novel (Katkov considered that I had presented an apotheosis of *The Contem-*

211

porary in him).[3] The qualities attributed to him are not accidental. I wanted to make a tragic character out of him—there was no room in this case for gentleness. He is honest, truthful, and a democrat through and through—and you don't find any *good* sides to him? He recommends *Stoff und Kraft* precisely because it is a *popular,* i.e., an empty book;[4] the duel with Pavel Petrovich is introduced specifically as a visual demonstration of the emptiness of elegant gentry chivalry—it is presented in an almost exaggeratedly comic way; and how could he decline it; after all, Pavel Petrovich would have clubbed him. It seems to me that Bazarov constantly crushes Pavel Petrovich, and not vice versa; and if he is called a nihilist, then that ought to read as a "revolutionary."

(2) What was said about Arkady, about the rehabilitation of the fathers, and so on, only shows—I'm sorry to say!—that I haven't been understood. *My entire povest is directed against the gentry as a progressive class.* Take a close look at the characters of Nikolay Petrovich, Pavel Petrovich, and Arkady. Weakness and flabbiness or limitations. Esthetic considerations made me take specifically *good* representatives of the gentry so as to prove my point all the more surely: if the cream is good, what does that mean about the milk? Taking bureaucrats, generals, bandits, and so on would be crude, le pont aux ânes [stupid]—and inaccurate. Every true *negator* that I have known (Belinsky, Bakunin, Herzen, Dobroliubov, Speshnyov[5] and so on) came, without exception, from relatively good and honest parents. And therein is contained a notion of great significance: this takes away from the *activists,* from the negators, any slightest shade of *personal* indignation or personal irritability. They follow along their own path only because they are more sensitive to the demands of the nation's life.[6] Countess Salias is wrong in saying that characters like Nikolay Petrovich and Pavel Petrovich are our grandfathers:[7] Nikolay Petrovich is me, Ogaryov, and thousands of others; Pavel Petrovich is Stolypin, Yesakov,[8] Rosset—also are our contemporaries. They are the best of the gentry—and that is precisely why I chose them, in order to demonstrate their bankruptcy. To present bribe-takers on the one hand, and on the other—an ideal youth—that's a picture that I'll let others draw . . . I wanted something larger. At one place (I threw it out because of censorship) I had Bazarov say to Arkady, to that same Arkady in whom your Heidelberg comrades see a *more successful character:* "Your father is a fine, decent fellow; but even if he were the worst bribe-taker imaginable—you still wouldn't get any further than well-born meekness or rage, because you're a nice little gentry lad."

(3) Good Lord! Kukshina, that caricature, is the *most successful* of all in your opinion! I can't even reply to that. Odintsova is as little *in love* with Arkady as she is with Bazarov—how can you fail to see that!—she's the same sort of representative of our idle, dreamy, curious, and cold epicurean

212

gentry ladies. Countess Salias understood *that* character perfectly. She would like first to stroke a wolf's fur (Bazarov) as long as he doesn't bite—and then a little boy's curls—and continue lying, freshly washed, on velvet.

(4) Bazarov's death (which Countess Salias calls *heroic* and therefore criticizes) ought, in my opinion, to have put the final trait on his tragic figure. But your young people even find his death accidental! I'll finish with the following remarks: if the reader doesn't come to love Bazarov, with all his coarseness, callousness, pitiless dryness and harshness—I repeat—if he doesn't come to love him, then I'm at fault and have missed the mark. But I didn't want to "oversweeten things," to use his words,[9] though by doing so I would probably have had the young people on my side immediately. I didn't want to solicit popularity with concessions of that sort. It's better to lose a battle (and I seem to have lost it) than to win it by a ruse. I imagined a gloomy, wild, large figure, half grown out of the soil, strong, spiteful, honest—and one all the same doomed to perish—because that figure is nonetheless still in the anteroom of the future,—I imagined a sort of strange pendant [counterpart] to Pugachov[10] and so on—but my young contemporaries shake their heads and tell me: "Hey, brother, you made a boo-boo and even offended us: Arkady came off better—too bad you didn't work on him a little more even." All that I can do is "remove my cap and make a low bow," as in the gypsy song. Up until now Bazarov has been understood completely by, i.e., my intentions have been understood by only two people—Dostoevsky and Botkin.[11] I'll try to send you a copy of my povest. And now enough about that.

Your poems, unfortunately, were rejected by *The Russian Messenger*. That's unfair; your poems are at least ten times better than those by Messrs. Shcherbina[12] and others that are published in *The Russian Messenger*. If you'll allow me, I'll take them and have them published in *Time*.[13] Write me a couple of words about this. Don't worry about your name—it won't be printed.

I haven't yet received a letter from Natalya Nikolayevna,[14] but I have news of her via Annenkov, whose acquaintance she has made. I won't be travelling through Heidelberg—but I'd like to have a look at the young Russians there. Give them my regards, even though they consider me backward . . . Tell them that I ask them to wait awhile yet before they pronounce the final verdict. You can convey the contents of this letter to anyone you like.

I clasp your hand firmly and wish you all the best. Work, work—and don't be in a hurry to draw up conclusions.

Your devoted

Iv. Turgenev

Letter 155 (1240). To N. Kh. Ketcher.
June 13/25, 1862. Spasskoye.

Village of Spasskoye.
June 13, 1862.

Dear Ketcher, I'm writing to you with the following request: would you like to undertake to print *Fathers and Sons* at your plant—and could you tell me approximately how much it would cost? It turns out that the countryside will provide a very mediocre income this year and I need to make some money by other means. I could send you a carefully corrected copy of *Fathers and Sons* and as much money down as you request. You should use good paper and a type size that isn't too small. It would also be good if the edition were ready by the end of July—because I'll be coming through Moscow at the very beginning of August and at that time I could sell the whole printing to Bazunov or some other bookseller. I presume that that would be more profitable than to sell the edition rights right now. But you're a better judge of this than I am—and I also rely on you in the matter of the number of copies to be printed. I don't think that any preface is necessary—I'd just like to dedicate the work to Belinsky's memory—and perhaps add a few lines from the author.[1] Do me the favor of writing me a few words immediately—and I'll be very grateful to you.

I clasp your hand and send my regards to your wife[2] and all your good friends.

Your devoted

Iv. Turgenev

P.S. My address is: Oryol Province, City of Mtsensk.

Letter 156 (1253). To Pauline Turgeneva.[1]
July 17/29, 1862. Spasskoye.

Spasskoye.
July 17/29, 1862.

My dear Paulinette,

It's been less than a week since I wrote you—and if I'm doing so now, it's not that I have anything new to tell you—but I want to advise you that I'm leaving Russia sooner than I had expected. I'm leaving here in fifteen days. For the future—and until I let you know otherwise—write me poste restante at Baden (Grand Duchy of Baden). At the same time please let me know your definite opinion about Mr. Honsez[2] (I suspect that I know what it is)—since I have received a very polite and carefully written four-page letter from him in which he speaks of himself as a *man who is waiting*. Since it would be unjust to lead this man *by the nose* any longer, write me a quick *no,* which I will convey to him in all sorts of gilded wrappings. Or perhaps you're taken with Mr. Honsez?

Mr. Honsez writes me that Mme García has installed herself definitively and forever at Brussels.[3] I foresaw that a long time ago.

Farewell, dear Paulinette; I embrace you and press Mme Innis' hand cordially.

Your father,

I. Turgenev

Letter 157 (1269). To A.A. Fet.
August 18, 23/August 30, September 4, 1862. Baden-Baden.

> Baden.
> August 30, 1862.
> Amalienstrasse, 337.

Well, here I am in Baden, carissime [dearest]—and I've taken pen in hand in order to renew our correspondence and see your dear scrawl again. The trip was accomplished safely and I've rented a little apartment here on a quiet street where, by the way, there are about two hundred children between the ages of two and seven (Germans are modest but fruitful)—and I intend to stay here about a month... I was about to write "doing nothing"—but honesty demands that I write "continuing to do nothing." The area is marvellous, there's lots and lots of greenery, the trees are old, shady and covered with emerald-green moss, the weather is good, the views are beautiful, there are good friends here, my health is fine—what more could I ask?

> Sept. 4

Just after I wrote the last words, "What more could I want?", the news of the sad conclusion to Garibaldi's[1] undertaking reached me—and I couldn't write any more. Although I know very well that the role of honest people in this world consists exclusively of perishing with dignity—and that sooner or later Octavian will definitely finish off Brutus—nonetheless I felt very bad. I am convinced that man needs something above and beyond beautiful views and old trees—and surely you—an inveterate and raging conservative, believer in serfdom, and supporter of the old order— even you will agree with me if you recall that you're a poet at the same time—and therefore a servant of the ideal. Write me a few words about the hunting, about the crops and animals, about Stepanovka—and about Spasskoye. I haven't been receiving any news from home. For greater certainty, write me in Paris, poste restante.

Farewell, be well—and give my regards to your wife.

> Your devoted
>
> Iv. Turgenev

216

Letter 158 (1273). To M.A. Markovich.
September 16/28, 1862. Baden-Baden.

Baden-Baden.
September 28, 1862.
Amalienstrasse, 337.

Dear Maria Alexandrovna, I haven't written in a long time, i.e., it's taken me a long time to answer your letter—please forgive me. There wasn't really anything important to tell you anyway, though. Your friend Vasily Botkin arrived here a few days ago and is travelling with me to Paris, where we hope to be by about the 15th of October. I'll be very happy to see you.

I haven't been reading anything or doing anything. I've been eating, sleeping, walking—and I'm healthy. I'm even thinking very little. Things are much easier that way. You can't think about everything—and you won't think up anything new anyway.

What sort of person is Bakunin, you ask. I gave a rather accurate portrait of him in the character of Rudin: now he's a Rudin who *wasn't* killed on the barricades. Just between the two of us: he's a wreck. He'll still mess around a little bit and try to rouse the Slavs—but nothing will come of it. I feel sorry for him: the life of an out-of-date and exhausted agitator is a heavy burden. That's my frank opinion of him—but don't you go telling anyone.

A few days ago I went to *your* Heidelberg. I have to admit that it's an interesting city. When I leave here I'll spend two days there and take a look at the wild Russian youth.[1]

Good-bye. Be well. I kiss you "on your sugary lips"—on paper that won't anger you.

Your devoted

Iv. Turgenev

P.S. Give my regards to the Trubetskoys and Marianna[2] when you see them. And how's the Prince[3]—has he returned from Russia?

Letter 159 (1276). To A.I. Herzen.
September 26/October 8, 1862. Baden-Baden.

Baden-Baden.
October 8, 1862.
Amalienstrasse, 337.

Dear Alexander Ivanovich, the reason that I've taken long to answer is that I kept planning to write a *long* letter—but Luginin's[1] arrival gave me the impulse to write you—and I don't know whether the letter will turn out to be short or long. First of all, let me tell you that Luginin appeals to me in a way that no young person has for a long time; he is a decent, sensible fellow. I've already answered him in detail about the address—and you've probably received my reply.[2] I asked him to send it to you with all due haste. As regards my answer to the letters that you published in *The Bell*,[3] I've already drafted a few pages—I'll show them to you—but since everyone is aware that you're writing to me—I've suspended my writing— all the more so as I received a covert *quasi-official* warning not to publish in *The Bell*.[4] The public's loss is not really great, though it would have been important for me. My major objection was that as regards me personally you formulated the question wrongly: it is not out of epicureanism, nor is it out of tiredness and laziness that I retired, as Gogol says, to the *shaded streams*[5] of European principles and institutions, if I were twenty-five years old I wouldn't behave any differently—not so much for my own good as for the good of the people. The role of the *educated* class in Russia—to be the transmitter of civilization to the people—with the understanding that they themselves are to decide what to reject or accept—is a role that is really quite modest—although Peter the Great and Lomonosov[6] appeared in it, and although it is put into effect by revolution—that role, in my opinion, is not yet finished. On the contrary, however, you gentlemen (like the Slavophiles) use the German way of thought and on the basis of a barely comprehended and barely comprehensible substance of the people, you abstract those principles on which you suppose that they will build their life—and you're whirling in a fog—and what's most important of all—you are in essence *renouncing revolution*—because the people before whom you bow are conservatives par excellence—and even bear within themselves the embryo of a bourgeoisie in sheepskin coats, warm and filthy huts, with bellies eternally stuffed to the point of heartburn and with revulsion for any sort of civic responsibility or activity, that will go far beyond all those brilliantly accurate traits with which you portrayed the Western bourgeoisie in your letters. You don't have to go far to see it—take a look at our merchants. I used the verb "abstract" with good reason. The *zemstvo,*[7] about which you so ranted to me in London—that notorious *zemstvo* has turned out in practice to be just as much a product of fireside reflection divorced from reality as Kavelin's [8] *patriarchal way of life* and so on. During the summer I worked at Shchapov[9] (I really worked!)—and nothing can change my conviction now. *Zemstvo* either means the same things as any other equivalent Western word or it doesn't mean anything at all—and in *Shchapov's* sense it is incomprehensible to exactly one hundred peasants out of a hundred.[10] You'll have to search for a trinity other than the "zemstvo, artel, and commune" that you've found—or admit that that special structure acquired by state and societal forms because of the efforts of the Russian people has not yet been sufficiently elucidated for us, people of reflection,[11] to be able to label it with categories. Otherwise there's the danger of groveling before the people at one moment, distorting them the next, then crediting them with sacred and high convictions, and then branding them unfortunate and insane, all practically on the same page, as Bakunin has done in his latest brochure.[12] Speaking of him, he says on p. 21 that "In 1863 there will be a terrible disaster in Russia if the Tsar doesn't decide to convene an all-national zemsky *duma.*"[13] If he wants, I'll bet him anything he likes that the Tsar won't convene anything and that 1863 will pass *exaggeratedly quietly.* Es gilt? [Are we on?] I'm certain that this prediction of mine will come true, just as did the one (remember?) that I made this spring in London about the statutes. I was mistaken only insofar as I thought that by the end of the year half of them would have been introduced—but they've almost all been introduced.[14] Really, my old friend, believe me: the only point of support for living revolutionary propaganda is that minority of the educated class in Russia that Bakunin calls rotten, uprooted from the soil, and traitors.[15] In any event, *you* have no other audience. Well, that's enough for now. Dixi et animam meam salvavi [I spoke and saved my soul]. And I still love you from the bottom of my heart and clasp your hand firmly.

Your Iv. Turgenev

P.S. As for the address, I can only say one thing: the mere fact that Messrs. Bezobrazov[16] and Paskevich[17] can sign it is enough to keep me from doing so.

Letter 160 (1286). To Friedrich Bodenstedt.[1]
October 19/31, 1862. Paris.

Paris.
October 19/31, 1862.
Rue de Rivoli, 210.

My dear Monsieur Bodenstedt, I arrived in Paris two days ago and I was given the letter that you wrote me in May and which had to wait for a reply until now because it didn't catch me here. I had left for Russia, to my great regret, without being able to pass through Munich. I'm back here for the winter and hasten to resume correspondence with you.

I can't help but begin by speaking of your translation of my novella "Faust,"[2] though that may be a little egotistical on my part. I've just read it and I was literally *enchanted* by it—it is simply perfect. (I'm speaking of the translation, of course, not of the novella.) It's not enough to have a profound knowledge of Russian—one must also be a great stylist oneself in order to do something that is such a complete success. Such good fortune has made my mouth water—and here's what I'm allowing myself to propose. I would be very happy to have myself introduced to the German reading public through as superb and popular an intermediary as you— and if you would like to make a choice of my novellas for publication, I would be delighted to turn over for your disposal the sum that you would judge sufficient for your fees—because I know very well that editors nowadays are not terribly well disposed toward things Russian and that they won't obligate themselves to anything more than the costs of publication. If this idea seems acceptable to you, drop me a line.[3] As for me, I could easily go as high as a thousand thalers. That's not too much for having the chance to have oneself appreciated by a *public* the likes of yours. In any case, it would be very kind of you to let me know your opinion.

As for that unfortunate article that you sent to Petersburg—that's another matter.[4] I have to confess that we've had bad luck in this case. Within the space of a year that journal *(The Contemporary)* lost its two most influential editors due to their deaths,[5] two others were imprisoned (Chernyshevsky is to be tried by the Senate)[6]—and, finally, it was suspended for 8 months—which means forever.[7] Its *files* were always in a bit of disorder, but now they're in chaos—and I'm quite afraid that we won't be able to retrieve that article. Nonetheless a friend of mine is now trying to find it[8]—and I haven't yet given up hope. I'll write you just as soon as I have any positive news.

I hope that you are in good health and that your eyes are causing you no suffering. Please give my regards to your family and remember me to

Mr. P. Heyse.[9] If you see Mme Nelidoff,[10] tell her that I'm waiting for an answer to the letter that I wrote from Baden. I sent her a copy of my latest novel—*Fathers and Sons*—at the same time. Ask her for it, if you would be interested in reading it—or else I can send you one from here. I look forward to your prompt reply and clasp your hand cordially.

Your devoted

I. Turgenev

P.S. In your translation, p. 69, line 15 from the top, there is what's probably a misprint. In the original it is "zu starr ('pristalny'—*'fixe'*) für Kinderaugen" [too staring for children's eyes] instead of feurig [fiery], which would contradict what had gone before.[11]

Letter 161 (1288). To A.I. Herzen.
October 23/November 4, 1862. Paris.

Paris.
November 4, 1862.
Rue de Rivoli, 210.

Dear Alexander Ivanovich, your *short* letter made me *vastly* happy—as the author of *Les Misérables* would say[1]—and I wish to tell you that I arrived here a few days ago and have moved into my old apartment. I didn't think you were angry with me for my not agreeing with the address, but rather, because I hindered others from signing it—if only for a while.[2] Nor can I agree with what you say about my vacillation, confusion, and explanations: as I recall, it was quite resolutely and without any *"considérants"* that I announced my disapproval of the project as it was conveyed to me. I could have been mistaken—but I knew very well what my opinion was. I quite agree with you that I'm not a political creature;[3] but if it comes to that, I confess that it's better to be a non-political person such as I am than to be a political one in the style of Ogaryov or Bakunin.

As for your last letter[4] in *The Bell*—it is just like the previous ones—intelligent, subtle, beautiful—but lacking conclusions and usefulness. I'm beginning to think that in the oft-repeated antithesis of the West, beautiful on the surface and ugly underneath—and the East, ugly on the surface and

221

beautiful underneath, there is contained a deceit that is still maintained even by remarkable minds because, in the first place, it is uncomplicated and convenient, and, secondly, a l'air d'être très ingénieuse et neuve [it seems to be very ingenious and new]. But I can already see white threads and worn-out elbow patches on it—and all your eloquence won't save it from the yawning grave, where it will lie en très bonne compagnie [in very good company] along with the philosophy of Hegel and Schelling, the French Republic, the patrimonial way of life of the Slavs, and—I make bold to add—the articles by the great socialist Nikolay Platonovich.[5] That *samum*[6] of which you speak doesn't blow just on the West—it pours over us as well,—but during your nearly quarter-century (16 years) absence from Russia, you've refashioned her in your own mind.[7] The grief that you feel at the thought of her is bitter; but believe me, in reality it is even more bitter than you imagine—and in that regard I'm more of a misanthrope than you. Russia is not the Venus de Milo with a coarse body and in fetters; she's the same sort of girl as her older sisters—only her ass is a little broader and she's already <--->—and she'll sleep around just as they do. Well—her mug's no match for theirs, to use the language of Ostrovsky. You need to read Schopenhauer more attentively, my friend, Schopenhauer.

But that's enough for now. All the same, I'm impatiently awaiting your next letter and I press your hand cordially.

Your Iv. Turgenev

P.S. Khanykov isn't in Paris yet—I'll tell him that you wrote me.[8] Botkin is here—and he's reverently serving his weak stomach, his eyes, nose, thighs, and so on.

Letter 162 (1290). To A.I. Herzen.
October 27/November 8, 1862. Paris.

Paris.
November 8, 1862.
Rue de Rivoli, 210.

What a correspondence you and I have unleashed, dear Alexander Ivanovich! It may not be to your taste—but that's the sort of mood that's come over me. The present letter was provoked by your last letter to me in

The Bell. It's very remarkable, though written somewhat—well, if not exactly floridly, then too cleverly for many readers who won't immediately understand the conception from Pan or *pre-Punic*—but these are minor details.[1] You give an unusually subtle and sensitive diagnosis of contemporary humanity—but why does that have to be *Western* humanity and not "bipèdes" in general? It's just as if you were a doctor, who, after identifying all the symptoms of a chronic illness, announces that the whole problem is a result of the patient's being French. An enemy of mysticism and absolutism, you mystically worship the Russian sheepskin coat and see in it a great blessing and the novelty and originality of future societal forms—in a word, das Absolute—that same absolute that you so laugh at in philosophy. All your idols have been shattered—but one can't live without an idol—so you up and erect an altar to this unknown new god about whose blessings no one knows anything—and it again becomes possible to pray, and believe, and be expectant. This god doesn't do what you at all expect—but as far as you're concerned, that's something temporary and accidental that was forcibly grafted onto him by the powers that be; your god loves to the point of adoration that which you hate—and hates what you love,—the god accepts precisely that which you reject, in his name— and you avert your gaze and stop up your ears—and with the ecstacy peculiar to all sceptics who are fed up with scepticism—with that specific, ultra-fanatical ecstasy you go on about "vernal freshness, blessed tempests," and so on.[2] History, philosophy, and statistics—all of that means nothing to you; nor do facts, even if only, for instance, the indisputable fact that by virtue of our language and racial stock, we Russians belong to the European family, "genus Europaeum"—and consequently, by virtue of the most invariable laws of physiology, we must follow the same path. I have yet to hear of a *duck* that belonged to the species of *duck* and breathed with gills, like a fish. And meanwhile, because of your mental agony, your exhaustion, and your thirst to place a new droplet of snow on a dried-up language, you strike out at everything that ought to be precious to every European, and therefore to us—at civilization, at legality, at revolution itself—and after filling young heads with your not yet fermented socio-Slavophile ale, you send them, inebriated and fuzzy-headed, out into a world where they are fated to stumble at the first step. I have no doubt that you do all of this in good conscience, honestly, and sorrowfully, with passionate and sincere self-sacrifice—and you are certain that I have no doubt about that ... but that doesn't make things any easier. It has to be one of the two: either serve revolution and European ideals, as before—or, if you haven't reached the stage where you're convinced of their unsoundness, then have the strength of spirit and courage to look the devil in *both* eyes, and say guilty—in the face *of all European mankind*—and don't make obvious or implied exceptions in favor of the new Russian Messiah who is

223

yet to come and in whom you really believe as little as you do in the European one. You'll reply that that's terrifying and that you could lose your popularity and the possibility of further activity . . . I agree, but on the one hand, to act as you are now acting is fruitless—and on the other hand, to spite you, I presume that you have sufficient strength of spirit so as not to fear any consequences of your stating what you consider to be the truth. We'll still wait a bit, but enough for now.

Your devoted

Iv. Turgenev

P.S.   And your friend and favorite Panin?[3]
       Who (because of his height) reached hell and heaven—
        Fell![4]
       And the same thing happened to Chevkin.[5]

Letter 163 (1292). To Ye. Ye. Lambert
October 28/November 9, 1862. Paris.

October 28/November 9, 1862.
Paris.
Rue de Rivoli, 210.

Dear Countess, I hasten to thank you for your letter and, without further explanations or justifications, to renew our correspondence. Besides, what's the point of them, these justifications, between people who, like you and me, have long since recognized and, I make bold to add, come to love each other? We'll take advantage of the unhappy fact that we ended up on this planet at all—but we ended up here at the same time—and we won't let each other out of our sight: everyone needs help from everyone else—and from the first day of life to the last.

By the way, I have mentioned the first day of life. Today, October 28, was precisely that first day for me forty-four years ago. Almost my entire life is already behind me—and I can't tell you precisely with what feeling it is that I glance at the past. I'm not exactly sorry or vexed, and I don't think

224

that I could have lived it better if . . . ! I'm not afraid to look ahead—it's just that I recognize the power that eternal, invariable, but deaf and dumb laws have over me—and the tiny squeal of my consciousness means just as little as if I took it into my head to babble "I, I, I" . . . on the shore of an ocean flowing away irretrievably. A fly still buzzes—but in another instant—and thirty or forty years are also an instant—it will no longer buzz—instead the same fly, but with a different nose, will start buzzing—and so on until the end of time. The spray and foam of the river of time! But that's enough of that sort of philosophizing—and the more so as these comparisons and so on will scarcely be to your liking.

What you tell me about yourself touches me and makes me happy: I see that you have reached that tranquil self-negation which is just as blessed and salutary as the tranquility of egoism is sterile and arid. To desire and expect nothing for oneself—and to have profound sympathy for others is genuine holiness. I don't mean to say that you have reached it, but you're on the way, and that's already a great accomplishment. I hope that you'll understand that when I say "not to desire anything for oneself" I don't for a second mean to deny your concern for your soul: loving one's soul and loving oneself are two different things. You mention the "beneficial effect" that I once had on you: if I really was such a great person, then allow me to demand my reward: namely—that you should never entertain the idea of indifference when you speak of my feelings toward you.[1]

You don't write anything about your health—I hope that it's no worse than last year's. It was very nice to hear about your husband. As for Count Karl, one can't help feeling very sorry for him—and I imagine that that is severe punishment for his uncompromising soul.[2] Why do you imagine that Pauline (who sends you warm greetings) doesn't go to church? Not only have I "not taken God away from her," but I go to church with her myself. I wouldn't allow myself such an encroachment on her freedom—and if I'm not a Christian, that's my personal affair—and perhaps my personal misfortune. Pauline, on the contrary, is very religious.

Farewell, dear Countess; I clasp your hand firmly and cordially and remain

Your devoted

Iv. Turgenev.

225

Letter 164 (1294). To A.I. Herzen.
November 13/25, 1862. Paris.

November 25, 1862.
Paris. Rue de Rivoli, 210.

Dear Alexander Ivanovich, I'm very sorry that you changed your mind and didn't send me your *angry* letter: an angry letter all the same is better than an irritated one. But I don't want to enter into any sort of recriminations—and I'm glad all the same that you at least replied. I admit that I expected objections to my objections[1]—but I don't see why you should take offense and be wounded by my hints about Ogaryov—or better to say, his theory.[2] The remarks, as far as I recall, were hardly sharp and hardly disrespectful. I'm at fault, I agree: it would be better not to speak of this and I promise not to upset you with so much as a single word on this topic, which is such a sensitive one for you. I can only assure you that in my disinclination toward the above-mentioned theory there exists something far more sensible than the antipathy of a "pregnant woman." I could expound in detail my reasons for thinking the way I do, but I have no hope of convincing you, and I'm afraid of wounding you again. And so—may this whole question remain between the two of us like the idol at Saïs— under an impenetrable veil.[3]

I cannot accept your accusation of *nihilism* in me either. (By the way— there's fate for you: I'm the one who flung that stone—and now it's striking me in the head.)[4] I'm not a nihilist—if only because I, as much as is given to my understanding, see a tragic side to the fates of the *whole European* family (including Russia, of course). I'm all the same a European—and I love the banner and believe in the banner under which I have taken my stand since my youth. With one hand you're chopping down *its* staff, while with the other you're trying to catch on to an as yet invisible staff—but that's your business—and perhaps you're right. But you're less right when you attribute ulterior goals to me (such as the pleasure of feeding parasites)[5]—or nonexistent feelings, such as irritation with the young generation. What's the point of all this? Doesn't it resemble the reproaches that people make when they accuse you of speaking and writing out of vainglory instead of convictions and so on? That sort of conjecture and malicious gossip—I'll say frankly—is unworthy of you and me.

In conclusion, I clasp you hand firmly and wish you vigor and good health. I'm very glad that you love me, and I'm certain that when you think things over a bit, you'll see that you have no reason to be upset with me.

Your devoted

Iv. Turgenev.

Letter 165 (1301). To I.P. Borisov.
December 3, 22, 1862/December 15, 1862; January 3, 1863. Paris.

Paris.
December 3/15, 1862.
Rue de Rivoli, 210.

Incomprehensible are the fates of our . . . mail, dear Ivan Petrovich! Your two letters—one of October 26, the other of November 22—arrived in Paris practically on the same day! They brought me double joy—and I hasten to reply to you.

First of all I want to express my pity for poor Fet, to whom I'll definitely write in a day or two, even though he didn't answer my last two letters. How did this horrible thing happen? Did the villain Röderer have anything to do with it? In any event, I hope that there will be no further consequences—and that he'll be left with both of his beautiful arms.[1]

January 3, 1863/December 22, 1862

I'm at fault, dear Ivan Petrovich! As you can see, this letter lay around for 20 days. It's not that I was busy—but various unpleasant incidents got in the way. Now I'll pay my debt, if only in a few words.

I was sincerely happy to hear about Tolstoy's marriage and what you write of his wife,[2] whom I recall having seen at her father's, A. Ye. Behrs, when she was practically a baby.[3] I wish him happiness—peace and quiet. I wouldn't like to see him, but I've never ceased taking a lively interest in everything that concerns him—and now it would be especially pleasant for me to hear that he has again sat down to literary activity, which he ought never to have abandoned.[4]

227

The news that you give me about the progress of peasant affairs is altogether reassuring and coincides with the news coming in from other sources. I hope that in the spring everything will calm down permanently—and when I arrive at Spasskoye in May—the deed will have been done and a new life have begun.[5] But the old one won't be forgotten either, namely, trips to Novosyelki, Stepanovka, Röderer, and so on.

I'd like to tell you something about my literary activities, but there's nothing to tell. I'm absolutely unable to do anything—I have some things floating around in my head, but I can't get anything down on paper. I don't know what will happen later—but for now it's a poor harvest, like the one that I hear threatens us next year because of so little snow.

Good-bye, dear Ivan Petrovich. I clasp your hand—send my regards to your wife—and kiss Petya[6] on his bright little head. Be well.

Your devoted

Iv. Turgenev

NOTES

Letter 1

1. Nikolay Nikolayevich Turgenev (1795-1881), the writer's uncle.
2. Anna Ivanovna, a friend of the Turgenev family's.
3. The Gagarins, Moscow friends of the Turgenevs.
4. Fyodor Ivanovich Lobanov, one of the Turgenevs' servants.
5. Alexander Sergeyevich Pushkin (1799-1837), the greatest Russian poet of the nineteenth century, if not of all time.
6. A quotation from the False Dmitri's speech to Marina in Pushkin's play *Boris Godunov.*
7. Yakovleva, a friend of Turgenev's mother's.
8. Valentin ("Falantine" is probably a humorous corruption of the name), the German teacher for Turgenev and his brothers.
9. Platon Nikolayevich Pogorelsky, the mathematics teacher for Turgenev and his brothers.
10. Ivan Andreyevich Krylov (1768-1844), the most famous Russian composer of fables. Turgenev's quotation is slightly inaccurate.
11. Nikanor, one of the Turgenevs' domestic servants.
12. Dmitri Nikitich Dubensky (d. 1863), a professor from Moscow University who taught the Turgenev brothers Russian, history, and geography.
13. Gardorf taught the Turgenev brothers Greek.
14. Doublet (?) taught Turgenev and his brothers French.
15. Shchurovsky taught the Turgenev boys Latin and philosophy.
16. Probably Lev Yakovlevich Yakovlev (1822-1887).
17. Canto III of Pushkin's "Ruslan and Lyudmila."
18. Nikolay Sergeevich Turgenev (1816-1879), the writer's older brother.
19. *The Moscow Telegraph,* an influential journal of the time.
20. Meyer, Turgenev's tutor.
21. The young Turgenev has in mind temporary service in a branch of the armed forces resembling our National Guard.

Letter 2

1. Alexander Vasilievich Nikitenko (1805-1877), a professor at Petersburg University when Turgenev met him. A literary historian, critic, and censor, Nikitenko was later editor for the journals *Son of the Fatherland* (1840-1846) and *The Contemporary* (1846-48).
2. The dramatic narrative poem in question is "Steno," written in 1834 and first published in 1913.
3. Pyotr Alexandrovich Pletnyov (1792-1865), a poet and critic, was a professor of Russian literature at Petersburg University when Turgenev met him. Pletnyov was the editor of *The Contemporary* (founded by Pushkin) from 1838-1846.
4. Soviet commentators point out that Turgenev's "close acquaintance" with Nikitenko was occasioned by this letter and not vice versa.

5. Some scholars consider that "An Old Man's Tale" is actually "An Old Landowner," one of Turgenev's early poems.

6. The reference is no doubt to the Messrs. Grech, Bulgarin, and Senkovsky—a trinity of nastiness and reaction who ruled the journals of the day. "Our Age" is not extant.

7. Mikhail Petrovich Vrochenko (1801-1855) and Ivan Ivanovich Panayev (1812-1862), both of whom were responsible for Shakespeare translations. Panayev was later a co-editor with Nekrasov of *The Contemporary.*

8. None of these works is extant.

9. Pletnyov. See note 3.

10. It is not known to what work Turgenev is making reference.

Letter 3

1. Timofey Nikolayevich Granovsky (1813-1855), a historian and professor at Moscow University whom Turgenev met in 1835 when both were students at Petersburg University.

2. Nikolay Vladimirovich Stankevich (1813-1840), the influential leader of a Moscow philosophical circle in the 1830s. Members of the circle included Turgenev, Vissarion Belinsky, and Mikhail Bakunin. The best study of Stankevich in any language is Edward Brown, *Stankevich and His Moscow Circle* (Stanford, 1966).

3. Stankevich was ill with tuberculosis.

4. Karl Werder (1806-1893), German philosopher and dramatist.

5. Berta Sautr, Stankevich's mistress.

6. Belinsky was sent to Salzbrunn.

7. An inexact quotation from N.M. Yazykov's poem "The Waterfall."

8. Leopold Ranke (1795-1886) taught history at Berlin University (1825-1871). The work that Turgenev refers to is *Deutsche Geschichte im Zeitalter der Reformation,* Bd. I-II (Berlin, 1839).

9. František Palacký (1798-1876), Czech historian and an important figure in the Czech national revival.

10. Philip Strahl was a German historian. Turgenev has in mind Strahl's *Geschichte des russischen Staates,* 1-2 (Hamburg, 1832-1839).

11. Karl Ludwig Michelet (1801-1893) was a German Hegelian and a professor at Berlin University.

12. Sophie Löwe (1811-1866), one of the leading sopranos of the 1840's. *Jean de Paris,* comic opera by Boieldieu.

13. Meyerbeer's *Robert le Diable.*

14. Adolf Bäuerle (1786-1859), Austrian novelist and dramatist; Fritz Beckman (1803-1866), a noted comic actor at the Königstadt Theater in Berlin; Eichbaum was an actress at the same theater.

15. Turgenev has in mind Auber's opera *La Dieu et la bayadère* (1830).

16. Soviet commentators have been unable to locate this "citation" in Schiller's works.

17. A quotation from Goethe's ballad "Gott und die Bayadere."

18. Sharon Turner (1768-1847), English historian, published his *The History of the Anglo-Saxons from the Earliest Period to the Norman Conquest* in 1799.

19. Amadeus Gotfried Adolf Müllner (1774-1829) was a German dramatist.

20. Frantz Grillparzer (1791-1872), Austrian dramatist, wrote *Sappho* in 1818. Karl Ludwig Börne (1786-1837), a literary critic.

21. Emile Souvestre (1806-1854) saw his *L'homme et l'argent* published in 1839.

22. Turgenev is referring to the novel by Charles Bernard (1804-1850).

Letter 4

1. Varvara Alexandrovna Dyakova (1812-?), the younger of Bakunin's two sisters. In his last months she and Stankevich shared an "elevated" love.
2. Turgenev has in mind Lyubov Alexandrovna Bakunina (1811-1838), the eldest of Bakunin's sisters. She had been Stankevich's fiancée.
3. Turgenev quotes from the poem "On the Death of a Maiden" by Ivan Petrovich Klyushnikov (1811-1895), who had been a member of Stankevich's circle. The poem was set to music by L.F. Langer (1802-1885). What Turgenev has in mind in saying "He, too, died" is unclear, since Klyushnikov and Langer were both still alive and the cited poem is about a woman.
4. Nikolay Grigorievich Frolov (1812-1855), translator and publisher, was close to Stankevich's circle. His first wife, Elizaveta Pavlovna, died fairly young and Frolov then married Stankevich's sister, Maria Vladimirovna (1823-1850). Frolov was the prototype for Turgenev's "Hamlet of the Shchigrov District."
5. Maria Pavlovna Kenney (née Galakhova), Frolov's sister-in-law (see note 4).
6. Alexander Pavlovich Yefremov (1814-1876), was a friend of Stankevich's, as well as of Turgenev, Bakunin, and Belinsky.
7. Yanuary Mikhaylovich Neverov (1810-1893), a close friend of Stankevich's and Granovsky's. He made his career as a teacher.
8. Rahel Varnhagen von Ense (1771-1833), the wife of Karl August Varnhagen von Ense (1785-1853), a German critic and memoirist.

Letter 5

1. Bettina von Arnim (1785-1859), German writer with whom Turgenev had become acquainted in 1838 in Berlin while he was a student. This letter, in German, is an unfinished draft.
2. The quotation is actually from von Arnim's *Goethes Briefwechsel mit einem Kinde*, not *Die Günderode*.
3. This romantic formulation can be traced to Goethe.
4. Turgenev is paraphrasing a passage from *Die Günderode*.

Letter 6

1. In 1842 Turgenev did in fact earn his master's degree in philosophy and classics.
2. Rarely are Turgenev's prevarications as clumsy as here. Note that although Turgenev is too ill to visit Nikitenko, he could perhaps leave his room to arrange to get his books through customs. Illness is a constant motif and excuse in Turgenev's letters.

Letter 7

1. Tatyana Alexandrovna Bakunina (1815-1871), the youngest of the three Bakunin sisters. Turgenev had met her in the fall of 1841 and the two of them had struck up an elevated, ethereal romance that bore no relation at all to Turgenev's essential indifference to Bakunina. He finally found the courage to break off with her: the present letter represents his epistolary attempt to lessen the pain both for himself and for Bakunina. Though Bakunina was indeed an inspiration for some of Turgenev's early lyrics, he eventually caricatured her in "Tatyana Borisovna and Her Nephew."
2. Opera by Meyerbeer.
3. Tatyana Mikhaylovna Poltoratskaya (née Bakunina).

4. The works that Turgenev cites are no doubt his own. They have not survived.
5. The Russian word is *podruga*—a *female* friend.
6. The last four paragraphs of the letter are in German in the original.

Letter 8

1. Alexey Alexandrovich Bakunin (1823-1882) and Alexander Alexandrovich Bakunin (1821-1908) the sixth and fifth of Bakunin's brothers.
2. *Goethes Briefe an die Gräfin zu Stolberg.* August Luisa Stolberg (1753-1835) was well known for her extensive correspondence with Goethe.
3. Vladimir Konstantinovich Rzhevsky (1811-1885), figure in Russian educational circles.
4. See letter 4, note 3.
5. A free reworking of a line from Pushkin's poem "The Prisoner."
6. Friedrich Wilhelm Grund (1791-1874), German composer.
7. The first line of Pushkin's "Count Nulin."
8. Turgenev's word play is untranslatable.
9. The poem is not extant.
10. Tatyana Aleksandrovna Bakunina. See letter 8, note 1.

Letter 9

1. Pauline Viardot (née García) (1821-1910), the daughter of the singers Manuel and Joaquina García, one of the most important singers of the nineteenth century. (Her sister, la Malibran, was even more famous.) She married Louis Viardot in 1840. She appeared in Petersburg and Moscow during the 1843/44, 1844/45, 1845/46, and 1852/53 seasons. The Viardots and Turgenev comprised a *ménage,* though whether Turgenev and Pauline Viardot were ever in fact lovers is a question that probably will never be answered. It is clear, however that Pauline Viardot was the single most important person in Turgenev's life. For most of the latter part of his life he was never away from her for more than a few months at a time. The original French version of this letter is not extant.
2. *Allegemeine Theaterzeitung,* Vienna newspaper.
3. Turgenev is playing on "votre bonne ville de," an old French expression used in addressing the King.
4. There was a Petersburg circle of Russians fanatically devoted to Viardot.
5. Eugenio Pizzolato, an Italian singer who performed in Petersburg in the 1840's and 1850's. It is likely that Turgenev's reference to Eugène in the first paragraph is to Pizzolato.
6. Bellini's *Capuletti e Montecchi,* in which the role of Romeo is sung by a mezzo-soprano.
7. "Die Stadt," song by Schubert.
8. The songs mentioned are all from a collection by Viardot: *Album de Mme Viardot-Garcia* (Paris, 1843).
9. Pauline Viardot's eldest daughter Louise.
10. Turgenev spent the summer at a dacha in Pargolovo, near Petersburg.
11. Louis Viardot (1800-1883), French writer, husband of Pauline Viardot. He and Turgenev together translated many works of Russian literature into French.
12. Turgenev worked for the Ministry of Internal Affairs from June 1843 until April 1845, when he officially retired from government service.

Letter 10

The French original of this letter is not extant.

1. Joaquina García (?-?), Pauline Viardot's mother. None of García's letters to Turgenev or his to her has survived.

2. Three operas—*La Gazza Ladra,* by Rossini; *Ernani,* by Verdi; and *La Fille du Régiment,* by Donizetti.

3. Moltini was a second-rate Italian singer in Petersburg.

4. Guili Borsi (soprano), Guasco (tenor), and Collini (baritone) performed Italian opera in Petersburg.

5. Antonio Tamburini (1800-1876), well-known Italian bass.

6. Marra, an Italian singer who did not do well in Petersburg.

7. Andrey Mikhailovich Gulevich (?-1875), one of Viardot's most fervent St. Petersburg admirers.

8. One of the two Vielgorsky brothers, probably Matvey Yurevich (1794-1866), a dilettante and important figure in Petersburg's musical life.

9. Turgenev is referring to *The Contemporary* [Sovremennik], a journal that had been founded by Pushkin, but had then floundered in the doldrums until Nekrasov and Panayev renovated it. As later letters will show, Turgenev's association with the journal eventually proved to be painful in the extreme.

10. In the original letter the expression was undoubtedly "au revoir" (as opposed to the less optimistic "adieu").

Letter 11.

1. Vissarion Grigorievich Belinsky (1811-1848), the most influential Russian literary critic of the 19th century. He is usually praised or upbraided for having called for a socially-conscious literature, but his true merit probably lies in his having acclaimed the likes of Pushkin, Lermontov, and Dostoevsky. The best work on Belinsky in English is Victor Terras, *Belinsky and Russian Literary Criticism* (Madison, 1974).

2. Belinsky had been travelling through Europe, accompanied most of the time by Turgenev.

3. Pavel Vasilievich Annenkov (1812-1887), critic and memoirist, was one of Turgenev's closest friends. A major part of Turgenev's correspondence is with Annenkov, and "First Love" is dedicated to him.

Annenkov's memoirs, *The Extraordinary Decade,* edited by Arthur Mendel and translated by Irwin Titunik, were published by The University of Michigan Press in 1968.

4. Undoubtedly a pawnshop ticket, but whose fur coat was pawned, or why or where or when remains a mystery, largely because the letter from Annenkov is not extant.

5. A Russian expression meaning "subtle wit."

6. "Buzun" is unrefined lake salt, and Gogol seems not to have said anything of the sort.

7. Tirá de Malmor, French physician who specialized in lung ailments. Belinsky's premature death was brought about by tuberculosis.

8. Turgenev probably means two sketches for the cycle *Notes of a Hunter.* Belinsky encouraged him in this endeavor.

9. The sketches "The Office" and "The Steward" were published in *The Contemporary* in 1847. For information on Nekrasov, see letter 40, note 7.

10. Turgenev did not arrive in Petersburg until mid-June of 1850.

Letter 12.

The original French version of this letter is not extant.

1. There were two Kamensky sisters, countesses, who were admirers of Viardot and met with her in Dresden and other places in Western Europe.

2. Turgenev means the García family and himself.

3. Turgenev is referring to phrenology.

4. The song is really "La chanson de Loïc," which along with "La Luciole" was included in Viardot's 1850 collection *10 mélodies par Pauline Viardot*.

5. Gilbert Duprez (1806-1896), one of the most famous tenors of his day.

6. The "Academie," Paris' second opera theater.

7. Chimborazo, one of the major peaks in the Andes.

8. "Deguelando," a humorous formulation based on the French "dégueuler," i.e., "to vomit."

9. Manuel García (1805-1906), Pauline Viardot's brother, singer and vocal pedagogue.

10. Rossini's opera *The Barber of Seville* and Bellini's *Norma*. Viardot had a great success in both operas, and her father, Manuel García (1775-1832) created the role of Almaviva in Rossini's opera.

11. Etiénne Arago (1802-1892), French dramatist whose *Les aristocraties, ou les idées républicaines* was performed in Paris in 1847.

12. Rachel (1820-1858), whose real name was Elise Felix, renowned French tragedienne.

13. Jules Michelet (1798-1874), French historian, the second volume of whose *Histoire de la Révolution française* had just come out in 1847.

14. Louis Blanc (1811-1882), French historian and politician, emigrated to England after the 1848 Revolution.

15. Turgenev has in mind the García family.

16. Tampoux, Parisian music publisher.

Letter 13.

1. Most of the French original of this letter has been lost. See note 3.

2. Joaquina García, Pauline Viardot's mother.

3. The French text from this point on has been lost.

4. Léon Viardot (1805-?), Louis Viardot's brother, a portrait painter.

5. Hermann Müller-Strübing (1812-1893), philologist, archeologist, and revolutionary. A friend of Bakunin's, Turgenev's and other Russians in Berlin and Paris.

6. *La Juive,* opera by Halévy.

7. Eugénie Adélaïde Louise, the Princess of Orleans, died December 31, 1847.

8. Abd-el-Kader, Algerian rebel who was captured by the French December 22, 1847.

9. The historian Jules Michelet's lectures were forcibly discontinued because of what the government considered their inflammatory nature.

10. Le Roy d'Estoilles, the son of the well-known surgeon Jean-Jacques Le-Roy D'Estoilles.

11. *L'Elisir d'Amore,* comic opera by Donizetti.

12. Fanni Persiani (1818-1867), one of the outstanding sopranos of her time.

13. Nemorino is the country-bumpkin hero of *L'Elisir d'Amore.*

14. Eugène Scribe (1791-1861), French dramatist who provided libretti for most of the major Italian and French opera composers of his time. His name is synonymous with melodrama.

15. Anne Louise Lavoye (1823-?), French singer famous for her comic roles.

16. Alexandra Mikhailovna Karatygina (1802-1880), comic actress who abandoned the stage in 1844.

17. Those loyal to Count Armaniac were massacred in Paris in 1418.

18. Turgenev included a sketch of Mlle Lavoye's finger at this point.

19. The words "Much, very much," appear in English in the original.

Letter 14.

1. The French original of this letter is not extant.

2. Pierre François Rayer (1793-1867), French physician who treated Turgenev, Herzen, and Nekrasov.

3. Thomas Robert Bugeaud de la Piconnerie (1784-1849), a Marshal of France, a leading conservative figure in the Revolution of 1848.

4. Baron Julius Jacob Haynau (1786-1853), one of the leaders of the Austrian army sent out to crush the Hungarian revolt. The defeat of which Turgenev speaks was not at Presburg (today's Bratislava), but at Komoru.

5. Heinrich Dembinski (1791-1864), a Pole, was one of the commanders of the Hungarian army. The rumors about his loss at the hands of the Russians were false.

Letter 15.

1. Andrey Alexandrovich Krayevsky (1810-1889), well-known journalist and publisher.

2. Krayevsky published *Notes of the Fatherland* [Otechestvennye zapiski] from 1839 to 1868. Turgenev's *The Bachelor* was published there in issue No. 9 for 1849.

3. The censor had forbidden the publication of *The Hanger-On* [Nakhlebnik].

4. Krayevsky did send Turgenev a 50-day promissory note for 300 rubles. See the following letter.

5. Neither *The Party* nor *The Governess* was finished.

Letter 16.

1. See letter 15 for the details on Turgenev's request for a loan.

2. "The Diary of a Superfluous Man."

3. Faddey Benediktovich Bulgarin (1789-1859), one of the most unpleasant and most unscrupulous Russian publishers of the first half of the 19th century. For most writers his name was synonymous with utter vileness.

4. The article "A Few Words about Meyerbeer's Opera *Le Prophète*" appeared in the second issue of *Notes of the Fatherland* for 1850.

5. *The Governess* was never finished. *The Student* was reworked and appeared under the new title *A Month in the Country* in the first issue of *The Contemporary* for 1855.

6. Turgenev's mother had been displeased by his relationship with Pauline Viardot, and by the summer of 1849 she had ceased sending him money.

7. The printer's page for Russians in the 19th century meant a signature sheet of 16 pages.

8. Turgenev arrived in Petersburg in the second half of June (Old Style), 1850.

Letter 17.

1. See letter 16, note 8.

2. *Breakfast* was performed in the theater, but it did not appear in print until 1856, when it was published in issue No. 8 of *The Contemporary*. *The Hanger-On* had not been approved by the censors.

3. "A Correspondence" was not in fact finished until December 1, 1854. Turgenev then offered it to Nekrasov's *Contemporary,* whose censor rejected it, after which Turgenev gave it to Krayevsky, who published it in the first issue of *Notes of the Fatherland* for 1856.

4. Turgenev changed his plans. He returned to Paris, left from there in mid-May (Old Style), and sailed from Stettin on June 17 (29), 1850.

5. Krayevsky sent Turgenev a promissory note for 200 silver rubles.

Letter 18.

1. The original of this letter is in French.

2. At that time Gounod and his mother were staying at Courtavenel, the Viardots' estate.

Letter 19.

1. Alexander Ivanovich Herzen (1812-1870), Russian radical who spent the latter half of his life in exile in London, from where he published *The Bell* and *Polar Star,* "underground" periodicals that wielded enormous influence in the 1850s and 1860s. For a detailed study of Herzen's life and work, see Martin Malia, *Alexander Herzen and the Birth of Russian Socialism* (Cambridge, 1961). This letter is an example of the many services that Turgenev provided for Herzen over the years.

2. Herzen had just left Paris for Nice.

3. Maria Kasparovna Reichel, née Erne (1822-1910), the Herzen children's nurse. The Rothschild that Turgenev refers to is the banking establishment.

4. Because of Herzen's participation in the European revolutions of 1848-49, open correspondence with him from inside Russia was impossible.

5. Nikolay Platonovich Ogaryov (1813-1877), one of Herzen's closest associates. He, his wife, and Herzen eventually comprised one of the century's most distinguished ménages à trois.

6. Georg Herwegh (1817-1874), German poet with decidedly revolutionary leanings. Exiled from Germany in the 1840s, he was in France in 1848, where he was in close contact with Herzen and Turgenev. See letter 283.

Letter 20.

1. The French original of this letter is not extant.

2. Pauline (Pelegaya) Ivanovna Turgeneva (1842-1919), Turgenev's illegitimate daughter by Avdotya Yermolayevna Ivanova, a seamstress at his mother's home. He seems rather to have forgotten that Pauline existed until he ran across her at Spasskoye in 1850, after which he sent her to france, where she was raised by the Viardot family. In married life she was Pauline Bruere.

3. Mlle Robert, Pauline Turgeneva's governess.

Letter 21.

1. The French original of this letter is not extant.

2. Turgenev is describing his story "The Singers" [Pevtsy], probably one of the two best-known sketches from *The Notes of a Hunter.*

3. David Teniers, the Younger (1610-1694), Flemish artist who specialized in scenes from the daily life of the common people.

4. Turgenev was actually turning thirty-three.

5. Alexander Sergeyevich Komarov, military engineer and teacher. He introduced Turgenev to Louis Viardot.

6. Nikolay Nikolayevich Tyutchev (1815-1878), translator and a member of Belinsky's circle. He managed Turgenev's estate Spasskoye in 1852-1853.

7. What Turgenev requested of Viardot remains a mystery.

8. See the preceding letter.

9. Matvey Yurevich Vielgorsky (1794-1866) and Mikhail Yurevich Vielgorsky (1788-1856), leaders of Russian musical life. Both were accomplished amateur musicians.

10. Fidès, the heroine of Meyerbeer's *Le Prophète.*

11. Vera Vasilievna Samoylova (1824-1880), well-known dramatic actress of her time, performed in several of Turgenev's plays. The play in question is *The Provincial Lady.*

12. *A Month in the Country.*

Letter 22.

1. The French original of this letter is not extant.

2. Varvara Petrovna Turgeneva (1780-1850), by all accounts a monstrous, despotic woman, died November 16/28, 1850, in Moscow.

3. Mikhail Alexandrovich Yazykov (1811-1885) ran a "Commission Office for People in the Provinces."

Letter 23.

1. The French original of this letter is not extant.

2. See preceding letter, note 2.

3. Nikolay Sergeyevich Turgenev, the writer's older brother.

Letter 24.

1. The original of this letter is in French.

2. Turgenev's mother's papers had been sealed, pending the co pletion of legal formalities.

3. Turgenev's relations with his mother had grown worse during the last few years of her life. A domineering, despotic woman, Varvara Turgeneva had cut off all financial support in an attempt to force Turgenev to return to Russia, and more importantly, to break off his relationship with Pauline Viardot.

4. See letter 22, note 3.

5. *Les Huguenots,* opera by Meyerbeer. Viardot, who performed two roles in the opera, was an enormous success.

6. Turgenev is referring to Varvara Nikolayevna Bogdanovich-Lutovinova (1833-1900), Varvara Petrovna Turgeneva's daughter by E.A. Behrs, coincidentally the father of Lev Tolstoy's wife.

7. Mme Renard was the governess whom Pauline Viardot hired for Turgenev's daughter, Pauline.

8. Pauline was eventually given her father's last name.

9. Turgenev is referring to Mariquita Sitchès, Pauline Viardot's aunt.

10. Mikhail Semyonovich Shchepkin (1788-1863), the most famous Russian actor of the 19th century. He performed in several of Turgenev's plays.

11. Yelizaveta Vasilievna Salias de Turnemir (1815-1892), the dramatist A.V. Sukhovo-Kobylin's sister, wrote historical novels under the pseudonym Evgenij Tur.

12. Turgenev has in mind his story "The Singers."

13. *Sappho,* opera by Gounod.

Letter 25.

1. Yevgeny Mikhailovich Feoktistov (1829-1898) was a journalist and historian who wrote for *The Contemporary* and *Notes of the Fatherland* in the 1850s.

2. Vasily Petrovich Botkin (1810-1869), author of articles on literature, the arts, and philosophy. A friend of Belinsky's, he and Turgenev travelled in France together in 1845.

3. Ye. V. Salias de Turnemir.

4. Feotkistov had advised Turgenev to cease work on *Notes of a Hunter* and produce a long work of some kind.

5. Turgenev's review of *Poetic Sketches: An Almanac of Poems Published by Ya. M. Poznyakov and A.P. Ponomarev* was published in the March 1851 issue of *The Contemporary.*

6. Aleksey Feofilaktovich Pisemsky (1821-1881), one of the major minor realists of the 19th century. His novel *A Thousand Souls* [Tysyacha dush] is his major claim to fame. In this letter Turgenev is referring to Pisemsky's story "Sergey Petrovich Khozarov and Mari Stupitsyna, a Marriage of Passion." The best English-language study of Pisemsky is Charles Moser, *Pisemsky: A Provincial Realist* (Cambridge, 1969).

7. Turgenev would seem to have been irritated by Botkin's affair with Ye. A. Khrushcheva, Turgenev's cousin. Furthermore, in a letter of March 30, 1851, Feoktistov had described Botkin's having started up an unseemly argument with Ye. V. Salias de Turnermir at a recent party.

8. Turgenev means Ye. V. Salias de Turnemir's sisters S.V. Sukhovo-Kobylina and Ye. V. Petrovo-Solovovo.

9. Almost nothing is known of Turgenev's work on this unfinished comedy. Sergey Vasilievich Shumsky (1820-1878), an outstanding actor at Moscow's Maly Theater, was a student of M.S. Shchepkin.

10. Yelena Konstantinovna Bodisko, T.N. Granovsky's cousin, and A.V. Stankevich's wife. In a letter to Turgenev Feoktistov had described her approaching marriage.

Letter 26.

1. This is only the partial text of a letter, the original of which is not extant.

2. Feoktistov had written Turgenev a letter on July 11 O.S., 1851, in which he expressed irritation with the writer's sister-in-law, A. Ya. Turgeneva, who had read someone else's mail, in this case V.P. Botkin's letter to Ye. A. Khrushcheva.

3. Yelizaveta Alexeyeva Khrushcheva (née Turgeneva) (see letter 26) was having an affair with V.P. Botkin.

4. Mikhail Alexeevich Turgenev (b. 1829), Ye.A. Khrushcheva's brother, Turgenev's cousin.

5. Pyotr Nikolayevich Turgenev (1804-1865), Turgenev's uncle.

6. Anna Yakovlevna Turgeneva, née Shvarts (d. 1872), N.S. Turgenev's wife.

Letter 27.

1. Konstantin Nikolayevich Leontiev (1831-1891), one of the most colorful figures in 19th-century Russian literature. He eventually abandoned fiction for philosophy and criticism. See Nikolay Berdiaev, *Leontiev* (Orono, Me., 1968).

2. Turgenev is referring to Leontiev's *A Marriage for Love* [Zhenit'ba po liubvi].

3. Turgenev has in mind some chapters from Leontiev's novel *The Bulavin Factory*, which remained unfinished.

Letter 28.

1. Mikhail Petrovich Pogodin (1800-1875), professor of Russian history at Moscow University, writer, journalist, and publisher of the Slavophile-leaning *The Muscovite* [Moskvityanin] from 1840-1855.

2. Turgenev, a Westernizer, would have had little use for Pogodin's *The Muscovite*.

3. It is unclear which stories Turgenev has in mind.

4. Probably Orest Mikhailovich Novitsky (1806-1884), a professor of philosophy at Kiev University and a censor. It is unclear what information Turgenev is referring to.

5. There are only two known letters from Turgenev to Pogodin.

Letter 29.

1. Sergey Timofeyevich Aksakov (1791-1859), distinguished writer with Slavophile inclinations. Author of theater reviews, nature sketches, and memoirs. His *Family Chronicle,* a nineteenth-century Russian classic, is little known in the West.

2. *Notes of a Hunter from Orenburg Province* [Zapiski ruzheynogo okhotnika Orenburgskoy gubernii] came out at the beginning of 1852.

3. Turgenev had urged Aksakov to publish the work.

4. The first edition of *Notes on Fishing* [Zapiski ob uzhenye ryby] appeared in 1847.

5. Turgenev wrote two reviews of the work, one for the April issue of *The Contemporary* for 1852 and one for the January issue of the same journal for 1853.

6. Konstantin Sergeyevich Aksakov (1817-1860) and Ivan Sergeyevich Aksakov (1823-1886), S.T. Aksakov's sons, both leading figures of the second generation of Slavophiles.

7. The almanac in question was *The Moscow Collection* [Moskovsky sbornik], the first volume of which came out in March 1852.

8. Turgenev is referring to his story "Three Meetings" [Tri vstrechi].

Letter 30.

1. The original of this letter is not extant. This fragment came from the files of the Third Department (Tsarist Secret Police), which regularly intercepted and copied Turgenev's correspondence.

2. Gogol, for reasons which no one has ever quite understood, burned the second volume of *Dead Souls,* which he had been working on for twelve years.

3. Turgenev's article on Gogol (an obituary) though forbidden by the St. Petersburg censors, appeared in *The Moscow News.* The "illegal" obituary was soon to provide a convenient excuse for Turgenev's arrest. See letters 31, 32.

Letter 31.

1. The original of this letter is not extant. This extract came from the files of the Third Department (Secret Police). See letter 39, note 1.

2. Prince Lvov had written Gogol to ask him why he had published *Selected Passages from a Correspondence with Friends.* Gogol had replied that he had wished to elucidate his personal shortcomings through the feelings of shame that the book would cause. See Vladimir Nabokov, *Nikolai Gogol* (Norfolk, Conn., 1944) for more about this strangest of Russians.

3. The article was published in *The Moscow News*, whose editors were unaware that it had been forbidden by the Petersburg censors. The publication of the article led to Turgenev's arrest. See letter 32.

Letter 32.

1. The original of this letter is in French.
2. Nicholas I had been displeased by Turgenev's *Notes of a Hunter*, which was widely perceived as an exposé of serfdom, as well as with other Turgenev works. Turgenev is correct in stating that his article on Gogol only provided a pretext for his arrest: the government was out to punish him for his other "radical" works.
3. Turgenev's *Notes of a Hunter* was in fact published in a separate edition, but the censor who passed it was removed from his position.
4. Eugène Vivier (1817-1900), French musician and composer who played in the orchestra of the Bolshoy Theater. He was as well known for his wit as for his musical talents.

Letter 33.

1. The story "The Germans."
2. A povest is a Russian genre that falls midway between the long short story and short novel.
3. Leontiev's *The Marriage*. See letter 27.
4. Turgenev means his confinement to his estate, ostensibly for having published in Moscow an article on Gogol which had been forbidden by the Petersburg censor. See letters 30, 31, 32.

Letter 34.

1. *Notes of a Hunter.*
2. For more on Turgenev's "old manner," see letter 38.
3. Turgenev has in mind his *Two Generations* [Dva pokoleniya], a novel which was not finished.
4. Dmitry Vasilievich Grigorovich (1822-1899), a minor writer who shared many of Turgenev's esthetic and political views. Here Turgenev has in mind Grigorovich's novel *Village Roads* [Proselochnye dorogi], which Turgenev and Aksakov considered a failure.
5. Aksakov had called the intelligentsia "ape people" because of its mimicking of Western European mores.
6. Turgenev is talking about the differences separating the Westernizers and the Slavophiles.
7. See letter 29, note 7.
8. The second volume did not appear. It was not passed by the censors.
9. Abramtsevo was Aksakov's estate. At the end of the 19th century it became an influential artistic center.

Letter 35.

1. Aksakov's *Hunter's Notes* [Okhotnichi zapiski].
2. Konstantin Sergeyevich Aksakov.
3. Ivan Sergeyevich Aksakov.
4. Mikhail Nikolayevich Zagoskin (1789-1852), minor writer, author of historical novels.

Letter 36.

1. Turgenev is referring to the ninth of Annenkov's "Provincial Letters," which appeared in *The Contemporary*, No. 10, 1851.

2. Ivan Petrovich Arapetov (1811-1887), prominent liberal bureaucrat, was a friend of Turgenev's.

3. Annenkov was at work on a biography of Pushkin.

Letter 37.

1. This letter, written in French, was probably enclosed with a letter to Pauline Viardot.

2. Turgenev had been confined to his estate at Spasskoye for having published a forbidden article on the occasion of Gogol's death (see letters 30, 31). He did not know how long his confinement would last.

3. Pauline Viardot and her mother, Joaquina Garcia.

Letter 38.

1. Turgenev was in the midst of an artistic crisis motivated by his dissatisfaction with the small form and his fears that he was incapable of producing novels.

2. This name in the original letter is indecipherable.

3. In a letter to Turgenev Annenkov had complained of his difficulty in completing his Pushkin biography. The major difficulty involved details of the duel that ended Pushkin's life. Since the duel made all parties involved look very bad, and since many of those parties or their relatives were still alive, Annenkov was faced with a real dilemma.

Vasily Andreyevich Zhukovsky (1783-1852), poet of genius and Pushkin's master, was present at the poet's death. The story Turgenev refers to is the letter that Zhukovsky sent to Pushkin's father, in which he included a detailed account of the poet's tragic death.

Letter 39.

1. Turgenev is alluding to his exile.

2. Turgenev means Leontiev's *A Marriage for Love*, which had been forbidden by the censors.

3. Krayevsky had given Turgenev someone's translation of Lessing's "Laokoon" to look over. Whose translation this was is a mystery.

Letter 40.

1. Annenkov was preparing *The Works of Pushkin* for publication.

2. Turgenev's *Two Generations*. See letter 33.

3. Annenkov had complained that the position of district police officer [stanovoi] had not existed at the time in which "The Inn" is set.

4. A destyatina = 2.7 acres.

5. A verst = 3500 feet.

6. As of December 1852, Turgenev had been forbidden even to leave his estate at Spasskoye.

7. Nikolay Alexeyevich Nekrasov (1821-1877), poet, publicist, editor of *The Contemporary*, later *Notes of the Fatherland*. A contradictory personality, he was always a thorn in the side of the Tsarist regime. See Sigmund Birkenmayer, *Nikolaj Nekrasov: His Life and Poetic Works* (The Hague, 1968).

8. Turgenev is referring to Aksakov's *Notes of a Hunter from Orenburg Province*. See letter 29.

9. Mérimée's *Le Faux Démétrius, scènes dramatiques.*

10. Henry Chorley (1808-1872), the distinguished English music and literary critic, made Turgenev's acquaintance via Pauline Viardot.

Annenkov, then preparing a collection of Pushkin's works, was stumped by one of Pushkin's "little tragedies," "The Covetous Knight" [Skupoy rytsar'], which bore the subtitle: "Scenes from Chenston's Tragi-comedy 'The Covetous Knight.'" Annenkov suspected that the subtitle was a literary mystification, and he appealed to Turgenev to ask Chorley about this question. The whole issue is complex, but to make a long story short, Annenkov was right: there was no Chenston.

11. Leontiev's *A Marriage for Love*. See letter 27.

12. Turgenev sent Krayevsky Leontiev's "The Germans" (see letter 33); the "other piece" mentioned by Turgenev was Leontiev's "Summer on a Farm" [Leto na khutore].

13. Turgenev means Dostoevsky, of course, who was at that time still in prison. Relations between Dostoevsky and Turgenev were rarely less than strained.

14. Characters from "The Inn."

Letter 41.

1. Aksakov's article "About the Ancient Way of Life among the Slavs in General and Russians in Particular (Apropos of Opinions about a Patriarchal Way of Life)," published in 1852.

2. Aksakov's article included a polemic with Sergey Mikhailovich Solovyov (1820-1879), Professor of History at Moscow University.

3. Konstantin Dmitrievich Kavelin (1818-1885), one of the leaders of the Westernizers.

4. Solovyov had posited a patriarchal way of life for the early Slavs; Aksakov and Turgenev believed that the commune [obshchina] had been the basis of social organization.

5. The Slavophiles read folk songs as positive expressions of conservative traits; Turgenev saw the songs as an expression of popular misery.

6. Vaska Buslayev, a warrior hero from Russian folklore. Kirsha Danilov, a Siberian Cossack, is the presumed compiler of the first collection of Russian folk epics.

Turgenev in his letter has in mind Vaska's death, which is preceded by his confrontation with a dead head. The head warns Vaska that his head too will soon lie on the Sorochinsk Hill.

7. "The Inn."

8. *Two Generations.* See letter 33.

Letter 42.

1. Ivan Fyodorovich Minitsky, a friend of Turgenev's who occasionally took care of business matters for him.

2. Minitsky had gotten a job as the supervisor of a boarding house at an Odessa secondary school.

3. In George Sand's *Consuelo* (1843) Satan is portrayed as the bearer of positive qualities.

4. An inaccurate quotation from Pushkin's "Songs of the Western Slavs," where the journey is a long one, not a difficult one.

5. *Two Generations.*

6. Turgenevo had been Turgenev's father's estate; at this point it belonged to Turgenev and his brother Nikolay.

7. *Notes of a Hunter.*

Letter 43.

1. *Two Generations.*
2. Evgeny Fyodorovich Korsh (1810-1897), publisher, member of the Herzen Circle in the 1840's, acquaintance of Turgenev's.
3. Afanasy Afanasievich Fet (Shenshin) (1820-1892), one of the major Russian poets of the 19th century. He and Turgenev soon became close friends, though by 1874 Fet's political conservatism so disturbed Turgenev that he broke off relations. A correspondence between the two was revived in 1878, but it never regained its earlier warmth and cordiality.
4. Turgenev had mailed the first chapter of *Two Generations* to Annenkov.
5. An inexact quotation from Pushkin's *Eugene Onegin.*

Letter 44.

1. See letter 40.
2. The work was published there in 1855.
3. In 1853 Prince Menshikov was sent to Turkey on a diplomatic mission. His behavior so outraged the Turks that they broke off relations, a situation that helped make a Turko-Russian war unavoidable.

Letter 45

1. Turgenev's unfinished novel *Two Generations.*
2. The line from Pushkin's "Winter Evening" actually reads: "Let's drink a toast, my good friend!"
3. Turgenev means Pushkin's cycle "Imitation of the Koran."

Letter 46.

1. St. Petersburg and Moscow.

Letter 47.

1. Turgenev for some reason felt that the name Michael had special significance for him.
2. The "colonial" refers to European craftsmen invited to settle in Russia.
3. The Aksakov family estate.
4. A reference to the Crimean War, which had begun only recently.
5. Evgeny Abramovich Baratynsky (1800-1844), one of the major Russian poets of the first half of the 19th century. His wife was Anastasiya Lvovna Baratynskaya, née Engelhardt (1804-1860).
6. Turgenev failed to complete this projected article.
7. *Notes of a Hunter.*
8. Needless to say, the literal translation given here fails utterly to capture the majesty of the Russian original.
9. K.S. Aksakov.

Letter 48.

1. Yelisey Yakovlevich Kolbasin (1831-1885), writer and historian of literature, a contributor to *The Contemporary,* and a friend of Turgenev's.

2. Mikhail Nikolaevich Musin-Pushkin (1795-1862), a trustee of the Petersburg Educational district and the chairman of the Petersburg Censorship Committee. He was the very symbol of literary reaction at the close of the reign of Nicholas I.

3. Dmitri Yakovlevich Kolbasin (1827-1890), Yelisey Yakovlevich's brother (see note 2), often took care of Turgenev's literary and business affairs for him.

4. Tolstoy's continuation of "Childhood."

5. Maria Nikolayevna Tolstaya (1830-1912), Lev Tolstoy's sister, married Count Valerian Petrovich Tolstoy (1813-1865). Turgenev saw Maria Tolstaya fairly often after 1854.

6. Turgenev adored chess.

7. Nikolay Markovich Fumeli, an Odessa publisher whose anthologies included Kolbasin's povests.

Letter 49.

1. Turgenev's play *A Month in the Country* was published in the first issue of *The Contemporary* for 1855.

2. Vasily Vladimirovich Karatayev (1830?-1859), a neighbor of Turgenev's. He was the author of the povest "A Moscow Family," which Turgenev was originally hopeful of getting published. The povest was never finished, but Turgenev later used its plot as the basis for his own novel *On the Eve*.

3. A private epithet for P.V. Annenkov, the format of whose collected works of Pushkin had displeased Nekrasov.

4. Zakhar Nikolayevich Mukhartov (d. 1876), an acquaintance of Turgenev's (he had an estate in Oryol Province), married Alexandra Nikolaevna Yukhantseva on November 6, 1854.

5. Alexander Vasilievich Druzhinin (824-1864) minor writer who served briefly as the main critic of *The Contemporary* (1855).

6. Anton Antonovich Delvig (1798-1831), a poet, was one of Pushkin's closest friends. His brother, whom Turgenev mentions, was Alexander Antonovich Delvig (1818-1882).

Letter 50.

1. Nikolay Mikhaylovich Shchepkin (1820-1886), a publisher, was the son of the actor Mikhail Semyonovich Shchepkin.

2. Early titles for the play *A Month in the Country* which had been printed, with many passages censored, in *The Contemporary*. See letter 49, note 1.

3. Ivan Mikhaylovich Snegiryov (1793-1868) was, in addition to other things, the censor for the Moscow Censorship Committee. He had persuaded the Committee to forbid *Two Sisters* for publication.

Letter 51.

1. Olga Alexandrovna Turgeneva (1836-1872), a distant relative of the author. Turgenev briefly considered marrying her (see letter 52).

2. "The Inn."

Letter 52.

1. Turgenev had a short flirtation with Olga Alexandrovna in 1854.

2. There were rumors that Turgenev was going to marry Olga Alexandrovna.

Letter 53.

1. Valerian Petrovich Tolstoy (1814-1865) and his wife Maria Nikolayevna.
2. Turgenev had departed from Moscow.
3. Jenny Vergani was the governess for the Tolstoys' children.

Letter 54.

1. "Yakov Pasynkov."

Letter 55.

1. Count Alexey Konstantinovich Tolstoy (1817-1875), poet, had influential ties at Court. He had played a role in the termination of Turgenev's exile at Spasskoye.
2. Yazykov had lost most of his money on doubtful enterprises and needed financial assistance.
3. Sofia Andreyevna Tolstaya, née Bakhmeteva, later Miller (1825-1895), wife of A.K. Tolstoy (her second husband), was an intelligent, educated woman who corresponded with Turgenev, Dostoevsky, Goncharov, Fet, and other writers.

Letter 56.

1. Count Vladimir Alexandrovich Sollogub (1814-1882), minor writer best remembered for *Tarantas*.
2. Turgenev's *Two Generations,* which remained unfinished.
3. Turgenev is referring to Aksakov's *Family Chronicle* and *Recollections,* which were published in Moscow in 1855.
4. Ivan Sergeyevich Aksakov.
5. Konstantin Sergeyevich Aksakov.

Letter 57.

1. The povest in question is an early version of *Rudin.*
2. Vladimir Nikolaevich Beketov (1809-1883), the censor for *The Contemporary* in the 1850s.
3. The story appeared in Krayevsky's *Notes of the Fatherland* in 1856.
4. Botkin was working on translations of various of Thomas Carlyle's essays.
5. Ivan Vasilievich Bazunov (1786-1866), a Moscow bookseller, was the Moscow commissionaire for *The Contemporary.*

Letter 58.

1. Druzhinin and Grigorovich.
2. The work in question is *Rudin.*
3. In "A.S. Pushkin and the Latest Edition of His Works" (published in *Library for Reading,* No. 4, 1855), Druzhinin argues that there is too little poetry in the works of Gogol's realist disciples, that Pushkin can serve as an antidote to the excessive realism of contemporary Russian literature. Druzhinin's article helped create the widespread opinion in the 1860's and 1870's that Pushkin was an art for art's sake poet, while Gogol was a critical realist. Both interpretations are deeply flawed.

4. Countess M.N. Tolstaya.

5. A quotation from Crébillon the Elder's tragedy *Rhadamiste et Zénobie* (1711).

6. The play in question is the farce *The School of Hospitality*. See reference to "home-grown farce" in letter 56.

7. Arlt's, a Moscow bookseller.

Letter 59.

1. The Belenkov brothers were Turgenev's neighbors. Turgenev had asked Annenkov to help arrange to have them enlisted in the nobility because of their heroic performance at the Defence of Sevastopol.

2. Feoktista Petrovna Volkova, a peasant girl who had become pregnant and accused Turgenev of being the father. He vowed that he was not the father and broke off relations with Volkova. Annenkov had suggested that Turgenev ask Kolbasin to take Volkova under his wing. See letters 82 and 183.

3. E. Narskaya, pseudonym of Natalya Petrovna Shalikova (1815-1878). The povest in question is "First Acquaintance with Society" [Pervoye znakomstvo so svetom].

4. Nikolay Gavrilovich Chernyshevsky (1828-1889), literary critic, author, radical martyr. The work cited is his M.A. dissertation, *The Esthetic Relation of Art to Reality*, in which he averred that art, at best, was a didactic imitation of reality. Turgenev was grossly offended by the work, which signalled the politico-aesthetic polarization of the late 1850s-1860s. Before his arrest in 1862 and exile in 1864, Chernyshevsky was for a short while editor of *The Contemporary*. His radical, anti-esthetic stance alienated Turgenev, Tolstoy, and others. See Evgenii Lampert, *Sons against Fathers* (Oxford, 1965).

5. The six-volume *Pushkin's Works* came out in 1855.

6. Turgenev is referring to his recent pseudo-romantic involvement with Maria Nikolaevna Tolstaya.

Letter 60.

1. See letter 59, note 3.

2. See letter 59, note 4. Chernyshevsky had published a review of his own book (in the sixth issue of *The Contemporary*, 1855) under the initials "N.P." Turgenev had mistakenly assumed that the author was Aleksander Nikolayevich Pypin (1833-1904), a well-known historian of literature.

3. Tolstoy's "Sevastopol in December" was published in the sixth issue of *The Contemporary* for 1855.

4. "Wood Felling" [Rubka lesa].

5. Tolstoy was in active service at the time.

6. Turgenev was mistaken about the alleged misprint. Nekrasov was a proponent of socially relevant poetry, not "pure" art.

7. Pavel Stepanovich Nakhimov (1802-1855), an Admiral, directed the defense of Sevastopol in 1854-1855.

8. Avdotya Yakovlevna Panayeva (1819-1893), Panayev's wife and Nekrasov's mistress. She wrote under the pseudonym "N. Stanitsky."

9. Panayev had written a very negative review of Leontiev's "Summer on a Farm," which was published in *Notes of the Fatherland*, No. 5, 1855.

10. Mikhail Larionovich Mikhailov (1829-1865), a radical author and critic, was a regular contributor to *The Contemporary*. He was arrested in 1861 and died in prison. The reference to his haircut and Turgenev's reaction testify to the popularity of long hair among Russian radicals of the 1850s-60s.

Letter 61.

1. See Letter 59, note 3.
2. See Letter 59, note 4.
3. *Rudin.*
4. Nekrasov has asked Turgenev to select some poems by Burns and provide Nekrasov with prose translations of them so that he could try turning them into rhymed translations.
5. Maria Vasilievna Belinskaya, née Orlova (1812-1890), the critic Belinsky's widow. Belinskaya had lent money to Turgenev when he was on his way to exile at Spasskoye.

Letter 62.

1. Sevastopol had fallen.
2. The Prussian Army was defeated at Jena in 1806.
3. K.S. Aksakov's *About Russian Verbs* was published in Moscow in 1855.
4. Ivan Sergeyevich Aksakov.
5. Nikolay Vasilievich Kireyevsky (1797-1870), wealthy landowner and devoted hunter.
6. M.N. Katkov's *Russian Messenger* [Russky vestnik], the first issue of which came out in January, 1856.

Letter 63.

1. The original of this letter is in French.
2. As long as the Crimean War was going on, Turgenev could not think of going to France.
3. Mme Harang, the director of the *pension* where Pauline Turgeneva was a student.
4. Peace was concluded in March 1856. On July 21/August 2, 1856, Turgenev left Petersburg for Western Europe.

Letter 64.

1. The novel is probably *Two Generations,* never finished.
2. Ye. Ya. Kolbasin's "Academy Lane."

Letter 65.

1. Maria Nikolayevna Tolstaya.
2. After the fall of Sevastopol Tolstoy and his battery were transferred first to Kermenchuk, then to Fotsal.
3. N.N. Tolstoy, Lev's brother.

Letter 66.

1. The Turkish fortress of Kars surrendered to Russian forces in November, 1855.
2. Nadezhda Nikolayevna is probably the Polish woman mentioned earlier in the letter.

Letter 67.

1. Lev Tolstoy.
2. Konstantin Alexandrovich Islavin (1827-1903) a good friend of Lev Tolstoy's, the uncle of his future wife, Sofia Andreyevna Behrs.

3. Edward Ivanovich Totleben (1818-1884), a military engineer, had directed the construction of fortifications at Sevastopol.

4. Apollon Nikolayevich Maykov (1821-1897), a noted poet of his age. Posterity has not been particularly kind to his reputation.

5. Boris Semyonovich Yakobi (1801-1874), a distinguished physicist and inventor, had probably made untoward remarks at the dinner because of his displeasure with the military establishment, which had refused to adopt several of his inventions.

6. Angelina Bosio (1824-1859) sang four seasons in Petersburg. During the fourth season she caught a cold and died. Her tragically short career continues to fascinate Russians. See letter 103.

7. Yelisey Yakovlevich Kolbasin.

8. Ivan Ivanovich Martynov (1771-1833), philologist, publisher, and erudite translator.

9. Nikolay Nikolayevich Tolstoy (1823-1860), Lev Tolstoy's brother, an author in his own right. His *Hunting in the Caucasus* was highly esteemed by Turgenev, Nekrasov, and others.

Letter 68.

1. Yekaterina Alexeyevna Ladyzhenskaya, née Duklu (1828-1891), a writer who published her works under the pseudonym S. Vakhnovskaya.

2. Scholars have been unable to ascertain who the Gagarina in question is.

3. Alexey Nikolayevich Ostrovsky (1823-1886), a major and prolific Russian playwright. Though hardly known in the West, his plays retain a central position in the Soviet repertory. Janáček's opera *Katya Kabanova* is based on Ostrovsky's best-known play, *The Storm* [Groza].

4. Maria Fyodorovna Shtakenshneider (1811-1892).

5. See letter 56 on this "home-grown farce."

6. The Grand Princess Maria Nikolayevna (1819-1876), was Alexander II's sister and the President of the Academy of Arts. The performance in question took place at her palace.

Letter 69.

1. Lavrenty Lvovich Dobrovolsky (1822-1862), secretary of the office of the Minister of Popular Enlightenment.

2. Yegor Petrovich Kovalevsky (1811-1868) traveller, writer, and public figure.

3. The Minister of Popular Enlightenment signed the release for "Mumu" May 31, 1856. The story, one of Turgenev's most bathetic, portrays a despotic serf owner, probably modelled on his own mother.

4. Ivan Alexandrovich Goncharov (1812-1891), the author of *A Common Story* [Obyknovennaya istoriya] and *Oblomov,* among many other works, was also a censor. He and Turgenev were originally on very good terms, but Goncharov later became obsessed with the notion that Turgenev was stealing his ideas, and by logical extension, his works. For a full description of this bizarre abberation on Goncharov's part, see Vsevolod Setschkareff, *Ivan Goncharov* (Wurzburg, 1974).

Letter 70.

1. Pavel Nikolayevich Ignatiev (1797-1879), an Adjutant-General.

2. Princess Olga Stepanovna Odoyevskaya (1797-1872), the wife of the writer Vladimir Fyodorovich Odoyevsky (1803-1869).

3. Count Sergey Stepanovich Lanskoy (1787-1862), Minister of the Interior from 1855 to 1861.

4. The Tolstoys in question are Valerian Petrovich and Maria Nikolayevna. The "relative" is Ye. Ya. Kolbasin.

5. Alexey Ivanovich Davydov was a bookseller and publisher who ran the Petersburg office for subscriptions to *The Contemporary*.

6. Turgenev is referring to the second volume of S.M. Solovyov's *History of Russia Since Ancient Times*.

7. The journal *For Light Reading* was published by Davydov. See note 5.

8. The story in question is Kolbasin's "Academy Lane."

9. Porfiry Timofeyevich Kudryashev, Turgenev's illegitimate half-brother. He served as a doctor in the Mtsensk District.

Letter 71.

1. *A History of Greece* by George Grot (1794-1871), the English historian, was published in 1845-1855.

2. Konstantin Sergeyevich Aksakov.

3. The *mir* was the commune which stood at the center of Russian peasant life and agriculture. Individual peasant families were responsible not so much to themselves as to the *mir*. Slavophiles such as K.S. Aksakov saw the *mir* as a potential model for all Russian political and social life. Turgenev, who was skeptical about the supposed virtues of the Russian peasantry, was never in favor of anything other than a Western socio-political model for Russia.

4. Prince Viktor Illarionovich Vasilchikov (1820-1878) headed a commission to expose abuses in the commissaries of the Southern and Crimean Armies. Vasilchikov sent Ivan Sergeyevich Aksakov to the Crimea to conduct a personal investigation.

5. Turgenev quotes, somewhat inaccurately, two lines from one of Ivan Sergeyevich Aksakov's poems.

Letter 72.

1. Countess Yelizaveta Yegorovna Lambert, née Kankrina (1821-1883), the wife of I.K. Lambert. An educated woman of great refinement, she and Turgenev conducted a lively, lengthy correspondence. Turgenev's letters to Lambert generally find him at his most philosophical; many of his letters to her are in fact keys to Turgenev's works. All in all, however, one cannot help but conclude that Lambert was rather a prig and ultimately a source of irritation to Turgenev.

2. These are references to Pushkin's *Eugene Onegin,* in which the ingenuous, but not-so-simple Tatyana, who lives in the country, falls in love with the wordly-wise and world-weary Onegin.

3. Lambert had mistakenly thought that the woman in question was Pauline Viardot.

4. In the 19th century many upper-class Russians, especially women, knew French better than they did their "native" language. This is but one measure of the abyss that separated the privileged elite from the broad masses.

5. Lambert had written Turgenev that she feared Pushkin because reading him aroused dark, stormy passions in her.

Letter 73.

1. Turgenev had sent Herzen his story "Faust" for the latter's critical comments.

2. Herzen had moved to Putney, a London suburb.

3. *The Polar Star* was a historico-literary journal published by Herzen (abroad) from 1855-1868. It gave special attention to documents relating to the Decembrist movement.

Letter 74.

1. Nikolay Nikolayevich Turgenev.

2. See letter 75.

3. A quotation from Pushkin.

4. The "Adjutant" is the Tolstoys' son, Nikolay Valerianovich (1850-1879). Olga Petrovna Okhotnitskaya was probably the Tolstoys' housekeeper. Nastya was another servant.

5. Tolstoy was at Yasnaya Polyana, his family estate, until the very end of 1856.

6. Valerian Petrovich Tolstoy.

7. Katkov, the editor of *Russian Messenger,* apparently envious that Lev Tolstoy was publishing in *The Contemporary,* was filling the air with rather nasty complaints and reproaches addressed in Lev Tolstoy's direction.

8. Katkov mistakenly thought that Turgenev's "Faust," published in *The Contemporary,* was the story "Phantoms," which Turgenev had promised to *The Russian Messenger.* Turgenev had received word that *The Russian Messenger* was planning to "expose" Turgenev by publishing the letter in which he promised "Phantoms" to *The Russian Messenger.*

Letter 75.

1. *The Cossacks.*

2. Nikolay Nikolaevich Tolstoy's "Hunting in the Caucasus" was published in *The Contemporary* in 1857.

3. "Faust," which Tolstoy did like.

Letter 76.

1. The complete text of this letter is not extant.

2. Stepan Semyonovich Dudyshkin (1820-1866), a critic for *Notes of the Fatherland.* He and Turgenev were never particularly close.

Letter 77.

1. Maria Nikolayevna Tolstaya.

2. Nikolay Nikolayevich Tolstoy.

3. The Viardots.

4. What follows are Turgenev's reactions to Chernyshevsky's series of articles, "Essays on the Gogolian Period in Russian Literature."

5. Annenkov had written Turgenev and expressed his dissatisfaction with Chernyshevsky's articles.

6. Varvara Valerianovna Tolstoya, later Nagornova (1850-1921), the daughter of Maria Nikolayevna and Valerian Petrovich Tolstoy.

Letter 78.

1. In 1856, Turgenev, Tolstoy, Grigorovich, and Ostrovsky had all agreed to publish future works only in *The Contemporary,* which was under Nekrasov's proprietorship.

2. Turgenev probably means Chernyshevsky's approval of Belinsky, if not his general insistence on a radical, socially-conscious Russian literature.

3. Turgenev is referring here to Krayevsky's exploitation of Belinsky.

4. Druzhinin's article is "Criticism of the Gogolian Period in Russian Literature and Our Attitude toward It." The article is a reaction to Chernyshevsky's series of articles on the so-called Gogol period.

5. Alexander Alexandrovich Bestuzhev-Marlinsky (1797-1837), one of the most popular Russian prose writers of the first quarter of the 19th century. His stories reveal the influence of the French *école frénétique* and abound in Romantic clichés and frenzied plots.

6. In "Literary Reminiscences" (1834) Belinsky had proclaimed the then enormously popular Bestuzhev-Marlinsky a worthless writer. History has largely confirmed Belinsky's testy evaluation.

7. Vladimir Grigorievich Benediktov (1807-1873), an enormously popular third-rate poet whose reputation, like Marlinsky's, was dealt a death-blow by Belinsky.

8. Turgenev here is arguing for a more socially-conscious Russian literature.

9. The former story is "A Meeting with a Moscow Acquaintance in a Military Detachment," the latter is "A Landowner's Morning."

Letter 79.

1. The pseudonym comes from the way Karuzov, the hero of Kolbasin's "In the Country and in Petersburg" (1855), laughs.

Letter 80.

1. Turgenev is referring to M. Du Camp's *Les Chants modernes* (1855).

2. Lecomte de Lisle.

3. Henri Delaveau (?-1862), French critic who translated Turgenev and Herzen; he wrote articles about Nekrasov, Turgenev, *et al.* for *Revue des deux Mondes* (1854-1858).

4. *The Childhood of Bagrov's Grandson* was published in 1858.

5. Prince Nikolay Ivanovich Trubetskoy (1807-1874), a liberal Slavophile who opposed the Tsarist regime, left Russia in the 1850's and settled in Paris. He figures as "Prince Coco" in Turgenev's *Smoke.*

6. Konstantin Sergeyevich Aksakov.

7. Prince Alexander Illarionovich Vasilchikov (1818-1881), liberal economist and public figure. His brother, Viktor Illarionovich, had headed an investigatory commission in which Ivan Sergeyevich Aksakov took part. See letter 71, note 4.

8. Ivan Vasilievich Kireyevsky (1806-1856) and Peter Vasilievich Kireyevsky (1808-1856), Slavophiles and friends of the Aksakovs, both died in 1856.

Letter 81.

1. Maria Nikolayevna Tolstaya.

2. There were rumors in Russia that Louis Viardot had died and that Turgenev would soon marry Pauline Viardot.

3. Nikolay Nikolayevich Tolstoy.

4. Tolstoy in later life rarely missed a chance to dismiss Shakespeare as a greatly over-rated author.

5. The woman was Princess Yekaterina Nikolayevna Meshcherskaya (1838-1874), the man—Heinrich Oppenheim (1819-1880), at that time a radical who knew Herzen. He eventually became one of Bismarck's staunchest supporters.

Letter 82.

1. *The Hanger-On* was published under the title *Another's Bread* in *The Contemporary*, No. 3, 1857.

2. Podlinsky, a university friend of Ye. Ya. Kolbasin's.

3. The "relative" is Ye. Ya. Kolbasin, who had promised to send Turgenev monthly reports on literary and socio-political life in Russia.

4. Kolbasin's povest "Academy Lane" was eventually published in *The Library for Reading*, No. 8, 1858.

5. In a letter of February 7/19, 1857, Ye. Ya. Kolbasin wrote that people were not rushing to buy Turgenev's book, though everyone was waiting for *Notes of a Hunter*.

6. Feoktista Petrovna Volkova was a peasant girl with whom Turgenev had been intimate. He gave her financial support before her marriage and later when she became a widow. See letters 59, 183.

Letter 83.

1. See letter 74, note 8.

2. Mikhail Yevgrafovich Saltykov (pseud. N. Shchedrin) (1826-1889), a radical publicist and exposé author whose best-known work is *The Golovlyov Family*—a stark indictment of the gentry.

3. Turgenev, Tolstoy, Ostrovsky, and Grigorovich had obligated themselves to publish all their works exclusively in *The Contemporary* from 1857 on. The above-mentioned authors all broke with *The Contemporary* in the early 1860s, when that journal's editorial board became radicalized and anti-estheticized.

4. Turgenev did not carry out this intention to translate *Don Quixote*.

5. Botkin's article about Fet's poetry was published in *The Contemporary*, No. 1, 1857.

Letter 84.

1. Count Vasily Alexeyevich Bobrinsky (1804-1874), a wealthy and influential land-owner.

2. Stepan Petrovich Shevyryov (1806-1864), professor at Moscow University, arch-conservative figure.

3. Alexander Dmitrievich Chertkov (1789-1858), the Moscow Marshal of the Nobility from 1846-1855. An archeologist and historian, he possessed a huge collection of books on Russian history.

4. The Iverskaya Chapel (torn down in the 1930s) stood near Red Square in Moscow. The people who gathered around it during the 19th century would have included drunkards, bums, and generally unsavory types.

5. K.S. Aksakov's article on Russian folk warrior heroes appeared in *Russian Conversation*, No. 4, 1856.

6. Robert Peel had recently made a series of anti-Russian speeches.

7. Shevyryov's wife was illegitimate.

8. The first Count Bobrinsky was the illegitimate son of Catherine II.

9. Count Arseny Andreyevich Zakrevsky (1783-1865), the Governor-General of Moscow from 1848-1859.

10. Zakrevsky did indeed telegraph Alexander II.

11. The subject under discussion is Princess E.R. Dashkova's memoirs of Catherine the Great, which were published in Russian translation from English in London in 1859. Herzen wrote the introduction to the volume. The phrase in question was the characterization of governmental power as "native mother, executioner, and sergeant."

Letter 85.

1. Vladimir Nikitich Kashperov (1827-1894), a composer of whom Turgenev thought highly, was M.I. Glinka's pupil.

2. Mikhail Ivanovich Glinka (1804-1857), the composer of the operas *Ruslan and Ludmila* and *Ivan Susanin,* generally considered the father of Russian music. The latter years of his life were not very productive, a circumstance which Turgenev mentions in the present letter.

3. Pyotr Mikhailovich Gribovsky, a landowner acquaintance of Annenkov's and Turgenev's.

4. Stolevsky, an acquaintance of Kashperov's, Turgenev's, and Annenkov's.

Letter 86.

1. Annenkov's comment on "The First Day" of "Journey to the Woodland."

2. Annenkov had written that I.I. Panayev had developed a cancerous lip.

3. An allusion to Stanza XXXVIII of Chapter II of Pushkin's *Eugene Onegin.*

4. The Russian word *sglazit'* has no English equivalent, but means to bring on bad luck by boasting of good fortune or wishing one good luck.

5. An allusion to a poem by A.F. Merzlyakov.

6. The first part of Annenkov's "N.V. Stankevich" appeared in the February, 1857 issue of *The Russian Messenger.*

7. The continuation of Saltykov-Shchedrin's *Provincial Sketches* had appeared in those issues.

8. Turgenev is referring to "The First Day" and "Second Day" of his "Journey to the Woodland." A third day was never written.

9. Daniel Douglas Hume, an American spiritualist and medium who began a successful tour of Europe in 1855. In 1856 he went to Russia.

10. Olga Alexandrovna Turgeneva.

Letter 87.

1. See letter 85.

2. Nikolay Alexandrovich Melgunov (1804-1867), a writer and music critic who was especially close to Herzen until 1861.

3. Turgenev means that he doubts Melgunov will be able to pay back the debt.

4. Johann Schönlein (1793-1864), a noted German physician of the time.

Letter 88.

1. The permission was granted February 7/19, 1859.

2. Discussion about the rights to the second edition continued into 1858. The rights ultimately remained with Turgenev.

3. Herzen had sent Turgenev a letter for Nekrasov which he threatened to publish in *The Bell* if Turgenev could not arrange delivery.

4. The Grand Duke Konstantin Nikolayevich (1827-1892), a liberal reformer whom Herzen wanted to attack in *The Bell*. Turgenev felt such an attack to be unjustified.

5. Herzen was irritated with Nekrasov on account of the so-called "Ogaryov Affair," a very messy tale that concluded with Ogaryov's inheritance being appropriated by N.S. Shanshiev and A. Ya. Panayeva. For details of the scandal see Ya. Z. Chernyak,*Ogarev, Nekrasov, Gertsen, Chernyshevskii v spore ob ogarevskom nasledstve* (M-L, 1933).

In his remarks about "beating one's own people" Turgenev is referring to Herzen's threat to publish an exposé of the "Ogaryov Affair" and what he saw as Nekrasov's role in it.

6. Lang was a London gunsmith. Herzen had taken care of money that Turgenev owed both Delaveau and Lang.

Letter 89.

1. Turgenev did go to Baden. Tolstoy, instead of travelling with Turgenev, went home to Russia to help sort out family difficulties. See letter 90.

Letter 90.

1. See letter 89.

2. The later reference to a doctor's instructions and pills suggests that the omitted word or words describe a disease or illness, the exact nature of which Soviet modesty chooses not to disclose.

3. Maria Nikolayevna Tolstaya.

4. Nikolay Mikhailovich Smirnov (1807-1870), the governor of Kaluga and later of Petersburg. His wife, Alexandra Osipovna Smirnova (1809-1882), was the prototype for Darya Mikhailovna Lasunskaya in *Rudin*.

5. Tolstoy's "Lucerne" (1857).

Letter 91.

1. That letter seems not to be extant.

2. See letter 88.

3. Nikolay Nikolayevich Turgenev.

4. This entire paragraph refers to Turgenev's relations with Pauline Viardot. Nekrasov was against Turgenev's going to Courtavenel to see Viardot.

5. "Asya."

6. Turgenev has in mind the quantitatively poor performance of Grigorovich, Ostrovsky, Tolstoy, and himself, who had bound themselves to submit their contributions to *The Contemporary.*

Letter 92.

1. Belinsky's widow was opposed to the project, so Nekrasov's plan was never realized. Turgenev's "Recollections of Belinsky" were published in *The Messenger of Europe* in 1869.

2. The reference is to the seventh supplementary volume of Annenkov's edition of *Pushkin's Works.* The volume came out in 1857.

Letter 93.

1. Annenkov has asked Turgenev to write some letters about his Parisian and English acquaintances for Korsh's new journal *Atheneum*. Turgenev wrote only one such letter, "From Abroad. The First Letter," which was published in *Atheneum*, No. 6, 1858.

2. Alexander Andreyevich Ivanov (1806-1858), well-known Russian painter who lived the greater part of his life in Rome. He spent more than 20 years working on his canvas "Christ's Appearance to the People"—the work to which Turgenev makes reference here.

3. Karl Pavlovich Bryullov (1799-1852) was a well-known Russian painter of a Romantic tendency. Like A.A. Ivanov, he lived in Italy many years. Turgenev disliked his work intensely, comparing it to Marlinsky's prose.

4. Prince Grigory Grigorievich Gagarin (1810-1893) had recently (in 1853) painted the Zion Cathedral in Tbilisi in the Byzantine style.

5. Yevgraf Semyonovich Sorokin (1821-1892), painter, became an academician in 1861 and was made a professor of historical painting in 1878.

6. Turgenev mentions this in his work "A Trip to Albano and Frascati (A Memoir of A.A. Ivanov)."

7. Olga Alexandrovna Turgeneva.

8. Prince Vladimir Alexandrovich Cherkassky (1824-1878) and his wife Princess Ekaterina Alexeevna Cherkasskaya (1825-1888). The Prince was a noted liberal figure, his wife a writer of children's stories.

9. Turgenev has in mind the seventh volume of Annenkov's *Pushkin's Works* (see letter 92, note 2), his book *N.V. Stankevich: His Correspondence and Biography* (M. 1857) and Annenkov's "Reminiscences of Gogol," the second part of which appeared in *Library for Reading*, no. 11, 1857.

10. See letter 90 for the details of Tolstoy's sudden return to Russia.

11. The story "Lucerne."

12. *Römische Geschichte*, vols I-III, by Theodor Mommsen (1817-1903) was published in 1854-1856.

13. Turgenev was worried that Bazunov had lost money on Turgenev's *Povests and Stories* (Petersburg, 1856). As Nekrasov and Annenkov were quick to point out, the volume had sold well and Bazunov had made a profit.

Letter 94.

1. V.P. Botkin.

2. As many of Turgenev's letters for 1856-1857 show, those years were a time of crisis in his artistic and personal life.

3. Turgenev discusses the theme of Russian ennui in his "From Abroad. The First Letter."

4. Turgenev has in mind rumors about preparations for the abolition of serfdom in Russia. Turgenev's hopes were premature, but by the beginning of 1860 he had transferred his peasants at Spasskoye from corvée to quitrent and hired labor.

6. Sofia Yakovlevna Verigina, née Bulgari (d. 1898), a friend of Lambert's and an acquaintance of Turgenev's.

7. Lydia Yevreinova, a children's writer.

Letter 95.

1. The original of this letter is in French.
2. Princess Anna Andreyevna Trubetskaya, née Gudoviçh (1819-1882), the wife of Prince N.I. Trubetskoy.
3. Pauline Viardot was on a concert tour of Germany.
4. Nikolay Sergeyevich Turgenev.

Letter 96.

1. Turgenev means Herzen and Ogaryov's *December 14, 1825 and the Emperor Nikolay,* an analysis of M.A. Korf's *The Ascension to the Throne of Nikolay I* (pub. 1857), a pro-monarchist treatment of the Decembrist uprising.
2. *Charivari,* a French satirical magazine.
3. Preparations for the abolition of serfdom.
4. Turgenev is referring to three rescripts of 1857 which gave the first notice of Alexander I's intentions of abolishing serfdom.
5. Herzen had published in *The Bell* a large exposé article on Alexey Alexandrovich Timashev-Bering (1818-1893), the head of the Third Department (i.e., secret police) and infamous for his cruelty.
6. Turgenev is mistaken. Timashev-Bering was not forcibly retired until 1858, when he was replaced by A.I. Krapotkin, rather than Alexey Petrovich Akhmatov (1818-1870), who did indeed become General Procurator of the Holy Synod in 1862.
Nikolay Pavlovich is Emperor Nikolay I.
7. Herzen published both *The Bell,* an emigré journal of contemporary events, and *The Polar Star,* a historico-literary journal named in honor of the Decembrists.
"The Zaltsmann Case" was published in the January 1858 issue of *The Bell.* The materials for the case, an exposé of Prince L.V. Kochubey, were transmitted to Herzen by Turgenev.
8. Alexander Mikhaylovich Geodonov (1790-1867), the Director of the Imperial Theaters from 1833 until 1858.
9. Turgenev is referring to his "A Journey to the Woodland."
10. The painter A.A. Ivanov.
11. Alexander II.
12. Herzen had written to tell Turgenev that his (Turgenev's) portrait was on sale in Russia.

Letter 97.

1. Frank (Franck?), a Paris Bookseller.
2. The sale of Herzen's publications was prohibited in Paris for the first two weeks in May, 1858.
3. Herzen's *Letters from Italy* were published in book editions in London in 1854 and in 1858.
4. Turgenev means affairs back home in Russia.
5. Vladimir Pavlovich Titov (1807-1891), the tutor to heir-apparent Nikolay Alexandrovich, was replaced by Avgust Teodor Grimm (1805-1878). Konstantin Dmitrievich Kavelin, who had been the heir's teacher, was removed from that position. Grigory Alexeyevich Shcherbatov (1819-1881) retired from his position as Trustee of the Petersburg Educational District. Ye. G. Kovalevsky had just been appointed Minister of National Enlightenment. All these actions represented a reaction to Alexander II's plans to abolish serfdom.

6. Alexander II.

7. Turgenev has in mind the forthcoming negotiations with his own serfs in connection with the coming liberation.

Letter 98.

1. Alexey Nikolayevich Apukhtin (1840-1893), one of the more popular Russian poets of the late nineteenth century. His reputation has suffered in the twentieth century, when he might have been quite forgotten had Tchaikovsky not set several of Apukhtin's poems to music.

2. Turgenev seems to mean that he found his own, unique voice only with *Notes of a Hunter*, the first sketch of which appeared in 1847, though his first major published work was the long poem *Parasha* (1843).

Letter 99.

1. When Turgenev was arrested and confined to Spasskoye for publishing the Gogol obituary, he sent two petitions (in 1852 and 1853) to Alexander Nikolayevich, then heir to the throne. Turgenev was convinced that his relatively brief tenure of confinement was the result of Alexander's personal sympathy for him.

2. Jósefat Ohrysko (1826-1890), an activist in the Polish liberation movement, began publishing the Polish-language newspaper *The Word* [Słowo] in Petersburg in 1859. At the end of February of that year, because of letters published by Joachim Lelewel, one of the emigré leaders of the Polish liberation movement, the newspaper was closed and its editor incarcerated in the Peter-Paul Fortress.

3. Turgenev's letter to Alexander II went unanswered.

Letter 100.

1. Nil Andreyevich Osnovsky (1819-1871) a writer and publisher.

2. N.A. Dobrolyubov's review of *Various Works of S. Aksakov,* published in *The Contemporary* (no. 2, 1859), was harshly critical of Aksakov's book.

3. Turgenev published his article "Hamlet and Don Quixote" in the first issue of *The Contemporary* for 1860, but that was his last work published there.

4. See Letter 99, note 2.

5. Vladimir Grigorievich Kartashevsky (d. 1876), a Petersburg civil servant whose mother, Nadezhda Timofeyevna Kartashevskaya (née Aksakova), was S.T. Aksakov's sister.

Letter 101.

1. The original of this letter is in French.

2. Clara Turgeneva, née Viaris (1814-1891), Nikolay Ivanovich Turgenev's wife. Clara Turgenev took a lively interest in Pauline Turgeneva's upbringing and education.

Letter 102.

1. The reference may be to F.I. Lobanov.

2. The Oryol Province Committee for Formulating Plans to Better the Life of Serfs was organized in 1858. Turgenev was not included in the Committee.

3. The new work in question is *On the Eve.*

4. *A Nest of Gentlefolk* had been received by the public very enthusiastically.

5. Countess Lambert oversaw a number of charities in Petersburg. The 75 rubles mentioned by Turgenev were presumably to go to some charitable cause.

Letter 103.

1. Goncharov was consumed by the notion that Turgenev had taken ideas for *Nest of Gentlefolk* and *On the Eve* from Goncharov's *The Precipice,* a work then in progress. By 1860 rumors of Turgenev's "plagiarism" were so rife in Petersburg that Turgenev turned the matter over to a court of arbitration, which ruled that any similarities between Turgenev's and Goncharov's works were purely coincidental.

2. Goncharov had reported to Turgenev a certain teacher's remarks to the effect that Turgenev's forte was the sketch, not the novel.

3. Goncharov accomplished a great deal of work on *Oblomov* while taking the baths at Marienbad in 1857.

4. Yekaterina Pavlovna Maykova, née Kalita (1836-1920) was a sort of literary assistant to Goncharov.

5. Count Grigory Alexandrovich Kushelev-Bezborodko (1832-1870), the publisher of the journal *The Russian Word.*

6. Pyotr Lukich Solyanikov, a civil servant and a translator.

7. Mitrofanushka is the preternaturally stupid protagonist in D.I. Fonvizin's play *The Adolescent* (1781).

Letter 104.

1. Turgenev obviously has in mind his relationship with Viardot.

2. "Siren," "tiger," and "polar bear" were nicknames given to Turgenev at various times.

3. Turgenev was working on *On the Eve.*

Letter 105.

1. Chernyshevsky visited Herzen in July, 1859, and Herzen did *not* like him.

2. Alexander Ivanovich Vegelin (d. 1860) was not actually a Decembrist, but the Decembrists considered him one of their own because of his imprisonment and exile in 1826 for membership in secret societies.

3. Prince Sergey Grigorievich Volkonsky (1788-1865), a Decembrist who returned from Siberia in 1857 after amnesty was declared in 1856.

4. Nikolay Yakovlevich Rostovtsev (1831-1897), a friend of Turgenev's and Herzen's.

5. Natalya Alexeyevna Ogaryova (1829-1913), Ogaryov's second wife, later Herzen's common-law wife. The threesome comprised one of nineteenth-century Russia's several famous ménages.

Letter 106.

1. Maria Alexandrovna Markovich, née Vilinskaya (1834-1907), an author who wrote under the pseudonym Marko Vovchok. Turgenev was a great admirer of her works, which were written in Ukrainian and Russian.

2. Vasily Mikhailovich Belozersky (1823-1899), a Ukranian activist and author who belonged to a circle of Ukrainian writers who lived in Petersburg. Afanasy Vasilievich Markovich (1822-1867) was a Ukrainian folklorist, ethnographer, and activist. His son by

Maria Alexandrovna, Bogdan Afanasievich Markovich (1853-1915), was a Populist, especially active in the 1870s and 1880s.

Letter 107.

1. Darya Ivanovna Yazdovskaya (d. 1883) was a widow who lived with the N.N. Tyutchevs and who occasionally undertook domestic assignments for Turgenev. Turgenev's letters to her are consistently bantering in tone.
2. Ruzanov owned a pharmacy in Petersburg.

Letter 108.

1. Count Alexander Dmitrievich Bludov (1817-1889) served as secretary at the Russian Embassy in London.

Letter 109.

1. Sergey Timofeyevich Aksakov died April 30/May 12, 1859.
2. *On the Eve.*
3. Turgenev is referring to *Russian Conversation,* a Moscow Slavophile journal.
4. Nikolay Nikolayevich Turgenev.
5. The *mir* was the peasant collective or commune. After the abolition of serfdom the land passed into the hands of the serfs only indirectly, through the intermediary of the commune among whose responsibilities were the division of land, collection of taxes, and so on. Most historians consider that the abolition of serfdom as much as left the peasants enserfed to the commune. Thus, it is hardly surprising that Turgenev's peasants were not eager to see the *mir* elevated to the status of an administrative body.
6. Olga Semyonovna Aksakova, née Zaplatina (1793-1878), S.T. Aksakov's wife.
7. Alexey Stepanovich Khomyakov (1804-1860), philosopher, theologian, and poet, was one of the leaders of the Slavophiles.
8. Alexey Andreyevich Yelagin (d. 1846) and Avdotya Petrovna Yelagina, née Yushkova (1789-1877) had a largely Slavophile salon in Moscow from the 1830s to the 1850s.

Letter 110.

1. The original of this letter is in French.
2. Didie was the nickname for the Viardot's second daughter, Claudie.

Letter 111.

1. *On the Eve.*

Letter 112.

1. Turgenev probably means his then unfinished article "Hamlet and Don Quixote," which he had promised to *The Contemporary.*
2. Lambert had confused two parallel, but not synonymous forms of the verb "to wander." Russian verbs of motion are notoriously sticky.
3. Gluck's opera *Orfeo* was produced in Paris, November 18, 1859 especially for Pauline Viardot, for whom the role of Orfeo was an enormous personal triumph. Turgenev was of course interested in the production and the opera, which may explain the earlier reference to "beloved green meadows," i.e., the Elysian Fields.

Letter 113.

1. Turgenev is referring to Leontiev's "Second Marriage," published in *Library for Reading,* No. 4 (1860).

2. Leontiev took Turgenev's advice in this matter, and it is indeed as an essayist that Leontiev is remembered today.

3. Baron Dmitry Grigorievich Rozen, an acquaintance of Turgenev's. Leontiev was then living on Rozen's estate as his personal doctor.

Letter 114.

1. The article was Dobrolyubov's review of Turgenev's *On the Eve.* The review was indeed published in *The Contemporary* (No. 3, 1860) and it led to Turgenev's breaking with the journal.

Dobrolyubov's article "When Will the Real Day Come" suggested that in the subtext of *On the Eve* was a call to revolution. Turgenev was horrified and disgusted by Dobrolyubov's interpretation. For an English version of the article see Ralph Matlaw, ed., *Belinsky, Chernyshevsky, and Dobrolyubov: Selected Criticism* (New York, 1962).

Letter 115.

1. Ivan Petrovich Borisov (1832-1871), one of Turgenev's neighbors in the Oryol Province. Borisov was married to Fet's sister, N.A. Shenshina.

2. Andrey Ivanovich Denier (1820-1892), a Petersburg photographer.

3. One of Turgenev's dogs.

4. Kalna was a summer house on Turgenev's estate, Spasskoye, that Fet was considering buying. Nothing came of the idea.

Letter 116.

1. Lambert responded that Zgurskaya was too young for the institutes.

Letter 117.

1. Annenkov, in Italy at the time, had very nearly purchased a ticket for a coach that was later attacked by bandits who shot one of the passengers.

2. Yakov Petrovich Polonsky (1819-1898), minor poet whose best verses on gypsy themes have held their own in the twentieth century. His first wife, Yelena Vasilievna Polonskaya, née Ustyuzhskaya, died July 8/20, 1860. His son had recently died, too.

3. Varvara Yakovlevna Kartashevskaya, née Makarova (1832-1902), played hostess to a group of Ukrainian writers and thinkers who used her home as a gathering place. Turgenev often dropped in on the group.

4. Nikolay Yakovlevich Makarov (1828-1892), V.Y. Kartashevskaya's brother, a journalist who belonged to the group of writers mentioned in Note 3.

5. Kilian, presumably a German doctor who prescribed waters for Kartashevskaya and her brother.

Letter 118.

1. The original of this letter is in French.

2. The reference is to Anna Nikolayevna Turgeneva (1857-1860), N.I. Turgenev's youngest daughter. See following note.

3. Nikolay Ivanovich Turgenev (1789-1879), a Decembrist who lived in Paris from 1824 on. He was the author of a number of works on Russian social history.

4. Delioux taught music at the school where Pauline studied.

Letter 119.

1. Turgenev uses the word *refleksiya,* which has no adequate English equivalent. It combines the notions of torturous self-analysis and excessive pondering over philosophical problems.

2. When Louis XIV complained that he had no teeth, one of the members of his court flattered him with the phrase that Turgenev cites.

3. Turgenev later used most of the two preceding sentences to characterize Pavel Kirsanov in Chapter VII of *Fathers and Sons.*

4. Turgenev spent the winter in Paris.

5. Fyodor Ivanovich Tyutchev (1803-1873), one of the three or four greatest Russian poets of the 19th century. Turgenev here quotes Tyutchev's poem "Don't reason, don't fuss."

6. Maria Petrovna Fet, née Botkina (1828-1894).

Letter 120.

1. Since Pauline Turgeneva was illegitimate, she would not have had full rights under the law in Russia.

2. Yakov Ivanovich Rostovtsev (1803-1860) had a very checkered career. In his youth he had denounced the Decembrists to Nikolay I. In later life he headed Alexander II's Commission for the Abolition of Serfdom.

3. This is the first reference in Turgenev's correspondence to plans for *Fathers and Sons.*

Letter 121.

1. The reference is to the draft plan for the Society for the Dissemination of Literacy and Primary Education; it was drawn up by Turgenev (with the help of Annenkov and N. Ya. Rostovtsev) in Ventnor on the Isle of Wight in August 1860.

2. Maria Alexandrovna Markovich.

3. Taras Shevchenko (1814-1861), the great Ukrainian poet of the 19th century. He was born a serf, but his freedom was purchased by a group of Russian literary admirers. Makarov wanted to break up Shevchenko's wedding, since the poet's intended—a servant named Lukeriya—was marrying Shevchenko only to irritate the Kartashevskys' other servants.

4. The plan came to naught.

Letter 122.

1. Fet had purchased Stepanovka, an estate 70 versts from Spasskoye.

2. A not quite accurate citation from Pushkin's "When I wander down noisy streets."

3. Andrey Ivanovich Podolinsky (1806-1886), a second-rate poet; Dmitry Yurievich Struysky (1806-1856), poet and music critic who used the pseudonym Trilunny; Fet; and Turgenev were all under critical attack at the time by N.A. Dobrolyubov and N.G. Chernyshevsky, the young radical editors of *The Contemporary.*

4. See letter 121.

5. Whether Fet expressed an opinion is not known.

Letter 123.

1. Turgenev is doubtless referring to his relations with Pauline Viardot.
2. Turgenev wrote half of *Fathers and Sons* during the winter of 1860-1861.
3. Insarov, the hero of Turgenev's *On the Eve*. A Bulgarian, he is consumed by a single idea—freeing his native land from the Turks.
4. See letter 121.
5. Nikolay Romanovich Tsebrikov (1800-1862), a Decembrist.

Letter 124.

1. As other letters testify, Turgenev felt obliged to stay in Paris until he could arrange his daughter's marriage.
2. Turgenev, though an admirer of Tolstoy's writings, considered that the latter indulged in excessive psychological detail.
3. See letter 113, note 1.
4. *Fathers and Sons.*

Letter 125.

1. The opening of this letter seems not to be extant.
2. Turgenev is referring to his daughter's governess, Maria Innis (d. 1879).
3. The work in question is *Fathers and Sons,* which Turgenev did not complete until the fall of 1861.
4. *The Age* (Vek), a weekly journal whose literary section was managed by A.V. Druzhinin. Turgenev published only one work in *The Age,* "A Trip to Albano and Frascati. Recollections of A.A. Ivanov" (1861).
5. Mikhail Alexeyevich Turgenev (1829-?).
6. The first line of Lermontov's poem "Gratitude."
7. The note is letter 126.
8. Nikolay Alexandrovich Dobrolyubov (1836-1861), one of the radical young critics on the staff of *The Contemporary.* He was extraordinarily hostile to most of the literati of Turgenev's generation, though in this case Turgenev was mistaken about the author of the article in question, who was actually N.G. Chernyshevsky. And Chernyshevsky did not mention Turgenev or the novel *Rudin* by name, though the object of his attack is nonetheless obvious.
9. Nikolay Tolstoy died September 20/October 2, 1860, in his brother Lev's arms. Details of Nikolay Tolstoy's final days eventually found their way into *Anna Karenina.*
10. See letter 117, note 2.

Letter 142.

1. Annenkov found *Fathers and Sons* a masterly work, but was critical of Bazarov and Anna Sergeyevna: they both seemed too ambiguous to him.
2. *Fathers and Sons* was to be published in Katkov's *Russian Messenger.*
3. Annenkov had written Turgenev about student protests and arrests in Moscow and Petersburg.
4. Nikolay Khristoforovich Ketcher (1809-1886), a doctor and translator, was a friend of Belinsky's, Herzen's, and Turgenev's.
5. Ketcher later wrote Annenkov that he had heard no rumors about Turgenev and Tolstoy.

6. In Chapter XXIV of *Fathers and Sons* Bazarov and Pavel Petrovich Kirsanov fight a duel.

7. This peculiar word appears in English in the original.

Letter 143.

1. See letter 142. The nature of Botkin's comments is a matter of conjecture.

2. According to Turgenev's later article "Apropos of *Fathers and Sons*," Katkov found Bazarov "practically an apotheosis of *The Contemporary*."

Letter 144.

1. The journal was Dostoevsky's *Time* (1861-1863).

2. The piece in question is probably "Phantoms," which finally appeared in Dostoevsky's second journal *Epoch (Nos. 1-2, 1864),* though Turgenev may have in mind the story "Enough."

Letter 145.

1. Turgenev cites part of Katkov's letter in his article "Apropos of *Fathers and Sons*."

2. By "present circumstances" Turgenev means the student demonstrations followed by arrests and the temporary closing of Petersburg University in the fall of 1861.

3. Katkov had wanted Odintsova's attitude in her discussions with Bazarov to be more archly ironic.

Letter 146.

1. The citation, in English in Turgenev's letter, is from *Othello,* Act,V.

2. Lambert's brother, Count Valerian Yegorovich Kankrin (b. 1820), died October 29/November 10, 1861.

3. Agrafena Ivanovna Mansurova (née Trubetskaya).

4. Turgenev probably has in mind the closing of universities and the unease in the countryside.

5. Nikolay Gerasimovich Pomyalovsky (1835-1863), the author of several grittily realistic sketches and novels which lie midway between journalism and prose fiction.

6. K.K. Lambert.

Letter 147.

1. Alexander Alexandrovich Bakunin visited London in mid-January, 1862, to see his brother M.A. Bakunin.

2. Turgenev reached London in mid-May, 1862.

3. Herzen's son, Alexander Alexandrovich Herzen (1839-1906), was interested in travelling to Russia. Herzen had asked Turgenev to find out whether such a trip was advisable. Herzen's son did not in fact go to Russia.

4. Alexander Vasilievich Golovin (1821-1886), Minister of Public Enlightenment from 1861 to 1866.

5. Prince Alexeydorovich Orlov (1827-1885), a general and diplomat, was an acquaintance of Turgenev's.

6. Mikhail Alexandrovich Bakunin (1814-1876) the nihilist revolutionary, one of Russia's most colorful figures. At the time of Turgenev's letter, Bakunin had recently escaped

from Siberia, travelled to Japan, crossed the Pacific, the U.S., and Atlantic, and turned up on Herzen's doorstep in London. For a detailed biography of Bakunin, see Edward H. Carr, *Michael Bakunin* (London, 1937).

7. Kozma Terentievich Soldatenkov (1818-1901), a publisher who Herzen thought might be in Paris.

8. Because of his father's émigré activities, Herzen's son had been fêted by the Russian students in Germany.

9. Golovin had recently been appointed Minister of Public Enlightenment.

10. Charles Mazades' "La Russie sous le règne de l'empereur Alexandre II" (January 15, 1862) devoted great attention to Herzen.

Letter 148.

1. Fet's estate Stepanovka.

2. The Russian *toska* can be rendered variously as "melancholy," "nostalgia," "home-sickness," "yearning," and so on.

3. A.N. Ostrovsky's play *Mini.*

4. See letter 146.

5. The heroine's name is Nadya.

6. No one has yet been able to identify the source for this quotation.

7. *The Hanger-On* was first staged in Moscow on January 30 O.S., 1862, then in Petersburg on February 7 O.S., 1862. Turgenev was upset because he thought that the main role would fall to F.A. Burdin (1827-1887), an actor whom he did not respect.

Letter 149.

1. Dostoevsky's letter, unfortunately, is not extant.

2. Ye. Ya. Kolbasin.

3. Turgenev reinstated the passage (Chapter XXV) when the novel was published in a separate edition in 1862.

4. A.N. Maykov was very enthusiastic about *Fathers and Sons.*

5. In 1855 Turgenev promised "Phantoms" to M.N. Katkov's *Russian Messenger.* Work on "Phantoms" dragged on, however, and instead Turgenev turned to "Faust," which appeared in *The Contemporary* in 1856. Katkov, believing that "Faust" was "Phantoms," accused Turgenev of breach of promise, which led to journal polemics between the author and the publisher.

6. The story "Enough."

7. Issues of *Time* usually came out late.

8. Maria Dmitrievna Dostoevskaya, née Konstant (1828-1864), Dostoevsky's first wife.

Letter 150.

1. N. Ya. Makarov married Olga Platonovna Chelishcheva in 1862.

2. P.V. Annenkov.

3. *Fathers and Sons.*

Letter 151.

1. Natalya Mikolayevna Rashet, née Antropova (circa 1830-1894), a translator and friend of many of the leading Russian writers of the mid-19th century. She spent most of the period 1860-1872 abroad.

2. Antonia Xaverievna, Bakunin's wife, was left in Siberia without means of support when Bakunin fled the country. Turgenev eventually arranged financial support for her.

3. The two Bakunin brothers arrested were Nikolay Alexandrovich (1818-1901) and Alexey Alexandrovich, not Ilya Alexandrovich (1819-1901) or Pavel Alexandrovich (1820-1900). When Turgenev returned to Russia in May 1862 he met with the two arrested brothers in the Peter-Paul Fortress in Petersburg.

Letter 152.

1. Fet's letter is not extant.
2. See letter 143.
3. Alexey Arkadievich Stolypin (1816-1858), a friend of Lermontov's, enjoyed the reputation of a "social lion."
4. The Rosset brothers, Arkady Osipovich, Klimenty Osipovich, and Alexander Osipovich, were all Officers of the Guard and social lions of Pushkin's time.
5. Turgenev left Paris May 22/June 3, 1862.
6. Turgenev means suitors for his daughter Pauline, who did not marry until 1865.
7. Vasily Petrovich Botkin.
8. Fyodor Alexeyevich Zinovyov (d. 1884) was the author of *Gentry Elections*.

Letter 153.

1. Henri Delaveau.
2. Nikolay Vladimirovich Khanykov (1822-1878), a geographer, orientalist, and ethnographer, lived in Paris from 1860 on.
3. The matchmaking was unsuccessful. Around May 13/25, 1862, Pauline Turgeneva and her governess, Maria Innis, left for Florence without Turgenev.
4. The composer's wife Clara.

Letter 154.

1. Konstantin Konstantinovich Sluchevsky (1837-1904), a poet whom Turgenev supported and helped early in the former's career. After 1866 Turgenev's attitude toward Sluchevsky cooled considerably. Sluchevsky is the prototype for Voroshilov, an ignoramus and careerist in Turgenev's *Smoke*.
2. Sluchevsky's letter is not extant, but it obviously contained a detailed report on the attitude of Russian students in Heidelberg towards *Fathers and Sons*.
3. See letter 143.
4. In Chapter 10 of *Fathers and Sons* Bazarov recommends that Arkady give Karl Büchner's *Stoff und Kraft* to his father to read.
5. Nikolay Alexandrovich Speshnyov (1821-1882), a member of the Petrashevsky Circle (to which F.M. Dostoevsky also belonged), returned to European Russia from Siberian exile in 1860.
6. Nation as in *narod*, i.e., "the people."
7. Here and later in the letter Turgenev is polemicizing with an article by Ye. Tur (pseud. of Ye. V. Salias de Turnemir) published in *The Northern Bee*, Nos. 91, 92 (1862).
8. Pyotr Semyonovich Yesakov (1806-1842), an officer of the Schlisselberg Chausseur Regiment and a social lion of his day.
9. See Chapter XXVI of *Fathers and Sons*.
10. Yemelyan Ivanovich Pugachov (c. 1742-1775) was the leader of a major peasant revolt that threw Catherine the Great into a panic (not without reason). Pugachov was

eventually captured and put to death on Red Square. For Russians he remains the symbol of a popular, i.e., peasant revolution.

11. See letter 149. Botkin's reactions are contained in N.V. Shcherban's memoirs (*The Russian Messenger*, 1860, No. 7, pp. 17-18).

12. Nikolay Fyodorovich Shcherbina (1821-1869), poet and translator.

13. The poems were not published in Dostoevsky's *Time*.

14. N.N. Rashet.

Letter 155.

1. The edition came out in September, 1862, with a dedication to Belinsky and a short preface by Turgenev.

2. Serafima Nikolayevna Ketcher.

Letter 156.

1. The original of this letter is in French.

2. Nothing is known about Mr. Honsez.

3. Joaquina García.

Letter 157.

1. Giuseppe Garibaldi (1807-1882) was wounded and taken prisoner by King Victor Emmanuel's troops on August 28, 1862.

Letter 158.

1. Turgenev used his impressions of the Russians in Heidelberg as the basis for the scenes at Gubaryov's in *Smoke*.

2. Marianna Turner, a friend of Prince N.I. Trubetskoy and his wife who lived with them in Paris.

3. Prince Nikolay Alexeyevich Orlov (1827-1885), a Russian diplomat, was married to the Trubetskoys' daughter Yekaterina Nikolayevna.

Letter 159.

1. Vladimir Fyodorovich Luginin (1834-1911), a friend of Herzen's and Ogaryov's, was a participant in the revolutionary movement of the 1860s.

2. The "address," which never fully materialized, was to be an appeal to Alexander II to convene a general Zemsky Sobor (Assembly of the Land) to lighten the peasant's burdens in the post-Reform era.

3. The reference is to Herzen's "Ends and Beginnings," a series of letters published in *The Bell* in 1862. The letters were a polemic with Turgenev.

4. Turgenev had thought of publishing his replies in *The Bell*, but was warned not to— probably by Count P.D. Kiselyov, the Russian Ambassador to France.

5. A quotation from Gogol's "The Inspector General."

6. Mikhail Vasilievich Lomonosov (1711-1765), one of the most remarkable men of his age, was a scientist, poet, grammarian, and all-around Renaissance man who, like Peter the Great, helped introduce Western ideas to Russia.

7. The *zemstvos*, legislative-administrative bodies of very limited self-government, were established as part of the Reforms of the 1860s. Peasants and landlords participated in the *zemstvos*.

266

8. For earlier criticism of Kavelin's theories, see letter 41.

9. Afanasy Prokovievich Shchapov (1830-1876), historian who was involved in the revolutionary movements of the 1860s. Herzen highly recommended Shchapov's writings to Turgenev.

10. Shchapov held that the governmental system of Russia up to the beginning of the 17th century was based on native institutions of self-government such as the *zemstvos*.

11. "Reflection" in the sense of intense intellectual analysis.

12. Turgenev has in mind Bakunin's "Romanov, Pugachov, or Pestel?"

13. A *duma* is a parliament.

14. Turgenev is referring to the major reforms involving and accompanying the abolition of serfdom.

15. Turgenev is paraphrasing a passage from "Romanov, Pugachov, or Pestel?"

16. Mikhail Alexandrovich Bezobrazov (d. before 1888), an arch-reactionary figure of the 1860s who attempted to dissuade Alexander II from abolishing serfdom.

17. Count Fyodor Ivanovich Paskevich-Erivansky (1823-1903) argued for giving the serfs freedom but no land.

Letter 160.

1. Friedrich Bodenstedt (1819-1893), German poet and translator. Some of his translations of Russian poets were set to music by Pauline Viardot.

The original of this letter is in French.

2. Bodenstedt's translation of Turgenev's "Faust" appeared in *Russische Revue* in 1862.

3. In 1863 Bodenstedt concluded a contract with the Munich publisher M. Rieger for a three-volume collection of selected Turgenev works. Sales were less than encouraging, and the edition was discontinued after two volumes.

4. Bodenstedt had sent an article "On Poetry in Germany after Heine" to *The Contemporary*, where it was lost for a while and eventually found in 1863.

5. N.A. Dobrolyubov died November 17/29, 1861—I.I. Panayev on February 19 O.S., 1862.

6. M.L. Mikhaylov was arrested September 14/26, 1862—N.G. Chernyshevsky on July 7/19, 1862.

7. The journal renewed publication in 1863.

8. P.V. Annenkov.

9. Paul Heyse (1830-1914), German writer who was much taken with Turgenev's works.

10. Olga Dmitrievna Nelidova (1839-1918), a translator.

11. The confusion had arisen because Bodenstedt used a French translation of Turgenev's "Faust" for his German translation.

Letter 161.

1. Turgenev very much disliked Hugo's style, which relies heavily on antitheses.

2. See letter 159 for details of the address to Alexander II.

3. The entire first paragraph of this letter is a response to Herzen's letter to Turgenev of November 1/13, 1862.

4. Turgenev is referring to the fifth letter in the series entitled "Ends and Beginnings." See letter 159, note 3.

5. N.P. Ogaryov.

6. A *samum* is a dry hot wind that blows through the deserts of Asia and Africa. In his fifth letter Herzen had compared the unhealthy socio-politico-moral atmosphere in Western Europe to a *samum* that he saw as a memento mori.

7. In his fifth letter Herzen spoke of Russia's young, healthy spirit—in contrast to that of a metaphorically dying Europe.

8. Herzen wanted Khanykov to send him his address.

Letter 162.

1. Turgenev is referring to Herzen's sixth letter in the series "Ends and Beginnings." In that letter Herzen uses "pre-Punic" to describe a society in decline; he also suggests that contemporary Western knowledge was concealing its impregnation by Pan instead of Jehovah.

2. From Turgenev's point of view, both Herzen and Bakunin idolized and idealized the Russian people.

3. Count Viktor Nikitich Panin (1801-1874), a Minister of Justice who had often been the target of attacks in *The Bell*, had recently been retired from his post.

4. Turgenev offers a slightly adapted quotation from I.I. Dmitriev's fable "The Oak and the Walking Stick." Panin was well-known for his height.

5. Konstantin Vladimirovich Chevkin (1802-1875) had lost his position of Chief of Travel and Communication for Russia.

Letter 163.

1. In her most recent letter Lambert had mentioned that Turgenev had taught her humility; in the same letter she suggested that Turgenev had recently grown indifferent to her.

2. In the same letter Lambert wrote that Karl Karlovich Lambert was hardhearted and unhappy.

Letter 164.

1. See letter 162.

2. In a letter of November 10/22, 1862, Herzen asked Turgenev why he was so intolerant of Ogaryov, adding that such weaknesses were permissible only in pregnant women.

3. An allusion to Schiller's poem "Das verschleierte Bild zu Saïs."

4. Turgenev is alluding to the fact that it was his novel *Fathers and Sons* that introduced the word "nihilist" into our modern philosophico-political vocabulary.

5. Herzen loathed the publishers with whom Turgenev regularly dealt.

Letter 165.

1. Fet had fallen down and sprained his arm. "Röderer" was a brand of German champagne.

2. Lev Tolstoy married Sofya Andreyevna Behrs (1844-1919).

3. The family of Andrey Yevstafievich Behrs (1808-1868), a doctor, lived in the Kremlin. Turgenev must have seen the young Sofya Andreyevna sometime in the 1850s.

Earlier, in the 1830s, Behrs had been the family doctor for Turgenev's mother, by whom he had a daughter. See letter 24, note 6.

4. Tolstoy often spoke of giving up literature.

5. Turgenev is referring to the reforms following the abolition of serfdom.

6. Pyotr Ivanovich Borisov (1858-1888), Ivan Petrovich's son.

INDEX TO VOLUME I

The numbers following names in this index refer to letter numbers, not pages. Italics indicates that the given person was the letter's addressee. Biographical information can usually be found in the notes to the first letter in which a person's name occurs.